It awaits your
discovery.

Praise for *Making ⋆ Contact*

"We cannot separate the earth from its greater cosmic environment. What is needed is a new story, and Alan Steinfeld's *Making Contact* is part of that story."
—Deepak Chopra, author of *Total Meditation*

"New Realities are upon us! Alan Steinfeld provides one of the most informed and open-minded overviews of communication with alien intelligence and the UFO/UAP phenomenon in his new book, *Making Contact*."
—Alex & Allyson Grey, cofounders and ministers of the Chapel of Sacred Mirrors

"In *Making Contact,* Alan Steinfeld has presented a fascinating compendium of views on the most important issue in the world today: the presence of extraterrestrial beings engaging the human race, and the pending confirmation of that presence by world governments. That confirmation, 'disclosure,' is close at hand, and this volume will help the reader to prepare."
—Stephen Bassett, executive director of Paradigm Research Group

"This is a serious book. *Making Contact* needs to be read by skeptics, advocates, and agnostics. Skeptics may not change their minds, but their responses will be a useful test for their belief systems. Advocates will find evidence for their perspective, and agnostics will find their worldview challenged. I have known a few of the authors in this anthology and will vouch for their sincerity, and we will see if history confirms their perspective."

—Stanley Krippner, Ph.D., coauthor
of *Personal Mythology*

"In this collection of finely written chapters by famous UFO researchers, the authors finally ask the right questions: What will human beings realize in finding themselves to be part of a larger cosmos? How come nonlocal communication involves subtle states of consciousness? Are we dealing with extraterrestrial beings or beings of a different nonmaterial order? My intuition aligns with the idea expressed here that humanity has to evolve from rational to intuitive beings for this momentous day to arrive. I highly recommend this exciting and very readable book to everyone with an open mind."

—Amit Goswami, quantum physicist
and author of *The Self-Aware Universe*

MAKING
CONTACT

---- ✳ ----

Preparing for the New Realities of Extraterrestrial Existence

---- ✳ ----

EDITED BY
ALAN STEINFELD

ST. MARTIN'S
ESSENTIALS
NEW YORK

First published in the United States by St. Martin's Essentials,
an imprint of St. Martin's Publishing Group

www.stmartins.com

Designed by Steven Seighman

Library of Congress Cataloging-in-Publication Data

Names: Steinfeld, Alan, editor.
Title: Making contact : preparing for the new realities of extraterrestrial
  existence / edited by Alan Steinfeld.
Description: First edition. | New York : St. Martin's Essentials, [2021] | Includes
  bibliographical references and index.
Identifiers: LCCN 2020053251 | ISBN 9781250773944 (paper over board) |
  ISBN 9781250773951 (ebook)
Subjects: LCSH: Unidentified flying objects. | Unidentified flying objects—
  Sightings and encounters.
Classification: LCC TL789 .M239 2021 | DDC 001.942—dc23
LC record available at https://lccn.loc.gov/2020053251

Our books may be purchased in bulk for promotional, educational, or business use.
Please contact your local bookseller or the Macmillan Corporate and Premium Sales
Department at 1-800-221-7945, extension 5442, or by email at
MacmillanSpecialMarkets@macmillan.com.

First Edition: 2021

10 9 8 7 6 5 4 3 2 1

In loving memory of Paula Gloria Tsaconas Barton, my spiritual muse and shining warrior of light and truth. She said to me while having a vision of ETs that they are here under the "**benevolent force of evolution.**"

This book is also dedicated to brave pioneers such as **Budd Hopkins, John Mack, Whitley Strieber, Linda Moulton Howe,** and many more who have devoted a lifetime of investigations to exploring the edges of the unknown. They are the giants whose shoulders I stood upon in order to give myself and the rest of humanity a deeper peek into forever. I want to give a special mention to the friendship and collaborations of Drs. **J. J. and Desiree Hurtak,** whose journeys into the awakening of consciousness have been enduring.

There is only one thing more powerful than all the armies in the world, and that is an idea whose time has come.

—VICTOR HUGO

CONTENTS

FOREWORD

George Noory, host of *Coast to Coast AM*

One of the things that has inspired me in the course of my life has been the desire to solve the great mysteries of the universe. I have always thought everything was possible. Even the most far-out ideas must be considered. From the beginning of my broadcast career, I've wanted to cover the stories that most media outlets would never touch: the strange, the mysterious, and the paranormal. I found that talking to people on the radio was the best way to explore these ideas, which I've been doing since I was twenty-one!

My efforts in broadcasting have been about working my way through the system, going from newscaster to executive producer in Detroit, then to news director in Minneapolis, and on to St. Louis. But I found that when truly interesting stories involving unusual occurrences came through the newsroom, most people in the business would shy away from them. What really bothered me, however, was when people at the station would joke about these reports. Adding to my frustration, when it came to UFOs, politicians, military officials, and scientists would scoff at the possibilities that had so fascinated me ever since I was young. Because of their mystery and oddity, UFOs remain, for me, the mother of all paranormal occurrences.

Wanting to look deeper into the mysteries, I started *Nighthawk*, a late-night radio program in St. Louis, Missouri, in 1996. Being one of the first news reporters to seriously consider UFO sightings, I was able to bring a sense of legitimacy to some seemingly outrageous stories. One of the reasons *Coast to Coast AM*, started by Art Bell, is so well respected is that it comes from a professional broadcast experience. Now with millions of listeners nightly, I feel my training and inquisitive nature have brought some degree of satisfaction to people looking for answers to the bigger questions of life.

At speaking engagements, when somebody asks how I got interested in the paranormal and UFOs, I say it goes back to my teenage years. At thirteen, my mother gave me the book *We Are Not Alone* by the great *New York Times* science writer Walter Sullivan, which opened a world of vast horizons. After I found the 1966 *Look* magazine article on the Betty and Barney Hill incident, I joined the National Investigations Committee on Aerial Phenomena (NICAP). Another book that brought me into a greater awareness of the phenomena was *The UFO Evidence*, edited by Richard H. Hall and published by NICAP. This is still one of the most valuable resources I have found, summarizing hundreds of NICAP investigations involving the unexplained sightings of military personnel, pilots, scientists, and engineers. The book clued me in to the bigger questions about UFOs regarding electromagnetism, radar tracking, sudden disappearances of craft, unusual vibrational presence, and the strange physical symptoms of close encounters. I am still looking into these unexplained topics, but as a young boy they created a need in me to find out more. It became my life's mission to talk to people who knew the secrets to these and other mysteries.

All of this led me to the first interview I ever did on the radio, with the godfather of Ufology, the late Stanton Friedman. You could say that interview with Stanton directed the course of my radio career. Now more than thirty years later, I am convinced that the extraordinary is real. It doesn't matter how far-fetched it may sound, there's always a chance to learn something new and consider more unknown possibilities, including such things as other dimensions, teleportation, and warp-speed travel. I feel that if we can think it, it can be created.

UFOs are still one of the favorite subjects for me and my audience. Throughout the years of doing interviews, as well as my own research, it is clear that the phenomenon has touched millions. Now finally it is all coming to the forefront as being more acceptable and media-friendly. Not laughing like they used to, people are starting to take it seriously, realizing "**Oh my gosh, maybe it is real. Maybe it is happening,**" especially now with the Pentagon's acknowledgment of unexplained aerial phenomena (UAP), as well as increased sightings worldwide as have been reported on my program over the years from such places as the National UFO Reporting Center out of Davenport, Washington. If aliens exist (and they seem to, based on what multitudes of callers have reported), they are not here to invade. They might be here to uplift us. It seems to me that whatever is out there is waiting for us to grow up and take some responsibility for the mess we've made. Taking all this into account, the fallacy of our aloneness in a vast universe (and perhaps other universes) is a no-brainer. How can thousands, maybe hundreds of thousands, of my guests, callers, military personnel, pilots, and the general public be wrong about what they have witnessed?

After years of interviewing and investigating, I am pretty much convinced that the cosmos is pulsating with life. However, I feel we're not going to have a news conference about it on the White House lawn. What I have said for years is that even when the government admits to a small kernel of truth, they are not going to tell us everything. The real truth is going to come from people like the late Edgar Mitchell, the Apollo 14 astronaut, and others who just say, **"Enough is enough. I'm going to tell it the way I see it. What I know. And I'm coming forward with it."** Real disclosure is in the process, and it is coming from people who are talking about their experiences. I am so happy my program has provided a forum for people to speak out. It feels like the movement is growing toward a paradigm-shifting vision of reality. Concerning UFOs and their occupants, the jury is still out as to the who, what, and why of their visits here. Whether these visitors are extraterrestrial, interdimensional, time travelers, or a combination of all three, is still something that needs to be discovered.

Whichever, the world is waking up to something that can no longer be denied. The glass ceiling of secrecy is cracking. Mainstream broadcasting outlets are now reporting on related topics like near death experiences, past lives, and psychic powers. *Coast to Coast AM* is no longer on the fringe. Now we are getting traditional scientists and academics coming forward, saying, *"I'm studying these*

reports and they are very interesting." This is what I envisioned in 1996 with **Nighthawk**. I wanted to plant seeds of
possibility in people's minds, and now the seeds are sprout-
ing. When the day finally comes for the official government
"*disclosure*" with the "*confirmation*" of alien bodies and
the remains of crashed saucers made public, my worldwide
listeners are the ones who are going to say to the skeptics: "*I
told you so.*"

This brings me to the reason I feel there is no better time
for a book like *Making Contact* to be presented to the world:
It is another necessary blow to the wall of denial, ridicule,
and ignorance that has separated us from the truth. **Alan
Steinfeld** has put together a well-conceived collection of
writings that covers all the bases. After reviewing its eleven
essays, I feel it is one of the best approaches I have found
to grasp the most jarring enigma humanity has ever faced.

There are a lot of people who claim to be experts in the
field, but because of my years in the business, I know right
away who has solid information. And I feel this book
contains the best of the best. I know because many of the
people represented here have been on my program over and
over again. What is remarkable is to find them all together
in one volume. It is as if my program were taking place in
overlapping hyper-dimensions all at once. Steinfeld's all-star
team is composed of some of the outstanding players in the
field whose knowledge I most respect. They share essential
information about what has defied explanation.

Let me take a moment to point out a few of the expert
contributors with whom I have had the pleasure of working
many times on the *Coast* program: **Linda Moulton Howe**
has had monthly appearances on the program for years,

with the latest reports from government insiders from her Earthfiles investigations. **Nick Pope**, the former assistant to the British Ministry of Defence, has always given us the behind-the-scenes strategies concerning the military cover-up. **Whitley Strieber's** accounts of his "**visitors**" have excited and terrified listeners, but his insights have pushed us to the edge of understanding aliens better than anyone I know. And I have to say that one of the writers whom Steinfeld has nabbed for the book is a person I certainly would have loved to have spoken with on my program: **Professor John Mack**. Despite his tragic death more than a decade ago, his studies on human–alien encounters remain one of the most important confirmations to date of alien abductions. Other distinguished guests who have also appeared on my show are **Mary Rodwell; Grant Cameron; J. J. and Desiree Hurtak; Darryl Anka;** and **Caroline Cory**. Each of their contributions gives the reader insights into the multifaceted intentions of our "visitors."

I wholeheartedly welcome *Making Contact* as a vital contribution to the literature that attempts to showcase the complexity of how UFOs and their occupants will affect all of us. But what makes this book such a valuable resource is that it provides detailed accounts of the phenomena from a variety of perspectives. For those who are unfamiliar with the idea of extraterrestrial existence, the book is foundational. For those already steeped in the field, there are some real gems here that have expanded my own lifelong study of the subject. Therefore, I recommend this as a manual for how contact will certainly shape each one of us in the future.

With the insights here, the world is better prepared. As I say on my Gaia program series, *Beyond Belief*: "**Something** *real is happening to people.*" Likewise, I feel the same about the reality of ghosts, near-death experiences (NDEs), and out-of-body experiences (OBEs). I have always felt connected to the familiar line from *The X-Files*: "*The truth is out there.*" When the human race ever gets to the place where we will understand that truth is another question. But I have faith in humankind. We are going to get through this difficult passage and build a civilization that will thrive within the harmony of the cosmos.

If we can dissolve the illusion of cosmic isolation and live into the new realities of extraterrestrial existence, we will need to know who, what, and why these beings are here. This can only happen when we open our minds as a race of Earthlings to a greater existence. In other words, we need this book! My listeners need this, humanity needs this, and our children and grandchildren need this, because "*making contact*" presents the opportunity to advance civilization. If we can meet the challenge and feel equal to these other beings, we have a chance to see the grander capacity of our human souls. When that happens, we ignite the magic of living in a world filled with adventure, hope, and unlimited possibilities.

My mission, ever since I talked to Stanton years ago, has been to help people figure out where they fit into the bigger reality. This is still my vision, because if we can embrace an expanded view of ourselves and our world, we might have a shot at the mysteries that have eluded us so far. I think we are closer than ever to figuring out some of it. I feel that becoming a spacefaring race bent on excursions throughout the Milky Way will mark the expansion of our God-given potential. I feel this is our destiny, and it could create the civilization that works for everyone. I feel that someday soon, maybe this decade, this century, or at some point in the near future, the conflicts that have plagued our species for eons will come to an end, and by "***making contact***" we will take our rightful place among the stars.

INTRODUCTION

Alan Steinfeld

*There are seasons in human affairs, of inward and out-
ward revolution, when new depths seem to be broken
up in the soul, when new wants are unfolded in multitudes, and a new and undefined good is thirsted for.
There are periods when the principles of experience need
to be modified, when hope and trust and instinct claim
a share . . . in the guidance of affairs, when in truth to
dare is the highest wisdom.*

—William Ellery Channing, *The Union*[1]

Let's face it, human civilization has been awash with the stunning achievements in the arts and sciences, coupled with the
most horrendous atrocities that a species can inflict upon
itself. We are now at a crossroads where, as the poet and ab-
olitionist William Channing stated above, *"New wants are
unfolded in multitudes."* These wants demand freedom from
tyranny, dogma, and the lies that have enslaved the human
race. We have lived with a hidden history that has resulted in
a crisis in "the season of human affairs," such as war with each
other, the Earth, and ourselves. To "modify the principles of

experience," we need to abolish these enslavements and rectify the falsehoods about who we are and our place in the cosmos. Now is the time when "thirsting for an undefined good" will lead us to "a season of inward and outward revolution" in the quality of thought and levels of perception. Now is the time when greed and manipulation can no longer threaten our existence. This will only come when we transcend our self-imposed limitations and connect to a greater truth, which has always meant a greater freedom. This is a book by and about people with a passion to take us beyond the confining ideas of a universe devoid of life. Their mission is the push for an expanded recognition of life on, above, and beyond the Earth because they instinctually know that "to dare is the highest wisdom."

THE NEW STORY

It is time to tell a better story about the whole pantheon of the unknown, their gods, miracles, angels, demons, aliens, and mysterious objects in the sky.
                    —Jeffrey Kripal, *The Super Natural*

One of the first writers to envision making contact with an alien race was H. G. Wells in 1898, with his earth-shattering novel, *War of the Worlds*. Years later in a more reflective mood he declared: ***"Civilization is in a race between education and catastrophe. Let us learn the truth and spread it as far and wide as our circumstances allow. For the truth is the greatest weapon we have."*** The veteran UFOlogist Stanton Friedman used to suggest that no one wants to deal with a species whose favorite pastime is "tribal warfare." Indeed, human history has been full of an ongoing series of aggression, hatred, and genocide leading to disaster. **"Dis-aster"** meaning in the ancient Greek "ill-fated star," has blocked the inclusion of other starry intelligences into our historical narrative. This exclusion is an out-of-date story creating an intolerable condition of global decay. We are at a juncture in the chronicles of civilization where we must say: **"Enough! It is time for something new and unknown to serve the greater humanity."**

The contemporary spiritual philosopher Deepak Chopra said: "Humans think only of what is good for me and mine without realizing that me and mine is entangled with all of existence. We cannot separate the earth from its greater cosmic environment . . . What is needed is a new story? If we don't create that story, which includes knowing our connection to all of existence, we are done!"[2] This is the present crisis: Disconnection from nature and each other has led to a narcissistic conquest to own what was never ours in the first place. Such abuses cannot be separated from the prevailing insistence of scientism (the *belief of science, not the facts*) that life on this paradise of a planet is an anomaly.

The new story of humanity remains to be written, but its prologue can be found in these pages. Hints of its upcoming chapters are sourced by the fact that we live in a time of astronomical discovery with an abundance of exoplanets coming into view. Perhaps the antiquated science-based pronouncement that we are *"the lonely freaks of a lifeless universe"* is coming to an end. In this context Arthur C. Clarke declared: "Two possibilities exist: Either we are alone in the Universe or we are not. Both are equally terrifying."

As anxious bystanders of either possibility, we have a

choice, like the storyteller in *The Life of Pi*. After being questioned by his inquisitors about whether his seaward journey with a tiger was real or not, he answered: *"Which story do you like better? The one with the tiger or the one being adrift in a vast ocean all alone?"* Well for us, I like the story *"with"* better. It offers a greater adventure of spirit, stretching us beyond our comfort zone, affording us the rewards of untapped creative thought. Potential encounters with other life-forms throughout the universe invites a grander perspective to be envisioned about ourselves and our place in the vastness of space. This is the evolutionary outlook at the source of *Making* Contact. The writings here present an enriching prospect that each of us is a part of a greater cosmic ecology. By laying out the likelihood that the universe is teeming with pulsating intelligence, we may find the courage to push beyond our barbarisms toward a prospective future and live freely, equally, and joyfully.

LIMITED WORLDVIEW

Every great advance in science has issued from a new audacity of imagination.

—John Dewey[3]

The suspicion that other sentient beings exist beyond our common humanity is not a new story. It is one of the oldest in history. Unfortunately, it has been institutionalized by religion or a material-centered science. In both cases, unfounded hyperbole has led us to a myopic view of reality. Conversely, what is expressed in these pages is based on empirical evidence—as it has been formally put forth as a means to gathering information that is not the results of laboratory settings. Rather, the information supplied in the present volume comes from direct observation and experience.

The volume argues that the notions of a mechanistic worldview have not gotten us very far in understanding "the what and who" of UFOs. *We cannot make sense of the seemingly irrational evidence that lies outside our ordinary realm of knowledge.* Preliminary considerations address three different levels of inquiry: First, could life, and for that matter intelligent life, exist elsewhere in the universe? Second, have more advanced intelligences visited and interacted with humans? Third, has an unsuspected presence been part of an untold story of humanity? If so, does this mean that we humans are part of something greater?

OTHER WORLDS

This investigation into the unreasonable begins with the reasonable statement about whether life is unique to Earth. Metrodorus of Chios was a student of Democritus, the man who in the fourth century B.C.E. first formulated the idea about atoms being the smallest measure of the microcosm. His younger colleague looked at the other end of the spectrum, the macrocosm suggesting "**to consider the Earth as the only populated world in the infinity of space is as absurd as to assert that in an entire field of seeds, only one plant will grow.**"[4] Advances in telescopes during the nineteenth century led to widespread public speculation about life throughout the universe, known as "**the Plurality of Worlds.**" One radical premise was proposed in 1844 by the American writer Edgar Allan Poe in the short story "The

Mesmeric Revelation." Poe expressed the idea that there are worlds that contain "*other rudimental thinking beings than man.*" "Rudimental" meaning basic physical beings. Taking a more spiritual angle he continued, "*the multitudinous conglomeration of rare matter into nebulae, planets, suns, and other bodies are for the sole purpose of supplying pabulum for the idiosyncrasy of the organs of an infinity of rudimental beings . . . Each of these is tenanted by a distinct variety of organic, rudimental, thinking creatures. In all, the organs vary with the features of the place tenanted.*"[5] Whether or not such "*thinking creatures . . .* [actually] *tenant a variety*" of planets cannot be confirmed at this point, but evidence for the plurality of worlds is more conceivable today than it has ever been. For instance, 99 percent of astrobiologists believe life exists somewhere in the cosmos. The current chairman of astrobiology for the Library of Congress, Steven Dick, said: "*I think the underlying principle is [that] the laws of physics and biology are universal . . . What has happened here is likely to have happened out there. The universe is an enormous place, too vast for life not to exist somewhere else.*"[6] This agrees with the views of one of the most well-respected scientists of our time, known for his contributions to Superstring theory, Michio Kaku: "*I think it's inevitable that we're going to find evidence not just of life but also of intelligent life because our galaxy has perhaps billions of Earth-like planets.*"[7] This is not a confirmation of extraterrestrial life, but an educated assertion. Dick concludes: "*The idea of life out there is very much at the forefront. The question is what are the implications?*"[8] Implications are what will be discussed in this text.

THE UNBELIEVED EVIDENCE

We may be in the universe as dogs and cats are in our libraries, seeing the books and hearing the conversation, but having no inkling of the meaning of it all.

—William James, *The Variety of Religious Experiences*

The book comes as a guide for shifting our conceptions about organic intelligence in the infinity of space. The sighting of strange objects in the sky and the notion of visitors coming to us from beyond this world stretches back to the dawn of civilization. Still, the phenomenon remains unacknowledged by the sincere scientists searching for life on the most distant stars. They have ignored such publications as Cheryl and Linda Costa's book, *UFO Sightings Desk Reference: United States of America 2001–2015,* which presents a compilation of more than 100,000 sightings of unusual objects in the sky within that fifteen-year period. A reviewer of the book for *The New York Times,* Ralph Blumenthal, wrote: **"People are seeing UFOs everywhere, and this book proves it."**[9] Moreover, the indexed reports reference only two national sources. My estimate is that only a fraction of sightings are reported, implying that the actual observations of strange craft are most likely significantly higher. Despite the great number of UFO witnesses, most scientists, like humans, in general, remain attached to their fixed beliefs, because their beliefs identify who they think they are. Aware of this fabricated sense of identity, the more enlightened physicist Max Planck declared: *"A new scientific truth*

does not triumph by convincing its opponents and making them see the light, but rather because its opponents eventually die and a new generation grows up that is familiar with it . . ."[10] Informally Planck's statement is often paraphrased as *"science moves forward one funeral at a time."*

Our attachment to personal beliefs has not changed since 1689, when John Locke wrote the essay *Concerning Human Understanding*: "Earthly minds, like mud walls, resist the strongest batteries: and though perhaps sometimes the force of a clear argument may make some impression, they nevertheless stand firm and keep out the enemy, truth, that would captivate or disturb them."[11] Locke's explanation is probably the best reason why most astrophysicists stand by the 1950 proclamation of the Fermi Paradox. This was proposed when the physicist Enrico Fermi, a pioneer in nuclear physics, looked around and realized that despite the uniformity of elements throughout the galaxy we have yet to meet an alien civilization. He shouted to his colleagues in exasperation: "Where is everybody?"[12] A response to this sort of ignorance came from one of the foundational researchers into alien–human contact. Budd Hopkins often said that the job of science is "to investigate the unexplained, not explain the uninvestigated." Nevertheless, the rallying cry of astronomers since Fermi has remained. Fermi asserted that "any civilization with a modest amount of rocket technology and an immodest amount of imperial incentive could rapidly colonize the entire galaxy."[13] But what if an ET civilization was not interested in colonization? Or better yet—what if the human race is exactly that, an outpost colony of an advanced alien race? Of course, Fermi and his fellow scientists must have missed the 1952 memo from the

CIA's Science Intelligence Deputy Director who acknowl-edged that there are "numerous other sightings of lights or objects which either in configuration or performance do not resemble any known aerial vehicle or explainable natu-ral phenomena."[14] Nevertheless, since Fermi, the lot of mainstream scientists, including those who have thus far fruitlessly searched the heavens for the well-funded SETI (Search for Extraterrestrial Intelligence) organization, still claim that we are alone. As recently as 2017, Space.com re-published an article titled "12 Possible Reasons We Haven't Found Aliens."[15] The central question remains: If profes-sional astronomers are looking "out there" for life, then how can hundreds of thousands of people (contactees) world-wide be claiming contact with beings so much closer to home, literally at times in their own backyards? This book directly addresses the reconciliation between the apparent lack of scientific evidence about life elsewhere with that cor-roboration from expert investigators and experiencers who are indeed being visited and interacting with other beings almost daily.

One explanation for the divergent views comes from the paradigm pundit Ken Wilber, who writes that *"Different world-views create not just different ideas about the world, they ac-tually create different worlds altogether."*[16] This is because people can only perceive what they believe exists. A perfect example came at the opening of Darryl Anka's essay on page 191 with "the paradox" about SETI is still looking for radio waves coming from some distant planet, while we ourselves have moved well beyond the radio age. Neverthe-less, there is a shift under way by innovative scientists like Avi Loeb, astronomer at Harvard University. His 2021 book, *Extraterrestrial: The First Sign of Intelligence Life Beyond Earth*, offers ample evidence that the object that flew by the Earth in October 2017 was an interstellar alien craft checking out our solar system. Loeb stated in a *New York Post* article: "*Some people do not want to discuss the possibility that there are other civilizations out there. They believe we are special and unique. I think it's a prejudice that should be abandoned.*"[17] Loeb explained how the skeptics are bending over backward to assign natural origins to the object "*Its weird properties don't stand up to scrutiny.*" The article goes on to say that the acceptance of an alien race making contact would trigger a serious search, leading us to scour the moon and Mars, for example, for debris that might have crash-landed thousands or millions of years ago. Loeb concludes that "*It would put us in perspective. If we are not alone, are we the smartest kids on the block? If there was a species that eliminated itself through war or changing the climate, we can get our act together and behave better? Instead, we are wasting a lot of resources on Earth fighting each other and other negative things that are a big waste.*"[18] The relevance of Loeb's forward-looking hypothesis defies the reasoning of the material-based science belief that surmises life is an anomaly in a lifeless universe.

The present collection is about entering a brave new world that gives insight into the workings of a greater life-affirming creation, by overcoming our socially conditioned skepticism. A way to consider without predjudice new and unusual situations originated with the philosopher Thomas Kuhn, a mentor to one of the prominent writers in this collection, Professor John Mack. Kuhn's thesis on *The Structure of Scientific Revolutions* states that the linchpin for conceptual changes must be the consideration of anomalies that have been disregarded in the present paradigm. According to Kuhn, anomalous discoveries are written off in the current scientific view because they challenge its basic assumptions. Kuhn wrote: *"In many ways, the established paradigm is the enemy of discovery. An anomaly may not be perceived for what it is, precisely because it is not expected."*[19] Anomalies are irrefutable evidence that the paranormal researcher Charles Fort called *"damned facts."* "Damned" because science just wants them to go away; they don't fit into scientists' well-formulated order of the world. As such, anomalous occurrences such as UFOs are uncategorizable in the current paradigm and have remained unidentifiable for almost a hundred years. In this regard Fort contended that the lack of knowledge about odd occurrences is covered over by authorities with terminology. The best example of this comes from calling something inexplicable in the sky a UFO (unidentified flying object) as if we know what it is. However, identifying something as *"unidentified"* is doublespeak and really means nothing at all.

Conclusively, in the 1930s the progressive psychologist Trigant Burrow said that *"whenever organic truth is denied its expression in the realm of reality, it will invent its expression in the realm of fantasy."*[20] If we take Burrow's insight into the nature of the psyche and apply it to the collective awareness of the species, we can see why some of the highest-grossing films of all time have been about off-world beings. This includes the *Star Wars* series, *Avatar*, and the Steven Spielberg classics *ET* and *Close Encounters of the Third Kind*; all are the obvious representatives of an organic truth whose expression in reality has been denied.

DISCLOSURE

The denials vanished on December 16, 2017. Before that date it was okay to call anyone who believed in UFOs "*a crackpot.*" The hour was struck when *The New York Times* turned the tide for a serious public awakening. The front-page headline proclaimed: "*The Pentagon's Mysterious U.F.O. Program.*" The article discussed the Senate's secret budget of $22 million to study what they called *Unexplained Aerial Phenomena*. Of course, unacknowledged government UFO programs into the phenomena have existed since the Roswell crash of 1947, with studies like *Project Blue Book* and the *Condon Report*. Even so, the *Times* article stated that in 2007 the Pentagon began the *Advanced Aerospace Threat Identification Program (AATIP)*. The online version of the article provided an official video released by the Pentagon of Navy pilots chasing a flying object that has been called a "*Tic Tac*" due to its shape and white color.[21]

The formal announcement was greeted by some UFO investigators as the long-awaited "**Disclosure.**" The proclamation was driven home when former AATIP investigator, Luis Elizondo, who said publicly: "*I think we're at the point now where we're beyond reasonable doubt that these things exist. We know they're there—we have some of the greatest technology in the world that has confirmed their existence.*"[22] While most researchers affirmed the importance of that "disclosure moment," others felt it doesn't become real until we have "**confirmation.**" This would be the action by the government of rolling out the alien bodies and the scavenged spaceships to provide the hard-core evidence of off-world visitations. Still, we moved a step closer to that on July 23, 2020, when *The New York Times* dropped another bombshell. It reported that the astrophysics consultant to the Pentagon's AATIP program, Eric W. Davis, gave a series of classified briefings to members of the Senate Armed Services and Intelligence Committees, and the Defense Department about **"*crashed retrievals of unexplained off-world vehicles not made on this earth.*"**[23] In a follow-up story, CNN reported that Senators Marco Rubio and Mark Warner confirmed that they were given information about the existence of advanced aerial vehicles of unknown origin having visited Earth. On the heels of that article came the announcement from the Pentagon's Department of Defense that further investigations are under way with the creation of the Unidentified Aerial Phenomena Task Force (UAPTF). Its ongoing mission is "to detect, analyze, and catalog UAPs in order to gain insight into the nature and origins of UAPs, and if they pose a threat to national security."[24]

THE INTELLIGENCE

Such slow-leaking government acknowledgments of "visitors" are only half the game. As in most sporting events, the defensive team (as in the Department of Defense) is met by the offensive players. What lies at the heart of this volume is the nature of the "offenders" of social order: the visitors and their confounding actions. Extraterrestrials (if that is what they are) who might at some point present themselves publicly has formally been called "**Contact.**" Unlike most opposing players, "confirmation" versus "contact" appears to be less at odds and more in collusion than it might first seem. Grant Cameron's *The Theory Wow,* pages 24 through

46, explains that the objective of both sides is not to shock people with an obvious presence but rather to plant seeds in our minds about a greater life in the cosmos.

Former Air Force officer and UFO advocate Robert Hastings theorizes that the steady approach on the part of "the ET intelligence" is for a slow and mitigated acceptance of otherworldly beings into our fragile notions of reality. In 2010 Hastings hosted a press conference with former military officers, testifying about UFO sightings over nuclear weapon bases. He eloquently summed up what might be the underlying strategy of the visitors: **"I am of the opinion that whoever they are, they have enough sense to know that if they interject themselves into our reality in one fell swoop, there could be very dire repercussions. Whereas, on the other hand, if they engage in an on again off again, cat and mouse behavior, that allows a slow psychological conditioning of humankind to their reality and to the presence of themselves. Then, when open contact, if that indeed is in the cards, occurs there will be far less trauma."**[25]

NOT A SPECTATOR SPORT

Every major competition of opposing teams is for the benefit of those watching on the sidelines. Yet Cameron emphasizes this is not a spectator sport. Those who seem like innocent bystanders are of direct concern to the phenomenon. In his essay he claims that **if someone sees a UFO it is not by chance; every sighting and contact experience is intentionally planned.** Whatever the players' game strategy is—something is certainly appearing in the skies on every continent to an increasing degree and interacting with the human population.

This is one reason I regard knowing the truth about UFOs as a serious business. The act of making contact seems to be a convergence of all three sides to create a coherent synthesis of awareness that will bring us (and maybe "them") to another level of perception. **Whitley Strieber** expressed this understanding in the final chapter of *The Super Natural*: "*They* [the visitors] *might need us to believe in them before they can become invested in our reality. If so, then the whole vast UFO and close encounter experience could be a sort of military operation designed to open the door in our minds from their side.*"[26] The mission of this book is to provide a key to that door from our side that will bring us closer to the threshold of making formal contact.

INTRODUCTION TO THE CONTRIBUTORS

Down how many roads among the stars must man propel himself in search of the final secret? The journey is difficult, immense, at times impossible, yet that will not deter some of us from attempting it.
—Loren Eiseley, *The Immense Journey*

Even though the phenomenon stretches back through the annals of recorded history, the brief background I've just laid out is enough of a foundation to contextualize the following essays. What will be covered is the widest overview ever proposed of the multifaceted phenomenon. More significantly, what I feel makes this anthology particularly exciting is the way the developmental structure of the essays progress from observation to knowledge to experience. Thus, the reader is able to proceed from the outer shell of the

material phenomena, advancing inward toward personal reflections, culminating in an understanding of how to merge
our consciousness with beings beyond the human realm.

In this respect, what is found in the following pages is
not from people for whom the idea of *"making contact"* is
a passing curiosity. The complexity of the subject being
explored is by some of the most intelligent and perceptive
people I have ever met; people not handicapped by ridicule,
fear, or contradictory reports. These pioneers have forged a
collection of unmatched acumen about the most bewildering circumstances humankind has ever faced. Many of the
writers have dedicated their professional lives to exacting
as much truth as they can convey about a mystery that has
yet to yield all its secrets. Nevertheless, such actions have led
some of these writers to face serious threats and open dis-
dain for speaking about their research and experiences. Yet
such occupational hazards have not prevented the majority
of them from publicly stating what they feel is of utmost concern to our human destiny and the fate of the planet. They
have stood firm in their resolve to step into the unknown
for the sake of knowledge. What is most valued from these
creative individuals are their original and well-informed insights whose purpose will catapult us toward an inconceivable future. They know that *"to dare is the highest wisdom."*

INVESTIGATORS

Specifically, the development of the text begins with **THE
INVESTIGATORS**. For lack of a better term, these are
people who look into the government cover-ups concerning the greatest secret never told. This area of study involves
the *"nuts and bolts"* hardware of the phenomena and ad-

dresses why the military insists on keeping the hard-core UFO evidence from the public. This level of inquiry can be equated to J. Allen Hynek's well-known classification of *Close Encounters of the First Kind*, which refers to only the sightings of unidentified flying objects.

Chapter 1: Nick Pope kicks off this compilation by laying out in the first part of his essay *"the government mindset"* and why top-secret materials are being kept from the public in the first place. As a government insider, Nick worked for more than two decades as the assistant at the British Ministry of Defence (MoD) assigned to researching and investigating the UFO phenomenon. He says that *"by using this inside knowledge what I hope to give is an informed assessment of what has been going on in the United States."* Getting down to the nuts and bolts, he talks about the need of "intelligence" strategies in evaluating possible alien craft and why the MoD considered UAP encounters as a real public threat. He also talks about the agency's investigation into the technology that extraterrestrial visitors would require to get here, and the possibility of back engineering this technology. Although still under an oath of secrecy from his government, he admits this essay *"is easily the most detailed account that I've given of my time investigating UFOs for the MoD, sharing my direct personal experience of the intelligence assessment of . . . UFO work."* In the second section of the essay, "Our Future Among the Stars," Nick speculates on "a roadmap to the stars," which is what might be in store for the human race with advanced engineering. This sort of optimism advances the reader toward a next level of consideration and leads into the next essay.

Chapter 2: Grant Cameron takes us deeper into the mechanics of the phenomenon with "The Theory of WOW." In this essay, he lays out the strategy that the intelligence behind the phenomenon might be taking to wake up a sleeping **planetary population.** Instead of the cliché about "landing on the White House lawn," he feels UFOs are performing spectacular aerial maneuvers to get people's attention so they can exclaim, "Wow, there must be more to reality than what I've been told." Their innumerable appearances, although fleeting at times, are meant to shake loose the workings of our conditioned mind and help us wonder about the larger scope of the cosmos. He asserts that if we truly understood the enormity of what we are facing we would realize that this is "**the Super Bowl of all stories.**" In recent years Grant has moved from the "nuts and bolts" investigations toward research on people who are "*making contact*." He has often said in interviews that he feels that while "*the story will eventually be told by government officials, it is the experiencers who have the direct knowledge on the subject*."

Chapter 3: Dr. J. J. Hurtak and Dr. Desiree Hurtak combine their knowledge of astronomy, environmental science, and UFO history to give an assessment of "Extraterrestrials and Multidimensional Nonlocality Reality." The overview starts with the various technological developments that will help us in "making contact." Their organization, The Academy for Future Science, researches advances in technology that we as a civilization need to develop for interstellar travel to become a reality. This includes the use of wormholes, stargates, and teleportation. Even though Dr. J. J. Hurtak was one of the first to present evidence of a crash retrieval spacecraft with photographs of alien bodies to the world press in 1979, the Hurtaks came to find that the phenomenon encompassed more than physical manifestation. Their research took them further into finding that life itself may have originated beyond Earth, and that nonphysical contact may include the presence of higher spiritual beings. Speculating on the nature of consciousness, they feel it is irrevocably "**connected to a nonlocal source**," as quantum physics is beginning to understand. They conclude that this evolved perspective is the most sophisticated way to understand the nature of all intersecting realities. In developing the right relationship between us and a universal consciousness we will be able to travel through the multidimensional realms of creation.

RESEARCHERS

THE RESEARCHERS again is a label that does not necessarily constitute the entire scope of the writers' work. It is only used to categorize the present material. These are people who look into the psychological and sociological implications of the phenomena. This includes various degrees of ET involvement and how each person's interaction can only be described from the level of awareness they are currently at. Presented in this section are two of the most respected minds in the UFO field. **Professor John Mack** and **Linda Moulton Howe** both agree that there are aspects to these non-human beings that seem connected to a more harmonious "*implicate order*." This extended look at the phenomena can be classified as ***Close Encounters of the Second and Third Kind***, investigating the ramifications of the alien presence.

Chapter 4: In "Contact in the Implicate Order," **Linda**

Moulton Howe dives deep into a personal accounting of her forty-plus years of research into the complexities of her ongoing investigations. What puts Linda in a unique position is that from her diligent **Earthfiles.com** reports, she can draw government whistleblowers into her trusted confidence. Her writing includes an extract of an eight-hour meeting with an unnamed official from the **Defense Intelligence Agency (DIA)** in Washington, DC. One of the facts that the individual revealed to Linda is that at least three competing ET races have participated in the evolutionary development of *Homo sapiens* on planet Earth. However, Linda agrees with the Hurtaks' speculation that *humans, given the chance to know the truth about who we really are, could achieve a greater destiny of mind and soul.*

Chapter 5: Having **Dr. John Mack's** "Studying Intrusions from the Subtle Realm: How Can We Deepen Our Knowledge?" is a real coup for its inclusion in this collection. The previously unpublished essay granted by the **John E. Mack Institute** profiles the unique position the late Professor Mack maintained in the study of those who interacted with the phenomena. As head of psychiatry at Harvard Medical School and with expertise in child and adolescent psychology as well as the psychology of religion, he helped many people cope with the reality of their contact experiences. Upon initially hearing about alien abductions, he considered the idea a form of mental illness. Only after conducting a large number of his own interviews with experiencers he concluded in his essay: "**No case has revealed that behind the reported** [alien] **experience is some kind of strange depression, or child abuse, or something else.**" Mack claimed that "abductions" were a logical development from his earlier work, which he said *"resides in the matter of identity—who we are in the deepest and broadest sense . . . the reported experience of the witness, and our clinical assessment of the genuineness of that report, may be the only means by which we can judge the reality of the experience."*[27] Despite his tragic passing in 2004, his work remains as current as ever in evaluating the effects of phenomena on the human psyche. Mack suggests that the very idea of alien abductions undermines the fundamental paradigm of the Western mind. His essay goes further in validating a nonrational, intuitive approach to reality.

EXPERIENCERS (ABDUCTEES AND CONTACTEES)

If the thousands of people who are already "making contact" were to come forward and be heard, it would totally grab the attention of our civilization. This is where the text gets highly personal, with writers sharing the intimate details of their interactions with other beings. In this regard, Grant Cameron comments that *if we really want to know what is going on, we have to talk to the people directly involved with the otherworldly beings.* These people can be broken down into two subcategories: *abductees* and *contactees*.

THE ABDUCTEES are people who claim to have been taken by aliens against their will for various invasive purposes such as genetic manipulation and vibrational upgrades. Alien abduction is considered a close encounter of the fourth kind. Unfortunately, this action has sometimes resulted in *PTSD effects*. Still, in many cases, not all, the feelings about forced abductions seem to shift later on in abductees' lives. Many people come to find that the disturbing events have increased a level of awareness in their lives that they might not have achieved any other way. This has manifested for a good number of abductees as **higher intelligence, increased creativity, psychic development, and healing powers**.

Chapter 6: Whitley Strieber's "The Return of the Visitors" is an excerpt from his 2019 book *A New World*. Whitley is probably the most well-known abductee in the world and one of the most profound thinkers on the topic. His breakthrough book on the subject, *Communion,* in 1987 was not only a worldwide bestseller but it also gave the planet the iconic face of an extraterrestrial. His writings since that time have been a continuous effort to contextualize his relationship with what he terms "**the visitors**." In this contribution he looks at the all-encompassing nature of what "*making contact*" really is. He offers a new way to integrate encounter experiences in terms of human awareness, but the caveat comes from the source of the title *A New World*. It seems that the United States Army Colonel Philip J. Corso told Whitley what an alien said to him when he asked what they can offer us. The alien answered, "*A new world, if you can take it.*" This is not a fearful projection but rather a challenge to shift the dynamics of human awareness.

Chapter 7: Alan Steinfeld's "Extraordinary Actuality: My Journey to the Stars" is one of the most intimate stories in the collection. It is about my lifelong compulsion with outer space. I begin my chapter with my childhood fascination with the stars and my love of science fiction books. In 1987 what I thought was fiction became an actuality, when

I experienced my own alien abduction on a cross-country road trip. This changed the direction of my life and academic interests. I became obsessed with all things UFO and ET related. Now, for the first time, I relay my hypnotic regression back to the 1987 abduction and the newfound understanding I retrieved about these other beings' efforts at "making contact." As I state in my essay, the dreamlike nature of contact is central to the ET experience. Trying to understand other ways of knowing has led me to look at the nature of perception, what is cognition, and how we can perceive new realities. This led me on a search around the world interviewing leading thinkers in science, art, and UFOs about the nature of reality. The possibilities of ET beings has helped me open a spiritual awareness of a cosmic consciousness that exists for everyone.

Chapter 8: "Something Moving" is the writer and performer **Henrietta Weekes's** biographical profile that communicates what cannot be said in words. The significant factor in the portrayal of her abductions is the way she showcases the nonlinear quality of her experience. Rather than telling us, her suggestive style illuminates the sensorial nature of the ET experience. By relating dreamlike fragmented memories and fragmented perceptions of her sometimes-fearful encounters, Henrietta stretches the reader to move into the feeling qualities of encounters. Her staccato phrasing allow a freer, more creative way to sense the multidimensions we all live in. The language conveys a method to shut down the analytical part of the brain. As John Mack expressed many times in his research, the phenomenon appears to be beyond the logic of the Western mind. In this way Weekes demonstrates how to activate new cognitive abilities to meet these beings on their own terms.

CONTACTEES. Up until this point it is fair to say that the contributions have all been contained within a worldview that may be doubtful to some, but intolerable to many. Contactees claim their interactions have been supremely intimate, and for the most part see the value of making contact. In some cases these people are converted abductees who have discovered the significance of their previous alien interactions. For instance, the *Edgar Mitchel Foundation for Research into Extraterrestrial and Extraordinary Encounters (FREE)* found that a large majority of the 4,200 experiencers in their online survey, many who had recalled past trauma of contact, years later looked upon their abduction as a beneficial force in their lives. Nevertheless, what I am referring to as "contactees" are generally people who have not suffered the traumatic effects of contact. As opposed to abductees, these people feel their encounters have been with benevolent beings who care about humanity, and often contribute to the contactees' well-being with uplifting, healing, and mind-expanding experiences. Mostly, these people feel that the ETs are here to evolve human civilization so that the Earth may become a more peaceful planet. Up until this point it is fair to say that the contributions have all been contained within a worldview that may be doubtful to some, but tolerable to many.

The more intimate nature of this next section, which can be classified as *"close encounters of a fifth, sixth, and seventh kind."* These last few chapters move the reader toward integrating the totality of the essays. I urge everyone to suspend their judgment of the possible and embrace the work of the next three writers as honest portrayals of their experiences and observations.

Chapter 9: Darryl Anka's "Telepathic Contact with Extraterrestrial Intelligence" specifically deals with one of the vital topics that was mentioned in seven out of the eight previous essays: *the use of mind-to-mind (telepathic) contact as the primary mode of extraterrestrial communication with humans.* Darryl is the perfect person to relay this information because for almost four decades he has had ongoing interaction with an extraterrestrial named Bashar. The entity is known to millions of people worldwide and by allowing Bashar to take full control of his body Darryl seems to have perfected a telepathic link with a member of an advanced civilization coming to us from 300 years in the future. Furthermore, Bashar is not just a channeled being; he is on a mission with his communications as a **"first contact specialist".** The contribution Darryl supplies is of his own journey working with the extraterrestrial in preparing the greater humanity for making contact.

Chapter 10: Mary Rodwell's "Awakening to Our Cosmic Heritage" is based on her investigations of 3,000 case histories with contactees. To her, "*making contact*" appears to be a global phenomenon, with aliens contributing to the new humans, whom she also refers to as "star children." Mary affirms there is a wide population of children who exhibit a maturity and wisdom beyond their years. They are known for their telepathic abilities and spiritual insights. Many of the children she quotes in her essay feel emotionally supported by their contact and have the ability to describe varieties of non-human visitors with a feeling that they are as familiar to them as their human family.

Her research also explores evidence of contact from a scientific, biological, psychological, anthropological, spiritual, and historical perspectives. Mary feels all this is part of a "genetic" engineering program to upgrade *Homo sapiens*. Her training as a nurse, midwife, and spiritual counselor has allowed her to look beyond the norm as many of these individuals demonstrate awareness of the nonphysical realms not understood by an older generation. Her work begins with an initial question: *"What will humanity look like when we realize we are part of a larger cosmos?"* Mary concludes with the sentiment that we are waking up to who we are as far as the truth of our cosmic heritage.

Chapter 11: This collection wraps up with an interview with **Caroline Cory** on "ET Lineages and Human Evolution." In this discussion with editor Alan Steinfeld, Caroline talks about how to live as someone who has fully assimilated the awareness of other realms into her daily life. While Mary Rodwell talks to children about their messages, Caroline is one of the few people who embody the ET mindset. In talking about the potential for the new gifts of consciousness, she touches on topics mentioned in previous essays, such as multidimensionality, the development of greater sensitivity and creativity. Specifically, her personal experiences have witnessed *a galactic grid linked to our brains, as well as explaining the way we can merge our energy fields with other beings. In acknowledging our lineage from the stars, we can align with those frequencies to activate the higher potential of our minds.* This will give the reader a valuable tool to move beyond the ordinary into the extraordinary. Caroline closes the interview by sharing how the ET connection is an evolutionary potential that will give us a more fulfilling human experience.

READER BEWARE

We set sail on this new sea because there is new knowledge to be gained, and new rights to be won, and they must be won and used for the progress of all people. I do say that space can be explored and mastered without feeding the fires of war, without repeating the mistakes that man has made in extending his writ around this globe of ours.

—John F. Kennedy[28]

Right off I have to say none of this will make any sense until there is a suspension of the logics of linear mechanistic view of reality. Whitley Strieber has made a specific argument in the past that "There is every implication that behind the supposed alien presence, there lies a completely new vision of reality that is at once larger and more accurate than the current rigorously materialistic scientific vision."[29] This is the reason for the myriad of perspectives being offered: to demonstrate that at this juncture in history there has yet to appear a monolithic truth of what "*making contact*" is all about. Einstein said: "**Whoever sets himself up in the field of truth and knowledge is shipwrecked by the laughter of the gods.**" For sure something unfathomable is happening in our skies, and there seems to be no comprehensive explanation coming any time soon. But one suggestion to keep in mind is found in *The Journal of Scientific Exploration* (1992): "***The phenomenon of Unidentified Flying***

Objects (UFOs) presently affords analysis [of] only pieces
of a hereto unknown whole reality. Because the whole is
not seen or understood, the visible pieces often appear to
be irreconcilable with one another and lead to hypotheses
which are in conflict."[30] This brings us to the point some
UFO investigators in the past have made that the situation
may be too dynamic for the government to admit they don't
understand what is going on. Linda Moulton Howe, com-
menting on the phenomena's intricacies, has said after her
nearly forty years of investigations: *"It is like a hall of mir-*
rors with a quicksand moving floor."[31] Nevertheless, the
reason this book is not a straightforward narrative is that
the nature of the phenomena appears to be a mosaic; a
myriad of impressions from which the reader can create an
educated hunch that adds to the collective cognition of a
new era of understanding. Nevertheless, the purpose of this
volume is to supply the foundation for interacting with a
situation that asks us to suspend our qualifications of reality and venture into the unknown.

NEW KNOWLEDGE

Let those who seek should not stop seeking until they
find. When they find, they will be disturbed. When they
are disturbed, they will marvel, and will reign overall.

—The Gospel of Thomas

In the process of letting go of our past qualifications so that
we can formulate a fresh take on the phenomena, we must
overcome two obstacles. First is the fact that UFOs and ETs
threaten our established way of thinking, because their

presence challenges our fundamental conceptions of the world. Our social conditioning wants us to live in a safe, secure, and predictable world. Even when something new and more expansive is offered, it is difficult to leave our comfort zone of what we think is real. Reality, as we know and trust, is more solid than the ground beneath our feet. If that is taken away, so are our predictable lives. Therefore, the biggest struggle that readers new and old to the subject have is confronting their own prescribed view of the possible, and not escaping into a stable position whereby they can say: "**Oh, now I know what UFOs and ETs are all about.**" This sort of conclusion isn't practical and maybe not even possible. The cultural historian Raymond Williams acknowledged his own resistance to new ideas in his book *The Long Revolution*: "*The effect of this new knowledge seems to me to be of the greatest importance, but I know from my own attempts to absorb it that it is so difficult to grasp and that its application must be met with all kinds of resistance and confusion.*"[32]

Even after we accept the fact that there are unknown objects in our skies, the second challenge is our capacity to know. I am reminded of what the philosopher Samuel Coleridge said about the nature of existence itself as being "**too profound for human insight.**" This sort of puzzlement was recently admitted to by the ex-CIA director talking about UFOs at the end of 2020: "**I think some of the phenomena we're going to be seeing continues to be unexplained and might, in fact, be some type of phenomenon that is the result of something that we don't yet understand and that could involve some type of activity that some might say constitutes a different form of life.**"[33]

Nevertheless, this is why I have assembled a team of admirable authors: because this enigma has never stopped the best of them from attempting to communicate what may indeed be beyond the reach of human comprehension.

In the following offerings I ask the reader to do what a curious John Mack did when first confronting the unbelievable claims of alien abductions. He approached his mentor, Thomas Kuhn, the man who coined the term "*paradigm shift*," to advise him on how to evaluate such an unknown situation. Kuhn suggested he just take it all in without trying to fit the information into a current belief system. After a few years of listening to many experiencers, Mack concluded that:

> *I was dealing with a phenomenon that I felt could not be explained psychiatrically yet was simply not passive within the framework of the Western scientific worldview. My choices then were either to insist upon a psychological explanation consistent with the prevailing Western scientific ideology. Or . . . open to the possibility that our conscious framework of reality is too limited and that a phenomenon such as this cannot be explained within its ontological parameters. In other words, a new scientific paradigm might be necessary in order to understand what was going on.*[34]

Mack contemplated what the public might soon be forced to contend with: how making contact with non-human intelligences could result in the evaporation of our current worldview, creating a global reset and cognitive realignment more drastic than the Copernican revolution. If this is true, then the radical nature of this material requires a suspension of belief to take it all in without judgment and afterward make an educated assessment of the situation. The German poet Rainer Maria Rilke wrote: "**We must accept our reality as vastly as we possibly can. Everything, even the unprecedented, must be possible within it. This is in the end the only kind of courage that is required of us: the courage to face the strangest, most unusual, most inexplicable experiences that can meet us.**"[35]

Hence, if the reader remains available to the considerations presented, they will find astonishing possibilities that even the most advanced scientific studies have yet to embrace. As Henrietta Weekes writes in her essay, it was only when she opened herself up to the idea of extraterrestrial contact that she was able to discover more of her own mind, more of herself, and the freedom to further her artistic explorations. In this way the adventure of absorbing the sequential development laid out here is to take the reader deeper down the rabbit hole of their own creative thought. In this manner the book is a primer for each of us to fashion a coherent understanding of a situation that has thus far evaded all categorization. And if none of this makes sense, then listen to the wisdom of Ralph Waldo Emerson, who, in the same year that Poe wrote "The Mesmeric Revelation," 1844, expressed the evolution of a mind confounded by the mysteries: "The state of science is an index of our self-knowledge. Since everything in nature answers to a [principled] power, if any phenomenon remains brute and dark, it is because the corresponding faculty in the observer is not yet active."[36]

In other words, if the reader has yet to reach a level of self-reflection, the phenomena described will remain inconceivable. New faculties of perception can be achieved only by putting aside everything we think, and avail ourselves to the creative force of the mind to, sooner or later, synthesize a new way of knowing.

POIESIS

Only by imagination can the world be known. What is needed is not larger and larger telescopes . . . but that the human mind should become increasingly aware of its own creative activity.

—Owen Barfield, *Poetic Diction*[37]

There are a few additional elements to consider before getting to the bulk of the book. The first is to see that **"*making contact*"** is a process, an ongoing action. It is not something that has happened or will happen only once. It is a happening and will continue to happen as an ongoing revelation of being. In this sense the word "making" is related to the ancient Greek word "*poiesis*," meaning to create, as well as the ability to receive new stimuli that had not been previously sensed. The German philosopher Martin Heidegger wrote "*poiesis*" is synonymous with a "bringing-forth into presence," an "unveiling" of the unknown.[38] "Making" *(poiesis)* is the drive of consciousness to evolve awareness for more inventive possibilities. Our survival depends on seeing a greater reconciliation of life and intelligence. The neurobiologist John Z. Young affirmed this effort, surmising that as a species we are hardwired for ongoing creative advancement. He wrote: *"The continuity of life depends on . . . the continuous invention of new ways of observing. This is man's special secret of living that the whole race will only be preserved if the individual contributes new inventions to the rules [of seeing] and passes that on to others."*[39]

Stretching the above sentiment to the possibilities of extraterrestrial existence, Whitley Strieber points out that "**it must never be forgotten that contact was not initiated by the visitors. It was initiated by the growing richness of the human mind.**"[40] In this way reading this book is a destining; an aspiration of our minds to reach outward while being matched by an equal power to receive new levels of awareness. Even if the information you are about to read defies everything you know, take a chance to venture into the unexplored by giving yourself the freedom to enlarge the context of your thoughts. The linguist Noam Chomsky, contemplating the human capacity to understand, suggested that *new levels of human cognition can only emerge at new levels of awareness*. In regards to the current topic, I take Chomsky's sentiment to denote that by extending ourselves toward the unknown, previously unrecognized perceptions can come into view.

THE POINT OF *MAKING* ∗ *CONTACT*

The universe is not made but is being made continually.
It is growing perhaps indefinitely.
                    —Henri Bergson, *Creative Evolution*[41]

One final point concerns the sage words of Professor Mack: "We're dealing with a phenomenon which violates our sense of reality, and which operates in this gray area between the physical world and the subjective, or mythic or other-realm world. We're being asked to prove this by the methods of the physical sciences alone. But those methods, in my view, will not yield its secrets, until we discover other ways of knowing."[42]

Other ways of knowing demand a suspension of our logical mind. So, while the phenomenon refuses to be known in any comprehensible, rational way, it can be apprehended in a more abstract sense.

Apprehending over comprehending is a movement toward a more open-ended, approximated awareness. It is a shift in how "to know." For example, the title *Making * Contact* is a clue to how apprehension can bring forth an expanded and more abstract sense of perception. Where words carry a specific meaning, symbols like the asterisk (*) provide a wider range of significance. It establishes an undefined presence, much like "the visitors" themselves. The writer/philosopher Johann Goethe contended that symbols are "*a living perceptible and instantaneous revelation of the unfathomable.*"[43] Their power lies in the ability to convey multiple meanings at once. The use of the * bestows a variety of obvious associations, such as a distant star as the possible origin of extraterrestrial existence, or it could mean a new star is rising to replace the ill-fated stars that have led to past disasters. On another level, its placement between "making" and "contact" is like the center point of a compass, representing the way consciousness reaches out in all directions. Whatever the reader's associations with the symbol, it is an initiation into a new way of knowing. It stands as a nonverbal communication, a silent transmission from mind to mind, like telepathy, mentioned in ten out of the eleven essays, as **"the point"** of making contact.

CONCLUSION

The time will come when diligent research over long periods will bring to light things that now lie hidden. There will come a time when our descendants will be amazed that we did not know things that are so plain to them.
—Roman writer Lucius Annaeus Seneca, *Natural Questions*, Book 7 (first century C.E.)

In addition to all the information stated above, the book arrives at a critical juncture in the government's ongoing disclosures on the reality of UFOs/UAPs. However, as it stands now, most scientists, politicians, and mainstream news outlets have no idea what to make of such reports, or the growing number publicly acknowledged contact experiences occurring on a global scale. The essential revelations covered here supply the needed clarification on the intent and intelligence behind the phenomena. Such perspectives provide a solid foundation for the *"preparation"* of the utmost challenge ever to confront humankind. This is the reason I ask the reader to take in everything presented in these pages, in order to acquire the mindset to adapt to the coming era.

Allowing each fragment, no matter bizarre, to work on welcoming fresh perceptual opportunities to be realized.

Find the courage to let go of the known in order to cognize an abstract awareness of a greater destiny. A teacher of human potential, Joe Dispenza, said, *"Knowledge is a precursor to experience. The more knowledge you have, the more prepared you are for the event."*[44] In this way, what you are about to read concerning *"the new realities of extraterrestrial existence"* is not a substitute for experience—it is a primer for one. Let the words liberate the infinitude of the human mind, where the principles of experience can be modified so that a new story of humanity can unfold. Now is the time to conceive the inconceivable and indulge in extraordinary dimensions of being. Take a peek into forever, where the spirit of adventure can transcend the boundaries of belief and reveal the unknown. It awaits your discovery.

1

GOVERNMENT MINDSET AND OUR FUTURE AMONG THE STARS

Nick Pope

Every story needs a villain. When it comes to the story of UFOs, the role of that villain is usually taken by the government. In this story, the government is sometimes seen as a single, monolithic entity, while other times, there's the suggestion that some sort of cabal exists within government, managing UFO secrets. In either case, a central belief among many in the UFO community is that a conspiracy exists to cover up the truth about an extraterrestrial presence. I have a somewhat different perspective on all this. I served for twenty-one years as a civilian employee of the United Kingdom's Ministry of Defence (MoD), and in the 1990s I was assigned to a division where my duties included researching and investigating the UFO phenomenon. In this chapter I'm going to use my previous experience to give readers an insight into why and how governments investigate UFOs, and the sorts of conclusions we reach. Some of this won't be popular, so perhaps this chapter can be seen as a sort of "minority report," and if the government is perceived as being the villain of the

UFO story, perhaps that makes me the villain of this book. Even if I am the villain, I still have a story to tell.

The first point to make is that governments look at the UFO phenomenon in a rather different way than the UFO community. They consider the topic—as they consider most issues—in the context of threats and opportunities. It's worth looking at this in a little detail, because this mindset contextualizes much of what follows.

It may surprise people to know that there's an equation that defines threat often used in various government, military, and intelligence community agencies. Threat is expressed as *capability* × *intent* (as an aside, risk is sometimes defined as *probability* × *harm*). When it comes to UFOs, we have some good data on capability. Not just eyewitness testimony from pilots, but radar data, FLIR (Forward-looking Infrared) films from military aircraft, and the associated MASINT (Measurement and Signature Intelligence) data from such films. Simply put, this data suggests an impressive capability, with very high speeds, rapid acceleration, and extreme maneuvers being frequently seen. In the context of our equation, this gives us a high value for capability. With intent, however, we quickly run into an obvious problem, namely a lack of definitive data in a situation where there are multiple competing theories about the nature of the UFO phenomenon. As a further complication, sightings would have to be individually assessed, because different incidents will likely have different causes. Some UFO sightings, for example, will be attributable to misidentifications of drones, meaning that intent could be assigned a value. Other sightings, however, will have no obvious explanation, which raises the question of how we could even begin to define intent. If we were dealing with technology from Russia or China, intelligence officers specializing in these countries could simply assess intent, drawing on their existing knowledge. But if we're dealing with something unknown—possibly even extraterrestrial—we can't even begin to make any assessment of intent. Thus, going back to our equation, no accurate value for intent can be given. So, if intent is unknown, even with good information about capability, no meaningful assessment of threat can be given. The threat is unknown.

This quote from a 1997 MoD document illustrates the thinking perfectly:

> *The second and critical question is do UAPs [Unidentified Aerial Phenomena] represent a possible threat to the defense of the realm. We could debate that (assuming for the sake of argument that something exists) they have never shown any hostile intent and therefore can not represent a threat. However, Russian aircraft attempting to penetrate the UK ADR [Air Defense Region] in the Cold War never showed hostile intent but they certainly represented a threat. Thus, the only logical conclusion that we can come to is that we do not know if UAPs represent a threat to the defense of the realm. We cannot eliminate the possibility.*

Not only can we not assess the extent of any threat, we can't say if one exists at all. This, however, allows us to more easily navigate territory in terms of understanding the government's mindset, because it's binary: Either a threat exists or it doesn't. The answer, of course, is simple. The military perspective is that it's better to assume a threat exists and be relieved when one doesn't materialize, as opposed to assuming there isn't a threat, and thus being unprepared if one suddenly emerges. While such a mindset isn't going to be popular with everyone, it is, perhaps, understandable to those with some knowledge about the way in which government works.

There's another factor to take into account here: money. In government, an excellent way to get a program funded is to highlight an actual or potential threat, and then put forward your program as being the way to mitigate or eliminate that threat. In relation to UFOs, the issue of threat is always going to be front and center. Indeed, it's almost an inevitable outcome, which highlights an interesting point about where one places a UFO program. Most nations that have run UFO programs have embedded them in the military (usually the air force), or in the Department of Defense. This placement, in and of itself, results in the approach described here. One exception to this rule is France, where their UFO program is embedded in the French national space agency. The other exception is the Pentagon's AATIP (Advanced Aerospace Threat Identification Program) project, which, while originally commissioned by the Defense Intelligence Agency, was largely conducted in the private sector. As we'll see later in this chapter when AATIP will be discussed in more detail, it's an interesting point that where you embed a UFO program has a discernable effect not just on mindset and methodology, but arguably on outcomes too.

If government looks at UFOs through the lens of threat

and opportunity, what of the opportunity? The answer can be summed up in two words: **technology acquisition**. It's an answer that better explains the reasons for UFO secrecy than the more clichéd theories doing the rounds. One sometimes hears, for example, the claim that governments are wary of disclosing an extraterrestrial presence because of some undefined fear of panic in the streets or the threat to world religions. The reality is that it's the possibility of technology acquisition that best explains the secrecy, and a UK MoD study with the code name Project Condign gives the best illustration of this. Because I was personally involved in this work, telling the story of Project Condign enables me to give a practical example of the points I've previously made. And because the final report has been partially declassified and released by the UK government, all this information can be verified in a way that isn't possible with a lot of material presented by alleged UFO whistleblowers. For those who may be wondering, the fact that the UK government has itself released most of its UFO files is the only reason I can talk about any of this. While I took early retirement from the MoD in 2006 (after a successful, interesting, and enjoyable twenty-one-year career), my secrecy oath is binding for life, and I wouldn't dream of divulging classified information. I'm not a whistleblower, so much as a commentator who can give an insider's perspective on how governments tackle the UFO issue. Project Condign encapsulates much of this.

Like the better-known United States Air Force program, **Project Blue Book**, the center of gravity of the MoD's UFO program was casework. We received several hundred sighting reports each year and investigated them to the best of our ability: Witnesses were interviewed, radar data was checked, photographs and videos—if we had them—were analyzed, and a painstaking series of cross-checks were made, attempting to correlate the description, location, and date/time with known aerial or astronomical objects and phenomena. We knew that aircraft and aircraft lights were often misidentified, so we could check commercial aircraft activity and military flight training to see if there was a match. The same was true for things like weather balloon launches, meteor showers, and a whole host of other things. At the end of this process we'd explained around 80 percent of sightings in conventional terms and had approximately 15 percent of cases where there was insufficient data to make a good assessment, leaving around 5 percent of cases unexplained. Unexplained meant unexplained, nothing more. We weren't claiming that these were extraterrestrial, but neither did we rule out the possibility. Our public position was that we remained "open-minded" about the possibilities of extraterrestrial life. In reality, some were more open-minded than others!

The work was interesting but could be frustrating. When I joined the MoD, each case looked different, but by the time I left, a lot looked the same. It was difficult to find the signal amid the noise. For every structured craft seen at close range by a trained observer there were dozens of vague lights and shapes in the sky, recalled by witnesses who were well meaning but often muddled in their recollections. Critically, our investigations were done on a case-by-case basis, with little or no trend analysis being performed. Simply put, nobody had taken a look at the data holistically and asked what it all amounted to. Project Condign was aimed at changing this.

One day in 1993 my opposite number in the MoD's Defence Intelligence Staff (DIS) came to see me. We talked through the problems, which had been brought to a head by a fascinating and unexplained series of sightings from March 30 and 31, when multiple UFO reports came in for a period of around six hours, from all around the United Kingdom, with many of the witnesses being police officers and military personnel. The intention of Project Condign was that, in parallel with our case-by-case investigations, we'd undertake what can probably best be described as an intelligence assessment of the UFO phenomenon itself.

In true UK civil service style, Project Condign took years to get off the ground, as a series of delays and controversies threatened to torpedo the study before it even began. Most of the documents have now been declassified and the struggle to get the study underway is interesting in and of itself, as one can see a skeptic-versus-believer battle taking place within the MoD, with some officials wanting the work done and others being less keen. It's worth looking at the reasons for the opposition. There were two, and they were very different. One objection was from a skeptical faction who felt that any such study was a waste of time and money. Their closed-minded view was essentially *"it can't be, so it isn't."* In parallel, they were concerned that any study of this nature would undermine the "no defense significance" soundbite that we routinely used in our dealings with Parliament, the media, and the public, as a sort of catchall evaluation for not only all individual sightings (even the unidentified ones!), but also the phenomenon in its entirety. While there was no intention to make the study public, there were understandable concerns about how it might be perceived within the MoD if it was discovered we were planning an intelligence assessment on something that we were publicly stating was of no defense significance. This was one reason why the security classification was high, the distribution list was small, and why no ministerial submission was ever drafted seeking authority from the Secretary of State for Defence or any of the other Defence ministers. As I recall, we wanted to ensure they were protected by the concept of plausible deniability.

The second objection was far more interesting but much more difficult to pin down, as the specifics of the objection were far too controversial to put into writing. It was from a small clique of officials who felt the UFO phenomenon was real but demonic in nature. This view seems to have its roots in a small passage in the Bible, in the Book of Ephesians, where Satan is described as "**the prince of the power of the air.**" One British proponent of this view was the Reverend Paul Inglesby, who circulated a pamphlet on this to a number of figures within the Establishment, including Admiral of the Fleet Peter John Hill-Norton, a retired five-star officer who had served as Chief of the Defence Staff (the UK's most senior military officer) and chair of NATO's Military Committee. If this sounds bizarre, a similar situation seems to have arisen in the Pentagon. Retired intelligence officer Luis Elizondo—point man for AATIP—reports that within the Department of Defense, serious study of the phenomenon got pushback for reasons that included religious belief. This pushback may have something to do with the idea that one shouldn't engage with anything demonic, as this feeds it and gives it energy, making it more powerful. If this applied to UFO research, it was even more likely to be a factor when that UFO investigation broadened out—as is claimed to have happened with AATIP—into more general paranormal research, conducted at the infamous Skinwalker Ranch in Utah.

Some MoD officials were more enlightened and Project Condign went ahead because such people carried the day. Writing in 1997, one MoD intelligence officer wrote, **"Being an objective, open-minded scientist, I do not dismiss out of hand the possibility of intelligent life evolving somewhere outside of our own solar system."** Another supporter, a senior Royal Air Force officer, was even more eloquent when he wrote:

> *Continuing discoveries of planets, and emerging knowledge of circumstances needed for at least non-intelligent life, lead to speculation that planets and life may commonly occur. With that change of perception, arguing that our rock alone is a teeming and verdant speck in a vast and sterile nothingness may soon be as unrewarding as the Church once found in continuing to enforce the idea that the world was flat; more so, with the knowledge that many suns are older than our own, and perhaps provide conditions for advanced evolution. Even though some experts argue very low probabilities for intelligent life, and allowing for barely imagined transit*

distances, requiring unknown uses of physics, we
cannot rule out entirely the idea of extra-terrestrial
observation/visitation, either covert or overt.

The open-minded faction won out and Project Condign went ahead.

The study was classified **Secret UK Eyes Only**, and to give an added layer of protection in terms of keeping it "off the radar," the work was contracted out to a defense company through the mechanism of an amendment to an existing contract. This mirrors the way in which AATIP was contracted out by the Defense Intelligence Agency to Bigelow Aerospace, which had two advantages for the government in terms of secrecy: It makes congressional scrutiny more difficult, and it takes much of the work outside the scope of the Freedom of Information Act.

While I was involved in the work that led to the study being undertaken, I'd been promoted and moved to another MoD division by the time the work began. But the MoD released a partially declassified version of the final report in 2006 so I can discuss some of the conclusions. A headline finding read as follows:

That UAP exist is indisputable. Credited with
the ability to hover, land, take off, accelerate
to exceptional velocities, and vanish, they can
reportedly alter their direction of flight suddenly
and clearly can exhibit aerodynamic characteristics
well beyond those of any known aircraft or missile—
either manned or unmanned.

Afterward, despite some good analytical work, the report's author unveiled what I can really only describe as his personal theory, which is that some of the best reports might be explainable in terms of exotic atmospheric plasmas, though he left the door open by saying, **"Although the study cannot offer the certainty of explanation of all UAP phenomena . . ."**

That perhaps the most sensitive parts of the final report related to technology acquisition was hardly surprising. A 1995 document about the potential benefits contained the revealing line **"We could use this technology, if it exists."** The implication was clear. While being careful in his wording, the intelligence official was essentially stating the possibility that if UFOs were extraterrestrial, there was self-evidently a technology involved, and a strategic aim should be to acquire this technology. It's an example of what is termed a **"low probability/high impact scenario,"** where even if you're skeptical about the chances, the potential benefit is so high that it more than justifies the effort. If we're discussing extraterrestrial technology, it's likely to be significantly ahead of anything we have, simply because viable interstellar travel is suggestive of a technology orders of magnitude beyond our current level. The nation on Earth that first acquires that technology will likely be the dominant force on this planet for the foreseeable future: militarily, politically, and economically. Those are high stakes indeed, and as I have said, I believe this interest in derivable technologies (irrespective of the true nature of the phenomenon) is the real reason for UFO secrecy. The US government was thinking along exactly the same lines, as will be explained when I discuss the Pentagon's AATIP program in more detail.

The specifics of Project Condign's areas of technological interest are intriguing, and should also be kept in mind
when looking at AATIP. One quote read: "**The relevance of
plasma and magnetic fields to UAP was an unexpected
feature of the study. It is recommended that further investigation should be** [undertaken] **into the applicability
of various characteristics in various novel military applications.**" Another extract, alluding to the race for this
technology by referencing Russian work in this area, said:
"**There is evidence . . . that scientists in the former So-
viet Union have taken a particular interest in 'UFO Phenomena.' They have identified the close connection with
plasma technologies and are pursuing related techniques
for potential military purposes.**" Finally, the report went
into some specific technological applications, listing "**very
high power energy generation, RF Weapons, Impulse
Radars, air vehicle drag and radar signature reduction
or control, and possibly for radar reflecting decoys.**" RF
weapons are radio frequency weapons—essentially, a directed energy weapon.

I now want to examine the twin stories of the Pentagon's
AATIP program and the US Navy UFO encounters, con-
textualizing this in the light of what I've revealed about government thinking on the subject in general, and in the light
of my work on the British government's program. AATIP is
still shrouded in mystery, and we have very little paperwork
on it. What we do know is this: In 2007 the Defense Intelligence Agency (DIA) expressed interest in undertaking a
study that would look at UFOs, but maybe some other fringe

phenomena too. This followed contact between a DIA scientist and billionaire Nevada businessman Robert Bigelow. Bigelow is a passionate UFO enthusiast who's had at least one UFO experience. In 2007 he owned a 500-acre property in Utah called Skinwalker Ranch, where a lot of UFO sightings and other paranormal phenomena were said to have been observed. (In Navajo culture, a skinwalker is a malevolent witch who has powers that include the ability to shapeshift into a variety of animal forms.) The DIA official supposedly visited the property and had a paranormal experience there, which led to the study. In August 2008 the DIA issued a contract solicitation and the next month a contract was awarded to Bigelow Aerospace, the sole bidder. Also involved was another friend of Bigelow's, former Senate Majority Leader Harry Reid. Reid, in conjunction with Senators Ted Stevens and Daniel Inouye, was instrumental in securing secret government funding for AATIP and the associated contract, known as AAWSAP (Advanced Aerospace Weapon System Applications Program). In all, the contract amounted to $22 million over the next few years. The exact timeline is disputed, as is the exact nature of the program, and even the status of the program—the Department of Defense (DoD) states that the program ended in 2012 when funding ran out and was not renewed, while some of those involved in the work claim it continues to this day under another name, either with different funding or with tasks being carried out at no additional cost using resources and capabilities already funded.

The existence of AATIP became mainstream media news on December 16, 2017, when *The New York Times* broke the story not only of AATIP but of the existence of FLIR

(Forward-looking Infrared) videos showing US Navy F/A-18 Super Hornet jets chasing unidentified objects of some sort. Two videos were published with the *New York Times* story and a third emerged a few days later, courtesy of the **To the Stars Academy of Arts & Science**, an organization fronted by rock singer Tom DeLonge, featuring a number of people—including Luis Elizondo—who had either been involved in AATIP or had government and military backgrounds. Of the three videos, two related to a 2015 incident off the East Coast of the United States, while the best-known incident dated from 2004 and involved a white, oval-shaped UFO dubbed the "Tic Tac," seen off the West Coast of the United States and chased by a pilot, Commander David Fravor, who went on the record for the *New York Times* story. "**I have no idea what I saw**," Fravor commented, but "**I want to fly one!**"

As part of the rigorous fact-checking for the story, a *Times* reporter met with a Pentagon official who confirmed the basics of the story, but there followed a debate that still persists about the true nature of the AATIP program. Before getting to that, it's worth making two points that tie in with what I said earlier about governments looking at the UFO phenomenon in terms of threats and opportunities. The first and most obvious point is that the T in AATIP stands for "threat." It's hard to think of a more blatant placement of the threat narrative. The second point is to highlight some quotes from one of the very few pieces of AATIP paperwork that have been made public—a June 24, 2009, letter from Harry Reid to Deputy Secretary of Defense William Lynn III. In a letter in which Reid sought Restricted SAP (Special Access Program) status for AATIP he argued that the "**technological insight and capability gained will provide the US with a distinct advantage over any foreign threats and allow the US to maintain its pre-eminence as a world leader**," while warning that these same technologies "**have the potential to be used with catastrophic effects by adversaries**." This is a perfect illustration of the point about technology acquisition being at the heart of UFO secrecy. The same letter lists some of these "**emerging disruptive aerospace technologies: advanced lift, propulsion, the use of unconventional materials and controls, signature reduction, weaponry, human interface, and human effects**." The overlap with the technologies listed in Project Condign's final report is telling. As we'll see, this isn't the only example of the British influence.

Almost immediately after *The Times* revealed the existence of AATIP, a media frenzy ensued. *The Washington Post* and *Politico* quickly followed up with stories of their own, and the story generated extensive TV coverage on most of the US networks, and indeed all around the world. This arguably was everything that the UFO community had wished for, short of disclosure: extensive mainstream media coverage in outlets that seldom touched the subject, on-the-record accounts of military pilots chasing UFOs that were tracked on radar and captured on video, the films themselves, revelations concerning the existence of a shadowy UFO program, and much more besides. It should be recalled that prior to December 16, 2017, the official line was that the US government was not involved in UFO investigations. Much of the UFO community had doubted that but were derided as conspiracy theorists when they argued that someone in government was investigating UFOs. The revelations seemed to vindicate this belief. For once, the conspiracy theorists were right. Or were they? At this point, the US Congress stepped in, and what happened next gets to the heart of the confusion and debate over what AATIP actually did.

On January 9, 2018, the DIA sent a letter to John McCain and Jack Reed, chairman and ranking member on the Senate Armed Services Committee, respectively. The letter began, "**Based on interest from your staff regarding the Defense Intelligence Agency role in the Advanced Aerospace Threat and Identification Program**"—the extra "and" in AATIP's title was just one of several different versions of the project's name being discussed in the early days of the mystery, with Aviation being substituted for Aerospace in some of the reporting—then went on to say that "**the purpose of AATIP was to investigate foreign advanced aerospace weapon threats from the present out to the next 40 years.**" Variations on this explanation have been used by various government public affairs officers since then, but the implication was clear, even if never explicitly stated: This was a program looking at things like Russian and Chinese aircraft, Iranian drones, and North Korean ballistic missiles. On one occasion a DoD spokesperson expanded this explanation to say that AATIP's role included the study of "**anomalous events (such as sightings of aerodynamic vehicles engaged in extreme maneuvers, with unique phenomenology, reported by US Navy pilots or other credible sources).**" I was the first person to obtain and publish this letter, via the DIA's Office of Corporate Communications. I'd asked for it in my capacity as a journalist, after a sharp-eyed UFO researcher had found reference to it in the *Congressional Record*. My request took months to process, and it was the letter's attachment that doubtless proved most problematic, because it cast doubt on the line that AATIP had anything to do with next-generation aerospace threats—conventional ones, at least!

The letter went on to say that a list of all products produced under the AATIP contract (that is, AAWSAP) was attached. Not a single one had anything to do with Russia, China, Iran, or North Korea. There was nothing about the political intentions, aeronautical engineering skills, or factory capacity of any other foreign nations. Nothing about drones, or drone swarms, or hypersonic missiles. Nothing that one would expect to find in any genuine program evaluating future air threats to the United States. The thirty-eight technical reports listed in the letter's attachment included studies into **anti-gravity, invisibility, stargates** (a concept arguably more science fiction than theoretical physics), **warp drive, and wormholes.** Many of the papers were clearly focused on technologies that would be required for interstellar travel, though even setting aside the paper on stargates, skeptics would doubtless label some of this material "**fringe science**," if not "**pseudoscience**." But was any of this enough to resolve the debate about the nature of the program? For those—including the DIA themselves—who were still trying to spin AATIP as not having anything to do with UFOs, perhaps it could be argued that aerospace technology might advance to the point where the use of warp drive and wormholes might be possible. Forty years is a long time, and some of the other areas covered had already been the subject of research. Both NASA and some aerospace corporations had previously studied the possibility of anti-gravity (NASA's fear of being seen as embracing pseudoscience led them to use the term "gravity modification"), while some defense analysts believe work into optical invisibility is quite advanced. Fortunately, there was one paper that so clearly had nothing to do with next-generation aerospace technology that its existence in AATIP resolved the debate in and of itself. The paper was on the Drake Equation—the sole purpose of which is to estimate the number of communicable civilizations in our Milky Way galaxy. It is difficult—arguably impossible—to argue that this illustrates anything other than an AATIP focus on extraterrestrials and, by extension, UFOs.

There was to be a further indicator. A May 2019 DoD statement to *New York Post* journalist Steven Greenstreet acknowledged that [AATIP] **"did pursue research and investigation into unidentified aerial phenomena."** This was doubly significant. Not only did it confirm the program was UFO-related but it was also further evidence of the British influence by virtue of use of the term UAP, which we'd adopted in the nineties in the MoD while seeking support for Project Condign. Indeed, a separate US Navy spokesperson acknowledged the term **"was borrowed from the United Kingdom."**

With this information now available, it becomes possible to hypothesize a scenario for AATIP, which seems to have been a UFO program. A very different one than Project Blue Book or the MoD's program. It seems to have been instigated by what I can only describe as a believer faction in and on the fringes of government, and taken as its start point the possibility that some UFO sightings were attributable to extraterrestrial visitation. It then asked two related questions: **What technology would extraterrestrial visitation require, and can we figure out any of this technology?** Its main formal output was the thirty-eight technical studies listed in the attachment to the DIA's January 9, 2018, letter to Congress, but the more informal output was clearly UAP-related. However, to keep much of the work outside the scope of the Freedom of Information Act and to give the government some plausible deniability (it should be recalled that while all this was going on, the government's line was that no UFO investigations were going on), most of the work was done by Bigelow Aerospace. What makes this even murkier is the fact that Bigelow was interested in this and spending money on it long before he got the DIA contract, through organizations that he funded, including the National Institute for Discovery Science (NIDS). Thus, there's a degree of uncertainty about UFO work done by Bigelow Aerospace after they got the AATIP contract, in terms of on what side of the line it fell. UFO-related information was certainly being sent to the DIA in progress reports, but was this wanted, and if so, why didn't it find its way into the thirty-eight technical reports? Was it something that the DIA had requested but kept off the books by treating it as outside the scope of the contract? Was it Bigelow's "passion project," meaning that his team offered up UFO material to the DIA in parallel with the contracted material as a sort of "extra," but with the DIA not acting on it?

In theory, with any government contract, a government employee is designated as the Contracting Officer Representative, responsible for ensuring that the contracted goods or services are delivered on time and on target, so nothing should be provided that isn't required. But lines can be blurry, especially with intelligence projects on sensitive subjects. And in government, few subjects are more sensitive than UFOs. The ultimate irony is that all the spin about advanced aerospace threats may not have been aimed at the public or the media, but at an internal, government audience. Just as we rebranded UFOs into UAPs to get the subject taken more seriously in the MoD, so the DIA may have done a similar thing to get past their own "gatekeepers" who might have nixed the project if they'd realized its true purpose. This would certainly explain why, years after the project was conceived, the DoD is having difficulty finding out what exactly was done in their name, with public affairs officer statements flip-flopping all over the place when it comes to explaining what AATIP did—and didn't do. As is so often the case with this subject, even if further documents emerge and other retired government officials speak out, the public is unlikely ever to know the full story.

This is easily the most detailed account that I've given of my time investigating UFOs for the MoD, sharing my direct personal experience of the intelligence assessment Project Condign and the MoD's more general UFO work, and using this inside knowledge to give what I hope is an informed assessment of what has been going on in the United States. While I've delved deeper into specific cases elsewhere, this is the clearest insight I've ever given into the mindset that government, military, and intelligence community personnel adopt when they approach this topic. It's not popular with everyone, particularly those who take a more New Age or spiritual view of the subject, but it is what it is. However, before closing, I want to set out a more personal manifesto. Call it, perhaps, a roadmap to the stars. I choose those words deliberately, echoing the motto of the UK's Royal Air Force: *Per ardua ad astra*, **meaning** *Through adversity to the stars.*

Humankind's destiny is out there, among the stars. We will voyage to the stars not simply out of curiosity and the human desire to explore, though the quest for knowledge for its own sake is arguably a key part of what makes us human. Above all, we will do this because we must. At present, humanity has all its eggs in one basket. Planet Earth is our home, but if disaster strikes, it will be not only where the human adventure begins but where it ends. Nuclear war, global pandemic, comet or asteroid impact, runaway climate change, and perhaps other perils may befall us. Even if we dodge all these bullets, one day our sun will expand, making life on Earth impossible. When this happens, in the far future, some have speculated that humanity might migrate to one of the outer planets, or perhaps to an artificial space station that could be placed in the sun's new habitable zone, even after Earth is no longer inhabitable. But such migration—within our solar system—only perpetuates the problem. Humanity will still have all its eggs in one basket, and any sufficiently major calamity would drive us to extinction. It's not just human beings, of course; Earth is home to a dizzying array of life-forms, all of them unique. All of them walking the same tightrope that we walk. Thus, the development of viable interstellar travel is an existential issue for humanity and indeed for all life on Earth.

The road may be a long and dangerous one, and the challenges are vast. At the sorts of speeds our current space probes can reach, it would take around 75,000 years to get to the closest star aside from our own sun—and we don't yet know if it has any habitable planets. Maybe there are sub–light speed technologies (propulsion systems utilizing nuclear fission or matter-antimatter annihilation have been postulated) that could dramatically shorten the journey, but we'd still be talking in terms of years. Perhaps some sort of suspended animation could be developed to deal with long journeys, or maybe gene editing could extend human life spans and make other changes that would enable us to deal with this problem. Or perhaps the "generation ship" concept can be developed, where distant descendants of the original travelers complete the journey begun by their ancestors. Given the sheer size of the universe (light takes around one and a half seconds to travel from Earth to the moon, around eight minutes to the sun, and over four years to the nearest star after the sun), viable interstellar travel may need faster-than-light travel. Our current understanding of physics suggests no object can be accelerated beyond the speed of light, though our understanding of the laws of physics constantly evolves and has been proven incorrect before. However, if light speed is an insurmountable barrier, maybe the laws of physics nonetheless permit a "workaround." That, of course, brings us back to AATIP and the papers exploring such concepts as warp drive, wormholes, and stargates. Whatever the journey looks like, it will probably be a journey of several steps. First, a permanent human presence on the moon; next, a colony on Mars; and ultimately, traveling beyond our solar system and establishing a human presence on planets orbiting other stars, so that never again will all our eggs be in the same basket here on Earth.

I hope that human ingenuity will deliver these outcomes, but it's worth mentioning two other possibilities that might get us there quicker than currently seems imaginable. The first possibility is that artificial intelligence results in quantum leap breakthroughs. AI might result in theoretical physics insights and practical engineering designs that would give us viable interstellar travel. The second, of course, is that other intelligences exist in the universe and that one of them could decide to give us a helping hand. This takes us to a related issue: Once humanity goes interstellar, what might we find? Unless we think there's something almost literally magical about Earth, we'll likely find our planet is quite ordinary. This is an example of the so-called mediocrity principle: Simply put, in this context, there's nothing special about Earth and there's nothing special about life. If true, this argues that the chances of there being just two civilizations in the cosmos are as vanishingly small as the chances of there being just one—that is, us. By reapplying the mediocrity principle, and the laws of probability, one is led to the inescapable conclusion that humanity won't be the most advanced civilization in the universe. Playing the odds, we're likely somewhere in the middle, which raises the intriguing question of what more advanced civilizations might look like. Science fiction movies often imply alien technology only a few hundred years ahead of ours. I suspect this is so that an inevitable defeat of an alien invasion doesn't seem too farfetched. Professor Stephen Hawking famously warned, "**If aliens visit us, the**

outcome would be much as when Columbus landed in America, which didn't turn out well for the Native Americans." The reality is likely to be quite different, if one considers timescales. In a universe nearly fourteen billion years old, the odds that the first civilization we encounter will be only a few hundred years ahead of us seem slim. What might a bigger gap look like? Depending on which estimate you accept, the ape/human split came somewhere between five and seven million years ago, but with our fourteen-billion-year timescale to play with, seven million years is just a heartbeat. What might a gap of several hundred million or a couple of billion years look like? The science fiction writer Arthur C. Clarke once wrote that "**any sufficiently advanced technology is indistinguishable from magic,**" and that's what we'll likely be dealing with. There may be other surprises.

In 2010 I attended two Royal Society discussion meetings in the United Kingdom. The first was titled "**The Detection of Extraterrestrial Life and the Consequences for Science and Society**" and the second "**Toward a Scientific and Societal Agenda on Extraterrestrial Life.**" Speaking at the first, former NASA chief historian Steven Dick speculated that we might be living in a "**largely post-biological universe**" where life-forms would include "**immortal thinking machines.**" There were no gasps of amazement from the audience at such a provocative statement. One could argue that he was preaching to the converted, but it's worth bearing in mind that this was more than ten years ago now, and a lot of water has passed under the bridge. The debate about a possible alien megastructure orbiting Tabby's Star and the speculation that the cigar-shaped object named 'Oumuamua might have been a derelict alien spacecraft speak to a new reality.

As increasing numbers of exoplanets are discovered, it seems that it's only a matter of time before we discover other Earths. Words such as "**astrobiology**," "**biosignatures**," and "**technosignature**" are now commonplace. Even UFOs, once derided as a fringe topic, have newfound respectability, courtesy of AATIP, the US Navy encounters, and the associated presidential and congressional interest. Some believe this is acclimatization, ahead of some official announcement— "**disclosure**," if you like. I think it's just progress. The inevitable, inexorable advancement of our science and technology, as we close in on the answer to one of the biggest and most profound questions that we can ask: "**Are we alone in the universe?**"

With the seemingly exponential march of progress and quickening pace of events, that question may be answered within a generation. And if humanity does realize that it shares this universe with other life-forms—biological and post-biological alike—with technologies that are indistinguishable from magic, what then? All I can say with any degree of certainty is that one chapter of the human story will end, and a new chapter will begin.

2

UFO DISCLOSURE AND THE THEORY OF WOW

Grant Cameron[1]

I am going to discuss my new theory about the UFO phenomena and alien disclosure. This will be a rundown of what the intelligence behind the phenomena is doing. I call it "The Theory of WOW."

On December 16, 2017, the front-page headlines of *The New York Times*, *The Washington Post*, and *Politico* confirmed that the American government had funded a secret research program on UFOs. It is not a coincidence that these three major news outlets in the United States decided on the exact same day to run a story about how the DoD (Department of Defense) in 2007 received $22 million of undisclosed (to the public) money from the Senate to study the phenomena. Looking at the depth of the articles, I can see that the story took about two months to put together. Therefore, the articles were planned to all be released at the same time. It was a setup. I maintain this is typical of what the US government has been doing all along: leaking material since the UFO phenomena went public in 1947.

The initial instance was with Kenneth Arnold, after he had the first public acclaimed sighting of what he called flying saucers over Mount Rainier in June of 1947. After Arnold reported the sighting, a government agency showed up and gave him two 8x11 photographs of UFOs from the Fourth Air Force, in order to convince him that what he saw was real. They did this because they wanted to be the ones to manage the story. More to the point, I maintain that sort of strategy has been part of a simultaneous government-run cover-up and a government-run disclosure. For instance, if they wanted to disclose the truth about UFOs, they would stand the president up and we would be told what's going on. But they're not disclosing, and they are not covering up. And at the same time, there have been a massive number of leaked government documents over the years to the UFO community. I think what they are doing is a controlled slow leak.

Interesting enough, the intelligence behind the phenomena is doing the same thing. They give us a little and then they take it away. Believe me, if "**the intelligence**" wanted you to know what was really going on, they would land on the White House lawn, so we would all know for sure that they are here. For whatever reason, they're not doing that. They're not covering up, and they're not disclosing either. They are doing something in between.

Another example of this incongruous policy can be seen in the December 16, 2017, articles. The *New York Times* piece said that the secret government program was called the **Advanced Aerospace Threat Identification (AATI)**. But in an article the same morning the *Washington Post* added the word "program" to their story, making the official name the **Advanced Aerospace Threat Identification Program (AATIP)**. Both papers have high-level sources inside the Pentagon and would not run a story unless they had conferred with the Pentagon. They would have asked their sources the name of the program and if it was for real. When the sources inside the Pentagon say, "**Yes, it is for real,**" only then can the writers run with the story. But when two different names are given to reporters for the program, I think that this sort of disagreement on the specific details makes the story unconfirmable.

This sort of doublespeak is something the government has been doing all along. They would release the same material a few times, but they change some small detail each time. By creating this confusion we remain uncertain if what they're putting out is true. A perfect example of this was how in their 2017 article in *The New York Times*, the photo and online video that were released say "**with permission from the Defense Department's Advanced Aerospace Threat Identification Program.**" The photo/video credit is clearly printed below the image: "**U.S. Department of Defense (DOD).**" However, the head of public affairs for the Pentagon said at the same time, "**We can absolutely assure you that we did not release any videos.**" *Wired* magazine quotes a Pentagon spokesperson as saying: "**The official who is authorized to release this video on behalf of DOD did not approve the release of this video . . . I stand firm that we did not release those videos.**"[2]

So now, if the government says they didn't release the videos, we are faced with the questions, who released the videos and are they real? I think if the government ever confirmed the release of real, honest information, it could mean official disclosure. That's game over; the cover-up falls apart. That is not happening, but what is happening is a gradual slow-leaking disclosure.

The government did the same thing with the Area 51 story. A man by the name of Bob Lazar came forward with a W-2 form indicating he worked for Navy intelligence, with the stories that there were supposed crashed flying saucers and a live alien there at the desert base. But like the *New York Times* story, there turns out to be no proof for any of this.

The government spokespeople denied the whole story. First, they said there is no Area 51, saying it is just a top-secret military base. Two decades later President Obama confirmed there was an Area 51, but wouldn't talk about it. They leak information and then deny it. They do this over and over again.

Take a look at the CIA. This was how an actual example of the process was described to me. If you are directing a movie in Hollywood about the CIA and they hear about it, they have two choices. One, they can either kill you, or two, they manage the direction they want you to go. What I was told they do is call you up and they say: "**I hear you're making a movie on the CIA. We would like to come by and see if we can help you get some background information on what you are doing.**" Then they start feeding you material to make sure you go in the direction they want. It's a "quid pro quo." That is how it's done. The Hollywood director ends up portraying the CIA as good guys who are seen as saving the world. This is obviously because the people in charge want to manage the media.

However, what I'm going to show you is that the intelligence behind the phenomena is doing exactly the same thing in their own way, and having fun with us at the same time. For instance, one of the bizarre elements of the video released by *The New York Times* showed pilots of the USS *Nimitz* aircraft carrier stationed off Southern California tracking a strange-looking object. What is seen in the online video is a few seconds of a white Tic Tac–looking thing exhibiting very bizarre behavior; such a drop from 80,000 feet to sea level in 7/8 of a second—impossible for today's jets.

The important question is why did the Tic Tac make this maneuver in front of the advancing fighter jets? It was obviously showing off its capabilities. Minutes later as the jets made another pass there was suddenly another object under the water, making it appear that a ship has just sunk. One can almost imagine the laughter of the UFO intelligence as they sent an object to make big bubbles for the observing jets.

It is evident that the UFO was playing with the jets. For instance, when the pilots were radioed to go to a certain flight location by the command post, all of a sudden they get a report that the Tic Tac was there instantly; meanwhile, the pilots were still twenty miles away from the target. They were saying, "**Hey, we know what you are doing and we are already over here.**"

When the pilots go "wow," the UFOs have accomplished their mission. The UFOs go away, and they haven't been seen since at that location.

It is this sort of behavior by the intelligence behind the UFO phenomenon that I call my analysis **The Theory of Wow**. When I came to this understanding of the wow aspect of UFO reports, everything started to make sense. The theory is that all they are doing is trying to get us to say "**wow**" to realize we are not alone. The idea was even expressed in a *New York Times* May 2019 article with the headline "**'Wow, What Is That?' Navy Pilots Report Unexplained Flying Objects.**" The whole UFO phenomenon may be just a plan to raise consciousness. Let me explain.

Conceivably it could all come down to this just being a science fair project on Alpha Centauri or Zeta Reticule. The teachers say to the children, "**Okay, we got these natives on planet Earth and we want to get their attention. What would you do?**"

So, the kids in grade one would say, "**Let's put lights on the craft.**" It seems like a joke. But it's not a joke, because why would UFOs need lights? You know why: So you can see them! Do you think we kept the lights on the helicopters when we went into Pakistan to get bin Laden? When you start looking at UFO reports you're going to see a wide display of lighting formations, and almost every one is different. The lights are not for them. They are for us. They want us to go "wow," and then go tell friends what we saw. A prime example is the August 1974 John Lennon encounter. He said he was so close to the UFO that he could have hit it with a brick. Lennon said, "**There were these white lights going around the edge of the craft with a red light on the top.**" The question arises, do you really think they need flashing lights around the edge and a red light on top to go through interstellar space? No! They just wanted to get Lennon's attention so he would know he is looking at a UFO and go "**wow!**" And the huge audience of people that follow his career would then know he saw a UFO.

The same thing happened with me when I saw my first

UFO lights in 1975. The observation threw me down the rabbit hole that I have never left. That was the same year there was a series of UFO incursions over US Air Force Strategic Air Command (SAC) bases, such as Loring Air Force Base in Maine, Wurtsmith Air Force Base in Michigan, and Minot Air Force Base in North Dakota, just south of where I was living in Canada. All these bases were housing nuclear warhead missiles, and the UFOs were in the restricted area where the nuclear weapons were. Did they turn off their lights as they came into the highly restricted, guarded area? No, and that should tell us something. Did the guards and the officials who had to investigate the incursions go "wow"? You can bet on it.

When UFOs appeared over their nuclear weapon storage areas with very bright lights, the military personnel started to freak out. They just hovered there. It was a message. They wanted us to think, "this cannot be ours. We must not be alone." The indirect message makes us think.

My experience happened the same year Travis Walton was abducted for five days. Why would they take him for five days? Were the alien abduction medical teams on strike? No. They kept him for five days because they knew that would get attention and a big wow. It worked. Walton to this day is still one of the most popular people on the UFO lecture circuit.

The messages are also an ever-evolving situation. Back in the 1950s, '60s, and '70s, UFOs used to be accompanied by what was called "angel hair." Most people today would not even know what angel hair is, but it used to be quite common in UFO sightings and UFO fly-bys. These very thin cotton-like strands, like spiderwebs, would slowly float down and hang off the trees or on the ground. People would pick it up and it would sort of melt away. It could never be analyzed because it would dissolve too quickly. If this was part of the UFO propulsion it would still be going on. It isn't, because angel hair was just part of an evolving circus act to get everyone to pay attention, go "wow," and then tell others.

In UFO history we see the pattern of making contact shifting too. People think that what is happening now happened then. I can guarantee you it's a completely different ball game. We see the ability to attract attention with weird actions as in the story of Budd Hopkins, the well-known alien abduction researcher. You might think that he had a rational idea and one day he thought: **"Oh, I think I want to study alien abductions."** No, that is not what happened.

Here's how he got wowed: At seven years old, maybe not by accident, Hopkins heard Orson Welles's *War of the Worlds* radio broadcast in 1938. He was listening with his parents and they started to freak out. A neighbor came over with a gun and said, **"We're going to the top of the hill to take on these Martians and defend our world."** The event presented him with all this intense emotion and interest around ETs. Twenty-six years later, in 1964, again maybe not by accident, he is on Cape Cod. It's midday, and he is driving his car with a few friends when they all see a craft hovering in front of the car. As they drive the object paces the car, almost like the craft was there because of them. Now obsessed, Hopkins goes back the next day to the same location and drives the same distance to see how long the object was with him. He starts reading all sorts of related material. Then to top it all off, in 1975, he goes into his corner liquor store, run by one of his buddies. Tell me this is random: His friend says, "**I had this weird experience yes-terday. I am driving along and there's this flying saucer off in a field, about a hundred yards from the road. There were these alien beings standing outside the craft and they were digging holes.**" Budd says, "**Really?**"

The next day he drives to that location and, sure enough, there are fifteen holes five inches deep in a field. He stops at a nearby apartment complex and asks the night watchman if he saw anything going on in that field the other night. The guy says, "**Oh yeah! There were these strange lights.**" And bam! He's sucked down the rabbit hole and ends up studying the abduction phenomenon. He writes one of the most famous UFO books ever, *Missing Time*. When was the last time you heard about aliens flying across the galaxy, and then standing around a craft with shovels digging holes? The whole thing was a setup. The purpose was to get Hopkins to go "wow" and get involved to help tell the story that we are not alone.

Another similar story involves Steve Murillo, who got wowed and ended up running the Los Angeles Mutual UFO Network investigation group. He was a Navy pilot who was with his wife at their rooftop pool in northern Los Angeles. He's just come home from doing karate, he is feeling worn out, so his wife goes down into the house to get him a glass of wine. She brings him a glass and then she says, "**Oh, I forgot my own drink.**"

She leaves, and that's when Murillo has the UFO experi-ence. They don't want her there. So, she forgets her drink and she goes downstairs while these five objects come shooting over his head. At first, he thinks they're geese. Then they fly right over his head in formation, then go off to the other part of the sky. He is watching them make another strange maneuver and they fly off. Now the question is: Did they have to make that movement? Did they have to come in a V-formation? I asked him directly, "**Do you think this was a random event? You just happened to be there?**" He said, "**No, I don't.**" It was planned, the whole thing. They let him have this sighting and he's dragged down the rabbit hole. Now he is totally into this stuff running the biggest UFO meeting group in California.

Let's look at what happened at the Ariel school in Rhodesia, Africa, 1994. A movie about this event is coming out soon. There were sixty-two schoolkids in a schoolyard at recess and an object landed. These sort of grey-type beings with real tight-fitting black suits appeared.

One of the witnesses was a girl from Hamilton, Canada, whose parents were missionaries there for the Salvation Army. She recalls running along the edge of the schoolyard, where there are logs, not fences. She and her friends are bouncing up and down on these logs and she sees in a flash out of the corner of her eye a grey-type alien being hovering above the ground. But he's not stationary; he is imitating them bouncing on the log. Then she looks toward the alien and, boom, it's right in front of her face.

She and the others are frozen while she experiences what is called "**rapid image cycling.**" This happens in a lot of cases. Suddenly the person looking at the alien starts to see quickly firing images coming into their mind, like a hundred a second. While that is happening, she starts getting ideas about technology. Basically, the message she received was: "**You've got technology but you could do better.**" She said the last image she saw was this giant sort of explosion. She said that didn't mean that the world was going to explode. The girl beside her was getting environmental images coming out of the alien's eyes. Images like we are destroying the world; the trees are going to die; that kind of stuff. There were also incidents at schoolyards in Ireland, in Russia where a ship landed in front of a bunch of kids, and in Australia involving 300 children. The question is, why does the intelligence land at a schoolyard? Most of these kids were between six and thirteen years old and many talked about receiving telepathic images coming into their heads. The question is: Are these kids telling the truth? If they are, look at the messages the aliens are trying to get across to us and the next generation.

Additionally, there is the idea that all UFO crafts have been the same since the first sightings. This is a fallacy. Let's go back to the earliest modern sightings in 1896 and 1897. What was seen then were huge wooden ships flying around with propellers on them. These were not one or two sightings; there were thousands, mostly on the West Coast. Then there was what was called Foo Fighters. Strange balls of light flying alongside the wings of both Germans and the Americans' planes during World War II. So, there was a huge change from these wood ships. Then after the war we saw a phenomenon known as ghost rockets around 1946, occurring only around Sweden. But if this is a random phenomenon, why would it not appear in other countries? Because the pattern is that they are doing different things at different time periods in different places.

The next shift in the pattern comes in the 1950s with George Adamski. From 1947 to 1952 there were lots of sightings but nobody was talking about aliens. Then in 1952

Adamski appears on the scene, a week after the detonation of the hydrogen bomb. He goes public with the statement that the ETs have given him a message for the world: "**Stop using nuclear weapons.**"

In 1961 the whole UFO story changes again, from friendly, beautiful humans to ugly, small grey beings. We have the beginning of the abduction scenarios with the Betty and Barney Hill case. The beings they encounter are wearing hats. Why would any alien from Zeta Reticulum wear a hat? The Hills see a classic UFO craft with windows around the sides, something that is very rarely reported about UFOs anymore. Like changing the pages of a book, their designs keep updating. Then on March 13, 1997, there was a remarkable sighting of the Phoenix lights. People all over the city saw a huge craft with lights on the edges estimated to be about a mile across. It floated a couple hundred feet off the ground right over the city like it was heading to get a case of beer. Ten thousand people saw it and everyone said, "**Wow, look at the size of that thing.**" But did the craft really need to be a mile across? No, but it all starts to make sense if you realized that maybe they're just trying to get our attention.

What about crop circles? Why would ETs make a crop circle and why are they all completely different from each other? Do aliens need to make symbols in the wheat fields of England? If they wanted to say they are here, they would just land and tell us what's going on. But if they want you to think deeper that is something else. The whole crop circle phenomena began in the early 1980s, with just simple round circles. Now there are about 4,000 of them from the 1980s, '90s, and into the 2000s. These were elaborate designs of symbols, mathematical equations, or complex Mayan designs all laid out in fields of either wheat, barley, and sometimes corn. When people see these on the ground or from aerial views, everyone goes, **"Wow, how'd they do that?"** No one can explain the legitimate crop circles or how these intricate overlaying patterns are made. In some instances, the growing crops have been woven together. The circle called **the Triple Julia Set** had over 400 concentric circles that appeared overnight in a rain storm. It was a progressive operation into the 2000s, which got more and more sophisticated each year, creating more "wow" moments!

I'm a good friend of Colin Andrews, who coined the term "crop circles." He has been quiet on the fact that he is also an experiencer and had been aware of aliens since 1950. One day in 1983, he is in England driving past an odd, flatted grass pattern in a field. This was his wow moment. He said, **"My old life was completely over. It changed as soon as I saw my first crop circle."**

However, for Colin something had already begun to percolate a few years earlier, in 1977. He was working in the communication business and had just bought one of those reel-to-reel tape recorders. It was sitting on the floor in his living room and he wanted to test it. He's plugged in a microphone, and the TV is going in the background. But as soon as he turns the tape recorder on, the TV goes blank and on comes a message with a very alien-sounding voice. Because he had just turned on the tape recorder at the same time, he was able to record the whole message. I think two million people in Britain heard this. This strange voice talked for about five minutes. The message basically says:

We come to warn you of the destiny of your race and
of your world, so that you may communicate it to
your fellow beings, the course that you must take to
avoid disasters which threaten your world and the
beings on our world and the beings on our worlds
around you. This is in order that you may share in
the Great Awakening as the planet passes through
the New Age of Aquarius. The New Age can be a time
of great peace and evolution for your race. But only if
your rulers are made aware of the evil forces that can
overshadow their judgment.

It goes on like that for about five minutes. Did Colin just happen to turn on his tape recorder as the message came on the TV? Was it just a coincidence, or another wow moment for his benefit and for the work he would do with crop circles later?

ITN (Independent Television News), the UK-based television production company that was broadcasting, was flooded with calls asking what's going on. People were asking, **"What happened to my TV? What was that alien message?"** The ITN network did two investigations into what and how something like this could happen. Then British government did a couple of investigations. The only thing they determined was that two TV towers sent a signal out toward Wiltshire county, the exact location where the whole crop circles craze would soon begin.

Speaking of crop circle formations, some experiencers report that they wake up with marks on their bodies. Some are like burn marks and cuts. There are many triangles.

Does an advanced intergalactic race need to put triangles on people's bodies? The more logical explanation would be that the experiencer goes, "Wow. How did that mark or cut get on my body while I was asleep in bed?" I say the reason you have this mark is because you could wake up from an abduction-type dream and say, **"It was just a dream; it didn't really happen."** But when you look at your arm and see this marking, you go, **"Oh, it wasn't a dream."** I don't think these markings necessarily have any meaning, except that they are signaling you to know: **"Yes, this is for real. It's not a dream**." If you didn't have the marks people would just say they imagined the contact experience. The physical marks are the evidence to prove it was real.

Another wow factor is the cattle mutilations. Almost all cattle mutilations are bloodless. Why are they bloodless? Because if they weren't bloodless, they would not have the mysterious wow factor. I think they drain the blood out of the cows, just so we can say, *"This is just amazing. Where did the blood go? There's not a single drop of blood. Wow, we couldn't do that."*

In one case the mutilated cow had no incision but its heart was missing. Why would the UFO intelligence do something so bizarre? They do it because the people who hear the story go "wow." In the same way the UFO comes back after mutilating the cow and drops it from one hundred feet into the farmer's yard where it is easy to find. Why would you go back and drop the cow? Why would you make bizarre, grotesque mutilations? They do it because they want that "wow." They want people to take pictures, do investigations, and tell people. Without the wow it is just a cow that died.

Here is the one story I love the best. A UFO lands and an alien comes out of the ship and asks a witness to get him a pail of water. I mean, seriously, this craft comes across the galaxy and it needs a pail of water? So, the guy goes off and gets a pail of water, gives it to the alien, and the UFO flies off. What's the point of that? The point is that it was something to raise awareness, to take notice, to think about it—to spread the message we are not alone.

I feel that eventually the consciousness will rise enough and there will be an awareness and openness to their presence. It will be like when gay people got the right to be recognized as equal human beings. Or when Black Americans got equal rights. Consciousness will reach a tipping point where the subject is in common discussions. At that point everyone will say, "**Yeah of course, there are aliens. I knew it all the time**."

Another major component of the phenomena is the misunderstanding that seeing a UFO is a random event. Let me absolutely assure you, it is not. If you see a UFO you are part of the game. There is no such thing as a random sighting. They are all intentional. Yet back in 1975 when you saw one, you thought it was a chance thing just flying by. You would say, "**Interesting, let's go for a beer**."

A good example of this is the *Nimitz* story that was leaked to *The New York Times*. The UFOs showed up over the aircraft carrier off the coast of San Diego in the southern Pacific. If it was a random event, it would have been there once. Yet they came back the next day and again for about a week. It is like that famous case, the Rendlesham Forest UFO landing in December 1980. For three nights in a row a lit-up craft landed in the woods next to a joint

US/UK air force base at RAF Woodbridge, England. We learned much later that the base housed unlawful nuclear missile warheads. But there is very little randomness and a whole lot of "wow" at the Rendlesham event.

Or take the Skinwalker Ranch, the now renowned paranormal place in Utah that the billionaire Bob Bigelow used to own. He had people there for seven years and all sorts of paranormal experiences occurred. There were space/time portals opening up. There were big giant wolves the size of a small horse walking around. There were also hundreds of sightings in the six years or seven years. However, when the reporter who broke the Area 51 story, George Knapp, went to investigate, he saw nothing. But when astrophysicist Eric Davis came to the ranch he had all sorts of paranormal experiences. The difference between the Knapp and Davis experiences is that they wanted Davis to have a "wow" daylight UFO experience just as he graduated with a Ph.D.

The fallacy is that we believe that there are external events that happen to us. We believe sightings and encounters are separate events. This is not a one-off. We don't realize that we are connected to them. We may be the ones manifesting them. On another level we may have agreed to be part of whatever this thing is. Once we have an experience, the phenomenon follows us around like a hitchhiker. Let me make it clear: There are no random events. It seems that almost 90 percent of experiencers have paranormal phenomenon as well. All of these are wow events. If this was random, why are these contactees experiencing things in their homes? Are they connected to a grander occurrence? They live in a world of wow.

When I got into the game after having my first sighting

in 1975, it was thought that if you saw one UFO in your lifetime, that was fine. But if you saw two you were considered crazy. Back then I would have thought you were crazy. Everybody thought that when you saw a UFO it was a totally arbitrary thing. You just happen to be in the right place at the right time, or you might consider it the wrong place at the wrong time. Now we know, in fact, some people are called "**lifers.**" For instance, if somebody comes up to me at a conference, and says they have had an abduction-like experience, I know it started when they were a child. This is why they are called lifers. The phenomenon continues throughout the course of their life.

My own UFO story is one filled with wow. My investigations got weird when I started to ask what was behind this whole phenomenon. This led to a major wow experience where I had a noetic-type download experience that told me the answer to the UFO mystery lay in understanding consciousness was the key, with the realization this whole phenomena was really "**all about consciousness.**"

When I started giving lectures on consciousness, the whole UFO community disowned me, like I had lost my marbles. They felt I should just stick with what I know, like the US presidents and FOIA documents. I said, "**No. If you want to know what is going on with this phenomenon, don't you think we should study people who have had experiences?**"

For instance, many contactees say that at one point during their experience, they knew the answer to everything in the universe. That is a bizarre thing to say. I would say, "**Well, how do you know about the far side of the universe?**" They say, "**I had a download experience so I know.**"

So, you get these people with a greatly expanded awareness, indicating that the phenomenon has taught them to shut down the left brain, rational ego mind, and give them the ability to access whatever information they want. It's all available. It is not that we have to learn anything, just a matter of developing the ability to connect to the higher self.

Now let's go a little deeper. In abductions people tend to black out. Most don't realize they're taken by aliens. Usually later in life something happens to wake them up. Suddenly they realize they have been having experiences their whole life. At first, it's very frightening, but in many hypnotic regressions back to the contact experience, the fear goes away. It is replaced by the realization that they feel they have a special reason for being on Earth. So the first question I ask every experiencer is: "**Do you believe you have a mission?**" They will say either "**Yeah, I know what it is**" or they say, "**I think so; I don't know what it is but somehow I think I've got a mission.**" It is as if they feel they have been chosen for something.

CONCLUSION

To sum it all up: This is not a random world. People chose to be a UFO experiencer. People chose to have a near-death experience to learn something. (Why is it that many UFO experiencers have had two NDEs?) I say researchers are making the wrong assumption. They assume it's one life. It is multiple lives. If we assume everything happening in the UFO world is random, nothing makes sense. Nothing happens by accident. If reincarnation is true, then everything changes, because we are living multiple lives, and you probably have an association with ETs in those other lives. (Incidentally, there may be more evidence for reincarnation than there is for the existence of UFOs.)

If it is one life, then as far as abductions, people are being taken against their will. But if we have multiple lives, these experiences and along with certain other things in your life, you have agreed to them and have to take personal responsibility for them. You can't say, **"I've got a terrible life."** You are the one choosing the cards. So, play the hand you have been dealt. Once you know you have multiple lives, then the idea of abductions changes. I asked Mary Rodwell, who has done 3,000 regressions. I said, **"Mary, is an abduction 100 percent a soul contract?"** She said, **"Absolutely!"** I believe if you regress all abductees back before this life, they all will say they agreed for this to happen.

Take the UFO contactee Kathy Marden, niece of Betty Hill and one of the researchers involved in **The Edgar Mitchell Foundation for Research into Extraterrestrial and Extraordinary Experiences** (FREE). She said, **"I don't know about agreeing to this experience. I can't believe this is true."** Then she had a past life regression and she said she couldn't believe the words coming out of her mouth: **"I chose this."**

It is the same with my friend Chris Bledsoe. Hollywood is doing a big thing with his dramatic UFO story. When he was hypnotically regressed by a psychiatrist from Harvard University, he was asked: **"When did you first encounter these beings?"** He said, **"They have been with me since before I was born."** This is the key. It is all part of a program that you've agreed to be involved in. It is there to either learn something or to teach other people. This is why these events don't just happen once to a person. It is something that you're either part of or you're not.

When you realize that UFOs are not random, you will understand that this is not a nuts-and-bolts phenomena either. That is the number one lesson I want to relay. If you think the UFO phenomena is just about hardware, you're never going to understand it. You need to know consciousness is the answer to the whole thing. Consciousness is *"the ground of being"* that changes all the rules about reality. Max Planck, Nobel laureate and the originator of quantum theory, spelled out the new reality this way: **"I regard consciousness as fundamental. I regard matter as derivative from consciousness. We cannot get behind consciousness. Everything that we talk about, everything that we regard as existing, postulates consciousness."**

Everything changes, and this is what they are teaching us. If the "intelligence" wanted to know what was going on they would come out and tell us, but they are not. They are giving us an indirect approach because they want us to think. They want us to reach a level of higher consciousness on our own. They are going at it slowly, attracting our attention with things that make us think deeply in order to blow our minds, and our normal way of thinking, thereby altering our beliefs and our notions of reality.

We won't be able to figure any of this out until we realize it is a demonstration of what can be called **"the nonlocal Mind."** When we all realize that essentially we are all aspects of that greater, infinite reality—it will certainly be a *Wow*!

3

EXTRATERRESTRIALS AND MULTIDIMENSIONAL NONLOCAL REALITY

Dr. J. J. Hurtak and Dr. Desiree Hurtak

"Beam me up, Scotty!" *Star Trek*'s Captain Kirk's teleportation depiction is not that far off from how those who have had extraterrestrial contact describe their experience of being taken onboard an alien spacecraft. There are numerous cases of human beings, and even cows and tractors, being "beamed" aboard spacecraft. An anti-gravity beam is the first thing that comes to mind, but in many cases humans have been taken through walls or windows. In the Smith-Thomas-Stafford abduction (January 20, 1976), which involved three women driving in a car in Kentucky, all three, and maybe their car, were picked up by a UFO. It started when they spotted a large red disc and then in minutes, a blue light engulfed their car and seized control. The local farmer confirmed their account by saying that he witnessed a flying aircraft that night shoot a beam of light at a car.

This is similar to the account of Garry Wood and Colin Wright in Scotland, who had an encounter on August 17, 1992, while driving on the highway near the Harperrig Reservoir. Above them they saw a large spacecraft and, although they tried to get away, they were engulfed by a **"curtain**

of white light." Then everything became a black void for what seemed like ten to fifteen seconds. Next, they found themselves driving on the wrong side of the road with several hours of missing time.[1] Could this be simple teleportation? Traveling by means of teleportation is currently being widely researched by quantum physicists.

Teleportation is what is described in *Star Trek*'s "**Beam me up, Scotty**" scenario, where the subject is standing on a platform one minute, and then instantaneously they "rematerialize" all their atoms in the exact same form in another location. How would this work? We know from quantum physics that changing the properties of one particle causes a related or "entangled" particle at a distant location to "*instantly*" react to the change, no matter how much space separates them. In fact, there is no limit to the distance over which quantum teleportation may operate.

In experiments conducted to prove this effect in 2017, from Ngari, Tibet, at an altitude of 5,100 meters (16,700 feet), photons, the smallest unit of measurable light, were teleported to China's Micius satellite at an altitude of ~500 kilometers. This allowed data to be transferred from a ground station to the satellite some 1,200 kilometers, or 750 miles, apart in space. So "outer space" allows for the same entangled configuration as we are finding on Earth.[2]

Quantum physicists are telling us that the universe is nonlocal and all space-time can be entangled, so traveling from one part to another if you have the right "sender/receiver mechanism" onboard a spacecraft could be literally instantaneous, thus "appearing" to move objects faster than light, but it's not a violation of the laws of the speed of light. It's Albert Einstein's "spooky action at a distance," and scientists all over the world are moving forward in studying this phenomenon.

Scientific researchers in China and Austria have transferred a symbolic image that existed in three-dimensional quantum states of something called a qutrit (tripartite unit of quantum information). Today, it is only information, and as much as four qubits were entangled and teleported between two chips.[3] Specifically, information was passed between the chips without any physical electronic cords or connections, but by quantum entanglement—that is, linking two particles using quantum physics.[4]

Nothing "alive" has ever been transferred, and many scientists feel it is impossible to do so. But this process is new and who knows what we can do in the future. It works because particles in the universe can be entangled, so all your atoms, theoretically, could instantly move to another place, and hopefully your consciousness along with them!

Although teleportation is an almost instant transmission of matter from one point to another, it may not be what is generally being described by many of those who have experienced close encounters with aliens, and especially those who have been "abducted," or transported to alien spaceships, usually in a defenseless or numbed state of mind. Here abductees report seeing aliens moving through walls, so it may not be teleportation at all. It may be that they can shift the molecules in their bodies into another frequency, even temporarily, so that they can pass through walls.

A witness named Petra in the Amy Rylance case of October 2001 watched Amy being moved out a window and toward a "huge spaceship" by a beam of light.[5] How does a physical form pass through a window? Moving bodies through walls and windows would involve the modulation of gravitational and matter waves of the body.

It seems that today there are two possible explanations for this occurrence. One is called "**quantum tunneling**," which focuses on electrons that are not just solid particles moving around the nucleus of the atom, but also act as waves in terms of quantum physics. As waves, electrons have the possibility of passing through a barrier without going around it. Scientists referred to them as probability waves or evanescent waves moving into propagating waves that can make it through the barrier. New research accepts that sometimes quantum bits can go through matter. Although there is only a very slight possibility that this can occur naturally, so much more if it was artificially controlled.

A second possible explanation comes when we recognized that there is also the possibility that the light beam witnessed in extraterrestrial encounters allows some of your electrons to rise to higher orbital levels so that you pass through the wall in a slightly different frequency state than the wall itself for a temporary period of time. This "higher frequency property of matter" is being researched in chemical and metallurgical laboratories today.

This last possibility may be the best explanation for what happened to John Velez, an artist who had several encounters and abductions by aliens from his bedroom. As usual, the aliens numb the body and/or the mind before the person is abducted. While remembering one of his encounters, John stated:

*I was taken from my bedroom one night. And I was
being carried out of the house. These beings have
the ability to literally walk through walls, doors,
solid objects. I don't know if it's some kind of a
mechanism, or whatever it is. And when we passed
through the back wall of my house, I momentarily
regained normal waking consciousness, and began to
fight them with all the strength I had.[6]*

So, there was some change of energy, at least related
to his consciousness awareness, in the process of going
through the wall during his abduction.

We could explain that this is taking place because atoms
are mostly empty space. The nucleus of an atom is about
10,000 to 100,000 times smaller than the entire atom. Most
of the atomic space is for the movement of electrons, which
exist outside the nucleus. So, the space of an atom is mostly
empty with tiny electrons moving around within it.

In fact, we know that it is the nature of electrons that
are involved with making things that appear solid. At the
lowest orbital level, there can be two electrons, each one
with a unique spin. By trying to put a third electron into
the lower orbital, one of the others has to leave or move to
a higher orbital level. But if one temporarily exchanges an
electron with that of the existing barrier, say electrons in a
glass window, a temporary exchange of particles could take
place without losing the original configuration of who we
are. So, your electrons simply exchange an electron temporarily with the wall and when you pass through it, you
either gain back the other needed electron or you go back

to the normal energy configuration that made you a solid.
Thus, these are two possibilities of how going through walls
might work, but until we actually get an explanation from
those who are using the technology, we will not know for
sure.

In many UFO observations, the alien spacecraft often
seems to materialize and dematerialize. This happens over
and over again. One of the most famous sightings is the
encounter associated with the Navy ship USS *Nimitz*, which
has been confirmed as a sighting of an "unidentified flying
object" by the Pentagon in *The New York Times* and other
news media on April 27, 2020: "**UFO Sighting: Ex-US Navy
Chief Reveals Moment Mystery Craft Vanished Before
His Eyes.**"[7] The story specifically noted that in November
2004 the Navy ordered two F/A-18 Super Hornet jets with
two Navy personnel in each to observe a UFO. Onboard
one jet was former commander David Fravor, a veteran
pilot who stated during his observation of them: "**As we approach it, and there is about 3,000 feet of altitude between
us, the thing rapidly accelerates and then—poof—it is
gone as it crosses our noses.**"[8] Is it reasonable to think that
the object was able to travel faster than what the "human
eye" or sophisticated cameras can detect?

There are many theoretical possibilities for how to travel
over vast distances in a spacecraft. One practical way often
proposed is to travel through hyperspace by using wormholes. In the popular media this has become known as traveling through "**stargates**," and there are some reports that
UFOs do use "portals" like stargates. Sounds like science
fiction? Stargates would cut years off the travel time if they
use an artificially created wormhole to temporarily travel

through hyperspace, where space and time bend together, causing two locations to meet.

How would a stargate work? A stargate is classified as an Einstein–Rosen bridge portal device. The theory of Einstein and Rosen was mainly to look at a Schwarzschild black hole. That was the historic start of the idea that was years ahead of its time when it was announced in 1935.[9]

Now in more modern times, movies like *Stargate* (1994) fantasize about what is called a two-way traversable wormhole, which was hypothesized in 1957 by physicist John A. Wheeler of Princeton University, who coined the term "wormhole."[10] A properly configured wormhole would allow people to come and go in both directions. He considered that "**the throat**," which is positioned between the two gates, connects normal space-time for almost instantaneous travel.

In 1988, M. S. Morris of Cal Tech co-authored a paper with Kip Thorne titled "**Wormholes in Space-Time and Their Use for Interstellar Travel: A Tool for Teaching General Relativity**," published in the *American Journal of Physics*.[11] This is a peer-reviewed journal. From here, the research kept going with more serious studies, and more unique movies were made as we moved up in our understanding of wormholes, such as the movie *Interstellar* (2014), which also added other dimensional realities.

The concept of traversable wormholes has certainly taken off in physics with peer-reviewed papers still continuing. We now think that Wheeler's traversable wormhole requires both a positive magnetic charge on one side and a negative one on the other to connect space and time at two or more different locations. Theoretically, some researchers believe there could be more than two wormholes within a single configuration.

Daniel L. Jafferis, associate professor of physics at Harvard University, has been leading the latest news. He pulls together string theory, supersymmetric quantum field theory, and quantum gravity. He prefers putting together black holes to make possible wormholes and says, "**From the outside perspective, travel through the wormhole is equivalent to quantum teleportation using entangled black holes.**"[12]

So, a wormhole actually could be two entangled black holes. Whether it is wormholes or black holes, scientists are seriously looking at these future possibilities. We, the authors, would claim it requires one black hole and one white hole entangled or joined together. A black hole is the way in and a white hole is the way out. So, with the two quantum entangled holes—most likely artificially formed—one could go forward and reverse, establishing wormhole travel.

This is because light rays must bend outward to escape on the other side of the wormhole.

Research might explain theoretically how such wormholes could work, but it's still just a theory. Some experiments have included the Casimir Effect, involving vacuum mechanics in making this work. Hence, physicists have derived an equation for wormhole possibilities, where the Einstein–Rosen bridge equals the Einstein–Podolsky–Rosen Paradox (ER = EPR). In layperson's terms, a zero point is created, allowing particles to move through a hyper-dimensional reality from one space-time to another. Wormholes are believed to hold a time machine effect, beginning from the time of their creation, where one opening would be in the past/present and the other could be in the future.

In addition to teleporting objects, or moving people through walls, aliens seem to have the ability to function in and out of the third dimension, as seen in some UFO sightings. Yes, some UFOs may be simply physical "nuts and bolts" craft flying locally in our interstellar neighborhood, but more and more accounts are describing UFOs that seem simply to vanish, but are they going just to another place in our universe through a wormhole, or literally changing dimensions? There are some UFO contactees who posit the latter. Wormholes may not just operate from one place to another in the universe; they may be dimensional doorways leading to other realities beyond our space-time.

As in the case of Commander Fravor from the *Nimitz*, many reports claim people see a UFO close by, and then suddenly the craft just immediately disappears. Is it simply the manipulation of light, like an invisibility cloaking device? Perhaps it may be more an actual "jump" into a type of fifth-dimensional reality. Whether we look at the existence of mini black holes[13] or not, the fifth dimension seems to be just on the other side of the veil of light, perhaps on the other side of the black hole and the white hole, as a threshold of the galactic portal. Moreover, if we were to consider the fifth to the eighth dimensions and the possibility of beings living there, we would get closer to the notion of time travel, as time—past, present, and future—would all be connected and completely nonlocal in these higher dimensional realities.

Hyperspace is only a hypothesis and thus has many definitions. But the idea of traveling through hyperspace implies the possibility of entering these other dimensions temporarily and then exiting them as needed.

Still, the fifth dimension is most probably another way to step beyond our space-time–matter reality and may be used by alien species as they appear and disappear from sight. We exist in the third dimension, which can be defined by the length, width, and height of any object. However, Einstein reported we also exist in the fourth dimension, which he associated with time. So, what about the fifth dimension or even the eighth dimension? String theorists believe that the universe may have ten or eleven dimensions, so why would life be stuck in just one or two?

In new scientific theories, such as the Randall-Sundrum "**braneworld model**," matter is confined to our dimensions, but gravity "leaks" into the other dimensions. We normally observe 3D matter and hence we can see physical reality, but light and gravity may not be limited to our dimensions.

It can be argued that the UFO phenomenon is pushing us into an understanding of new quantum possibilities, and even a multidimensional science. The declassified Majestic 12 documents, via investigators Robert Wood, formerly an aerospace engineer at McDonnell Douglas, and his son Ryan have given further evidence of a greater technical matrix behind the UFO experience.[14]

The path of "**making contact**" with extraterrestrials may be difficult to imagine with our current scientific understanding. There seems to be a variety of intelligences in outer space and, thus, likely a variety of technologies being employed. Perhaps most are not that hard to comprehend through the new avenues being experimented with quantum physics. However, we must choose our approach carefully, knowing that some new scientific theories point to the idea that we ourselves may be nonlocal and multidimensional inhabitants of a living planet, representing intelligent life as one of many throughout the universe.

As we grow in our own technological knowledge, there seems to be a move away from those like Donald Keyhoe, co-founder of the **National Investigations Committee on Aerial Phenomena** (NICAP), and Walt Andrus, the former head of the **Mutual UFO Network** (MUFON), who both sought only scientific investigations that had metallic evidences. We are now beginning to see that there is much more to the whole phenomenon than just what is called in the field of UFOlogy "**nuts and bolts.**"

DO EXTRATERRESTRIALS READ OUR MINDS?

Close Encounters of the Third Kind (1977) seemed strange to moviegoers when they watched the contactee constructing a mountain in his living room. Few understood the message that consultant Dr. J. Allen Hynek was trying to convey. For those who have had contact, there seems to be something placed in their heads. That is, once there is an encounter, even of the "first kind," it seems to create an ongoing connection.

Contactees claim they have been implanted, like we implant tags in cats and dogs to track them. Some implants appear to be small devices, but could it be that an alien species, as many witnesses claim, normally communicates telepathically? It is possible that this way they can establish a type of "signal alignment" within our brains that we have yet to understand. Enough to say that we are learning that the brain does not work solely by means of neurochemical reactions, but seems to also work via bio-photonic and electron oscillations as well as nonlocality. Many contactees report that communication during their extraterrestrial encounters was not by speaking aloud, but came to them telepathically. So, do the space aliens have the means to "get into our heads" and become consciously entangled with us?

According to journalist Linda Moulton Howe, in her "Citizen Hearing on Disclosure" report in Washington, DC, in 2013, a military officer was part of an arranged contact with an ET. When they got together, the information that was passed to the soldier from the alien was not just a brief "Hello" but seven levels of information that were fed into his brain. So much so that the strong, young soldier literally passed out. In addition, Howe points out that just as the information went into his brain, so information was taken out.[15]

This coincides with reports that we, the authors, have investigated of Carlos Diaz from Tepoztlán, Mexico. We personally interacted with Diaz to validate the claims he stated to both ourselves and other researchers. We also examined his photographs and the thermal imaging enhancements produced by other researchers. He told us he was in contact with not a nuts-and-bolts spacecraft, but one that appeared as a yellow-orange light. According to Diaz, the ship seemed to be made of a yellow plasma, like a glowing sphere. Something similar to what we have animated in our video *Merkabah, Voyage of a Star Seed*.[16]

On several occasions, he entered the ship and talked to the inhabitants, who were greatly concerned about how we were handling our planetary environment. On one occasion, he was taken into a cave that was being used by his alien associates but that in the past had been used also by the Mayans. He saw various "yellow spheres" in the cave and he was told that if the aliens touched his seventh vertebra, it would activate his neurons, allowing the aliens to "copy" many of his thoughts and store them, without doing him any harm. He experienced this himself when he picked up one of the yellow spheres in the cave and he realized he was experiencing the thoughts of an eagle.

Specifically, while standing in the cave, he experienced the eagle's consciousness while in flight, including seeing wings on each side of himself while flying high above an open plain. He could not determine if it was the eagle's current thoughts he was experiencing or those of the past. If past thoughts, the spheres were simply a library. Yet many contactees feel an immediate connection to the aliens they have encountered.

EXPLAINING TELEPATHY

How can we explain this? In recent research, the work of David Chalmers and Christof Koch,[17] to name a few, has dominated the scientific scene regarding the powers and potential of consciousness. Their work also takes into account the known biological facts that seem particularly pertinent to the mind-brain experience. Many researchers and scientists studying aspects of consciousness are gathering data showing that consciousness is not exclusively centered in the brain. Rather, it is a field of information around the globe that we can "tune into."

Remote viewing and other nonlocal abilities have confirmed this scientific hypothesis. We have personally written several papers with Dr. E. A. Rauscher, who cited John

A. Wheeler as one of her advisors while he was at Princeton and she was at UC Berkeley. In collaboration with others, Rauscher confirmed that the brain has the ability to receive and send information from a larger consciousness field.

Physicists, led by Heisenberg, Pauli, and Schrödinger, have all tried to explain consciousness and physics, which has led us to the understanding of a nonlocal entangled consciousness, which may not be limited to our local space and time. In our co-authored book titled *Mind Dynamics in Space and Time*, Rauscher wrote about psi, the ability to see beyond our five senses with the power of the mind. She stated:

> We have made giant advancements in our
> understanding of the nature and the properties of
> consciousness by applying the scientific method . . .
> I believe we are on the threshold of another great
> advancement in psi research that utilizes the
> scientific method . . . Psi is as old as human kind
> and beyond, extending to animals and plants. We
> are in a new and exciting era of a deeper discovery,
> which we are privileged to experience as we seek the
> scientific exploration of psi.[18]

Rauscher was able to say this because of the work she did at SRI (Stanford Research Institute, Menlo Park, California) with Ingo Swann, one of the government's top remote viewers. Remote viewing is generally about seeing distant targets around the globe, but Swann took it to another level. In April 1973, Swann and Harold Sherman, another remote viewer, did a laboratory test where they looked at off-planetary targets, specifically Jupiter, in terms of remote viewing, before any satellite probes were able to go there. Both men described exactly what future satellites were able to confirm. They saw harsh storms and gas clouds with rainbows, described rings around Jupiter, and specifically Swann saw **"crystals that glitter."**[19] Now we know Jupiter has rings and its upper atmosphere is divided into cloud belts and zones made up primarily of ammonia crystals, sulfur, and mixtures of the two compounds. In fact, Jupiter's white clouds consist of frozen ammonia crystals.

The very successful remote viewing studies carried out at the Stanford Research Institute from the early to mid-1970s were supported at first by the Defense Intelligence Agency (DIA) and later funding was continued by the CIA. Under the guidance of Russell Targ, Harold Puthoff, astronaut Edgar Mitchell, Ingo Swann, Joe McMoneagle, Hella Hammid, and Uri Geller, the institute provided a rich database of experiments with astonishing results. With strict scientific control, thousands of demonstrations involving remote viewing skills proved that the skeptics are wrong, the nonlocality of consciousness exists! Specifically, SRI research confirmed that nonlocal sensing is established as a viable way of knowing information acquired by the skilled practitioner. This was clearly demonstrated when the perceptual brains of the remote viewing practitioners continually received information from nonlocal targets, which exist in the quantum field.

Consequently, even within great, conservative institutions, shifts have been taking place in the understanding of human consciousness. New horizons of studies are introducing ways of understanding how nonlocality can contribute in unique ways to allow the human intellect to see and know more than the five senses. The brain is beginning to be seen as the instrument of, and not the generator of, consciousness.

Unfortunately, because the funding for the research came from intelligence agencies, specifically the CIA, many of the validating results have remained inaccessible. However, some declassified documents appeared in 2017, namely **"Project Stargate"** (and others, such as "Grill Flame"), which continued the work of the Stanford Research Institute but operating out of a military base in Maryland. This was a strictly government-controlled program that ran from the late 1970s to the early 1990s. Recently, more of this once-classified research has been released through film documents, as in Russell Targ's retrospective on his SRI days called *Third Eye Spies*.

The work shows the use of paraphysical "superpowers" used globally by sensitives finding amazing facts that can only be attributed to a sixth sense or psi. Rauscher and Targ believed their abilities were not limited to our 3D/4D reality, but that our own brains can work on multidimensional levels.[20] Here multidimensionality transcends the materialistic understanding of matter, energy, space, and time. Accounts have shown that aliens can look into our past or see our future, or display what we call "*precognition*." Humans also can draw from different time realities. We are proposing that both humans and extraterrestrials can draw from the same consciousness field existing in our dimension or in other dimensions.

If life abounds in the universe, then we can pick up on aliens just as they can pick up on us. The question is, do we want to, and if so, which aliens? Aliens seem to have the ability to know our mental signals, and if we align with them, then they can align with us, or vice versa. But researchers have shown that there are many different types of aliens with various agendas, and there are many other forces in the universe we can awaken to once we understand that "we are not alone."

Ultimately, each person has access to the same consciousness field, but our association with the field varies from person to person based on our unique attunements. This is not too different from the experience of George Van Tassel, who originally worked for Douglas Aircraft, Hughes Aircraft, and Lockheed as an aerospace engineer. In 1953, Van Tassel had a unique encounter with an alien who landed outside where he was sleeping in a hollowed-out chamber under Giant Rock near Joshua Tree in Southern California.[21] Although he did not hear a noise, when he went outside to get some air, he met an alien walking toward him, who was named Solganda. And looking beyond him, Van Tassel saw his landed spacecraft. In Van Tassel's recollection, he was taken aboard and given scientific information to help humanity regarding "time travel" and "longevity." After that, Van Tassel seemed to possess an ongoing sense of mental communication with Solganda that lasted most of his lifetime. We both came to know Van Tassel in the last decade of his life and admired his will to make a difference for humanity, especially in the construction of the famous domed structure called "**The Integratron**," which he developed as a rudimentary time machine.

So yes, advanced alien intelligences can know what

we are thinking. On another note of closer experience, a woman named Annie, who had encountered an alien intelligence while scuba diving in the area of the Bermuda Triangle, was told by the aliens not to talk about her encounters. Later, when she was talking about her contact, a shelf literally flew up, not down, off the wall in the kitchen, breaking all the bottles that were on it. She turned to her associates and said, "**I cannot talk about this.**" Therefore, we know from our work with remote viewing that there is absolutely a consciousness field, and this consciousness field is not limited to the Earth. In this way, we propose the possibility that all things can truly be known anytime and anywhere. In reality, there is no private information when we tune our consciousness to it.

HOW ARE WE LIKE THEM?

We mentioned the fact that there seem to be many different alien species. If you could examine a reptilian or a grey extraterrestrial as reported by many contactees, how different would they be? Although their DNA code would be different from that of our species on Earth, just as we are different from other animal species, it is our belief that their "coding" functions would work in a very similar fashion to ours. The DNA system is in actuality a code book of information that we believe is universal for organic lifeforms.

Two Kazakhstani researchers, physicist Vladimir I. shCherbak of al-Farabi Kazakh National University and astrobiologist Maxim A. Makukov of the Fesenkov Astrophysical Institute, proposed in a peer-reviewed study titled "**The 'Wow! Signal' of the Terrestrial Genetic Code**" that

our DNA is so sophisticated that it could not possibly have evolved just on planet Earth. They go on to assert that **life throughout the galaxy may have been spread by intelligent design. They further assert that it would be very difficult, if not impossible, to have our DNA develop solely by random processes.**[22]

On July 15, 1979, one of the authors of this chapter (J. J. Hurtak) had the opportunity to present pictures and give a critical overview of anatomical details regarding "**retrieved extraterrestrial bodies,**" now called EBEs, or Extraterrestrial Biological Entities, at the First National Parapsychological Conference in Mexico City. In describing the specifics of the ET aliens held by American authorities, Dr. Hurtak presented to the national press information that appeared in the newspapers *El Universal* (July 16, 1979) and on page two of *The News*, Mexico City, which reported the following details. Specifically documented under the provocative headline "**Parapsychology Meet Offers View of Aliens,**" the aliens were described as follows in *The News*: "**Hurtak's pictures of 'aliens' show 'humanoids of the lower type' about three feet tall, with no ears, no sex organs, and a thin mouth. They looked exactly alike as if coming from the same cookie jar and probably reproduce by cloning.**"[23]

More recent contact reports over the last forty years have substantiated the historic benchmark of Dr. J. J. Hurtak and his overview of the anatomical details now associated with "greys" and "grey-white" specimens from other parts of the universe. Of course, not every alien reported looks like this; many are different, while some are very similar to us. Grey aliens may be acceptable, but many report strange reptilian forms, insectoid beings, and even those that look like a walking, telepathically talking, praying mantis, to name a few. In our opinion, what should be most shocking are the space aliens who look like us. Are they "shape shifting" so as not to frighten us?

One popular report of a being that looked like us came from Elizabeth Klarer, who achieved international fame with her book, *Beyond the Light Barrier*,[24] which covered her meeting with a cosmic visitor identified as Akon in the 1950s in the mountains of Drakensberg, South Africa. She became a close friend and colleague to us while we were lecturing at South African universities in the 1980s and 1990s. We were most interested in the details of her contact story with Akon, who claimed to be from a planet called "Meton"—interestingly enough, a name that similarly appears in Dr. James Hurtak's book from 1973, *The Keys of Enoch.*®[25]

Elizabeth Klarer once worked with British Intelligence in South Africa, but she did not have the advanced schooling necessary for the mathematical and astrophysical insights that she provided to authorities in South Africa and Germany shortly after her experiences. Researchers were at first bemused by her claims until they saw the hard evidence of pictures and private notations shared by Akon. Soft-spoken and congenial, Klarer later was invited to speak privately to the House of Lords in the United Kingdom and at conferences on extraterrestrial science in various parts of Europe as more and more collaborative evidence was collected by other investigators of claimed human–ET contact.

Klarer described Akon as a Nordic-looking visitor

whose distinguished profile would be like that of a diplomat from any of the northern European countries. Klarer met him on several occasions before she claimed to be actually taken to his home planet, Meton, a planet orbiting the star Proxima Centauri. Unbeknown to Elizabeth at the time, the star is one of the closest to our sun. Akon told her his type of intelligence once lived here on Earth, but because of environmental and planetary changes they had to leave for a nearby star using spaceships with the ability to traverse "the light barrier." When she went with him to Meton, she witnessed a multi-level home that made use of levitation transportation from floor to floor. However, it was also the place where she gave birth to Akon's son through consent and by normal means. Her son, named **Ayling**, had to be left behind as she made her way back to Earth. Fantastic as this seems, this case needs to be placed in a real *X-Files* for ongoing study with so-called Nordic intelligence visiting our planet. It should by all accounts be the subject of fresh, declassified information from those higher-ups involved with exo-politics.

Other cases of alien contact are not always so physical. We know that they can come through walls and windows, but some don't even have to consistently keep their body form. An interesting, more intrusive alien case was reported on ufocasebook.com from Yuba City, California, on September 11, 2013. A husband and wife were in bed, when the man suddenly got the feeling that they were not alone. He reported:

> *I was lying on my right side with my wife to my back.*
> *I opened my eyes and the room was lit in a pale*

*orange glow. I rolled over toward my wife and that
was when I saw three typical grey aliens standing in
my master bathroom about five feet from my wife's
side of the bed.*[26]

The witness reports that he could not make out their faces, but they had big heads. As he was able to scream and his wife was awakened, he reported: "**The three entities dematerialized into three orange glowing balls and floated through the walls of the bathroom . . .**"[27]

So, some grey beings may be able to quickly morph into a completely different form, showing that the body is only one manifestation and that consciousness may be the most important aspect of life. We would be remiss in our reporting should we not account for such beings that are not necessarily completely physical. We talked about how spaceships can disappear, but does every life-form require flesh and blood or some other fluid to course through its veins? From our experience, the answer is no; there are many forms of life that can take on a different biological blueprint of existence, like we find in the caterpillar-to-butterfly scenario, only these beings can move into and out of their forms at will.

IS THERE ANYTHING BEYOND ETS?

There are numerous reports of beings in bioplasmic forms like those described earlier, but there are also beings who appear in even more rarefied light who clearly seem to operate beyond our normal dimensions. Since everything that occurs in the living universe is ultimately the result of one or more quantum mechanical events, the universe is inhabited by an almost unlimited number of rather discrete conscious systems, thinking and nonthinking entities that are responsible for the detailed workings of the universe.

Just a few hours outside Bangkok, Thailand, contact has been taking place since 1997. It started when a man living near Khao Kala hill, outside the town of Nakhon Sawan, was in a deep state of Buddhist meditation. He started receiving messages, and flying saucers were also seen in the area. Three years later he passed away, but not before passing on his ability of "contact" to his daughter, Wassanu. According to his information, he was in touch with two types of aliens. Wassanu reported: **"Pluto aliens are made of energy, can appear in physical form, and are able to teach humans. Loku, short for Lokukatapa-kadikong, aliens have a physical body and knowledge of high technology. They work together."**[28] The daughter also mentioned that the aliens are concerned about wars and environmental changes on Earth. They affirm that they are here to help and even transport people if needed.

What is important here is that this is one contact that confirms not only multiple alien types, but that some aliens are made of energy. It is this form of being that we are speaking about here. Pluto seems extremely uninhabitable to us, but Pluto could be symbolic of beings who are just on the fringes of our solar system watching us. Others in the past have talked about beings from Venus. We know that it would be difficult for life-forms like ours to live on Venus, but if they were energy forms, this would open up greater realms of possibility.

Regarding the Pluto contact in Thailand, much of the

information was received in meditations, but supposedly they are reported to have lived 10,000 years and "**travel through dimensions. It's advanced physics. I travel with my mind,**" the communique affirmed.[29]

These types of intelligences are very different from the ETs, who are generally involved in the mundane level of exploring and examining humans; these energy forms are of another category of "**out of this world**" visitors that many are now encountering. We call them the "Cosmic Others." These could be further classified into subcategories, two of which we will mention here, called the **Extra-Celestials** (ECs) and the **Ultraterrestrials** (UTs), both of whose appearance is generally in an energy form, which has been known at times to reveal the outline of a human body or a glowing face.

In a philosophical sense, Extra-Celestials can be called luminous, noncorporeal beings. In their nonmaterial form, they have the ability to come and go without technological structures. The ECs do communicate with humans and make it clear they are not gods. They also often speak generally of a Supreme Being whom they too revere. They express themselves in telepathic communication and use an energy field for sustaining contact, which they place around those individuals they are assisting. Sometimes you can see their faces, but they also appear as orbs or spheres, energetic geometries, and superluminal light bursts or sparks hovering around human bodies in singular or collective gatherings.

The Ultraterrestrials generally only appear to humans who are working to acquire specific states of consciousness. They do not live close to our Earth reality and only come to assist humans or to help prevent certain other extraterrestrials from taking advantage of our naïveté. Because of their different dimensional origins, their appearance can be overwhelming to the biochemistry of the human body. They are not subject to the laws of physical entropy, because their vibratory functions consistently operate on a higher plane of reality and consciousness awareness.

Dr. J. J. Hurtak had a unique experience in 1973 in which he traveled into other dimensions with one who was called an **Ophanim** messenger. This was not an ET but a UT being. There was no channeling or spacecraft involved, but it was a "Merkabah-type" experience, where he was literally taken into and shown other dimensions. When he returned and shared his experiences, paraphysical events began to occur around his body, and these were observed by him for up to a year after the experience. Hurtak was shown that these "Ultraterrestrials" do not need a spaceship and mainly travel by the power of the mind. The being he was in touch with explained that they are Cosmic Messengers, who are here to provide us with information about our planet, help us advance our own science, and understand that violence is not a way to a greater future.

The UTs and ECs can appear to be part-human and part-angelic. They can manifest in human appearances, so as not to frighten our species. Both forms allow for the Divine Will to manifest in a variety of ways and often act as intermediaries in assisting with the awareness of the higher-dimensional realities.

The phenomenon of the **Merkabah** is also not a UFO spacecraft but is a type of diamond-vehicle as spoken of in ancient Buddhist teachings. The term "Merkabah" is a Hebrew word that means "**vehicle.**" In the mystical literature, it is normally understood as a nonmaterial vehicle that creates a multidimensional overlap that takes the "rider" or traveler into other realms that are outside the vast third-dimensional universe that we live in. Here the traveler can choose to remain in those realms or return to assist in the mission that is generally given.

In another encounter in 1974–1975, information from the greater cosmic realms was experienced in a remote viewing session with Dr. Andrija Puharich and Dr. J. J. Hurtak. Both saw into the future that major planetary changes would occur. This included the focus on climate and human affairs for the first half of the twenty-first century, with a dominant role to be played by China. This session occurred inside a special Faraday cage built by Dr. Puharich for advanced research. UTs can show themselves as a human or light energy presence, and come also as thought-forms in some instances, advancing human evolution with wisdom, knowledge, love, and compassion.

One of the key questions should be: What is the relationship to God in all of this? And how large exactly is our cosmic family?

Of the numerous physical and spiritual planets and other realities that exist, there seems to be very little limitation in defining Life in the universe. Life truly spans the universe, and encompasses or perhaps is even generated by a "**Higher Consciousness Presence**" that is behind intelligent life in all its many forms.

More immediately, contact with cosmic cultures needs to be with those who will allow us to maintain our individual identity and will undoubtedly lead us in the direction of our own cosmic evolution. This requires an enlarged understanding of time—past, present, and future. Contact, thus, needs to be with those who will help us go beyond our own eventual extinction and provide an awareness of our own higher purpose in the universe as we become conscious of ourselves as multidimensional beings.

There is definite evidence that the Ultraterrestrial, and in some cases the Extraterrestrial, Intelligences have a greater conscious awareness, and there is evidence, too, that this ability can be shared and acquired by us. It would be entirely plausible that in certain circumstances, the mind of humankind should come together in a larger way, to realize the complex state of affairs in the universe and the greater reality of all of creation.

As our consciousness is awakened to the vastness of life, we are gaining the wisdom and understanding of the importance of cooperation, not only among ourselves but with other races of intelligence. We believe consciousness is a ubiquitous cosmological principle of the universe. The human mind is a complex system embedded in this totality. In essence, preparation is being made for us to realize that we are part of the cosmic citizenship in the heavens. However, we are also but one branch of Life, whereby we will continue as the new Adams and Eves in ongoing stages of evolution. Hopefully, we shall soon understand, firsthand, the references spoken of by the ancients, that this creation is a "House of Many Mansions."

Gathering new information from all sources is motivating us to look deeper for answers. This has resulted in new scientific insights into our true human destiny. The time is now to see ourselves and all of humanity as "**cosmoplanetary-quantum beings**." Inherent in the nature of the human mind is a fundamental spiritual component that allows degrees of absolute truth to be perceived and received. The ultimate goal here is for us to have a greater understanding of existence itself. We find it exquisitely exciting to be alive at this time and to keep moving forward in the ongoing discovery of our evolutionary role within the multifaceted, multidimensional reality of vastly higher intelligences within the ever-expanding multiverse we live in.

CONTACT IN THE IMPLICATE ORDER

Linda Moulton Howe

Ultimately, the entire universe (with all its "particles," including those constituting human beings, their laboratories, observing instruments, etc.) has to be understood as a single undivided whole, in which analysis into separately and independently existent parts has no fundamental status [in the implicate order].[1]
—David Bohm, Ph.D., quantum physicist and author
of *Wholeness and the Implicate Order*

My first vivid memory of contact with another physical place beyond Earth was in the summer of 1952. I was turning cartwheels in the big backyard of our small house on North 28th Street in Boise, Idaho. I was ten and my brother, Jim, was seven. Our dad, Chet Moulton, was a pilot who had taught others to fly in World War II and went on to become Director of Aeronautics for Idaho. Mom gave us all deep love and lessons in compassion when she scooped up spiders and moths in towels to free them outdoors.

I had finished fifth grade that spring and wanted to start an astronomy club because I loved looking at the moon and stars through a $49.95 Dynascope reflector telescope that Dad and Mom gave me for my birthday.

The sun had set, but the sky was still a twilight orchid as I came out of one cartwheel and aimed for the low branch of a crabapple tree. If I didn't put my hands down in the right spot and swing my legs just so, I would miss grabbing the branch behind my knees. But that time I didn't miss and felt the fun of swinging back and forth with my long, curly hair dragging on the grass.

I didn't like the feeling of blood running to my head. So, next I put my hands down on the grass to stop swinging and sprang backward in a stand-up. And there it was! A yellow-white full moon rising right above the crabapple tree. It never mattered how many full moons I had seen; every one always made me gasp at first sight.

I stood there staring at the beautiful round light. As I stared, all sounds faded away. The big moon seemed closer and closer. Then, like a jump cut in a movie, I was there! At the moon, on the moon, inside the moon. *It's hollow! And it's watching us.*

Then back—standing next to the crabapple tree, still staring at the full moon. And I knew **Something Else** was there. Maybe the blood rushing into my head when I hung from the tree limb opened up a brain part that can remote view long distances? Whatever happened, I was there and knew the moon is hollow, watching and listening to Earth. Then another knowing: Don't talk about it.

"IT'S NOT OUR MOON"

That was sixty-eight years ago from the summer of 2020, as I write for the first time about my lunar revelation.

But now, look at the following words in a book published posthumously in April 2020 titled *Selected by Extraterrestrials, Volume 2*, by William Mills Tompkins (1923–2017). He worked from 1942 through World War II and on to the NASA Apollo program for naval intelligence on advanced technology projects concerning UFOs. The book was edited and published by Robert Wood, Ph.D., a retired aerospace engineer at McDonnell Douglas, a major American aerospace manufacturing corporation and defense contractor that merged with Boeing in 1997.

Here's Tompkins on page 78:

It has been known for thousands of years that the Moon is not a planetary Moon. It is a hollow Moon "station" that was built out in the galaxy by one of the Federations, towed into Earth orbit and parked with one side facing Earth. It is just a solar system command center handling situation in this sector of the galaxy. First, it's not our Moon. Planet Earth is not our planet. We are just allowed to use it while working for them at slightly above the slave level. The Moon and Earth both belong to several entities out there.

Page 83:

We must accept that the planet that we live on is just a massive laboratory being used by possibly a hundred different entities with hundreds of agendas. One of which is that none of them will help or interfere with us . . . We really are just a big

*laboratory down here supporting their agendas . . .
They biologically control us to live this ridiculously
short seventy-five-year life span compared to their
300- to 3,000-year life spans. Some insect aliens don't
die at all.*

*[Praying-mantis beings have been described
by an American intelligence analyst to me as
living for billions of years while overseeing life and
terraforming experiments in solar systems.]*

According to retired naval engineer Tompkins in a four-hour recorded interview I did with him in May 2016, when he was ninety-three years old, there are actual "star wars" going on in the Milky Way galaxy between different intelligences, who battle with each other over territories and genetic creations. Their weapons include manipulations of gravity, time, minds, and invisibility. Tompkins told me, **"World War II was an extraterrestrial war fought through human bodies."** He also described Adolf Hitler and the Nazi SS as conspiring with "Vril-ya ET types"—tall, blond, blue-eyed Aryans—to take over the Earth with advanced Vril craft and to enslave certain human populations to do work for the Vril-ya overseers.

Allegedly, the Vril technology could neutralize gravity, which was the key to building Vril craft and the extremely large Vril interstellar spacecraft that could go to populated planets orbiting stars in this and other galaxies. Tompkins wrote that the Vril-ya had an urgent need to find livable planets because environmental conditions deteriorated on the original Vril-ya planets that orbited an old red binary star system called Aldebaran. There was an exodus to find new planetary homes and the Vril-ya ended up in this solar system where on Earth they found deep underground caverns beneath Antarctica and other parts of this world to inhabit. Those blond humanoids discovered they weren't the only ones underground. Large reptilian humanoids and smaller grey-colored humanoids were already based under deserts and inside mountains. Allegedly, all three alien species mixed and matched genes in already-evolving primates on Earth to produce various stand-up models, from *Homo erectus* to *Homo sapiens sapiens.*

That Big Secret of cosmic advanced beings manipulating genes behind the scenes was allegedly shared with elite power broker groups such as the Illuminati, Rosicrucians, Masons, and Bilderbergers.

We humans have deliberately been kept dumb and blind by the planetary manipulators. We are not alone in this universe and never have been, and, according to current military special ops whistleblowers, interstellar trade of metals and genes and cloned bodies is current throughout the Milky Way galaxy and beyond.

NOW EARTH IS LOOKING FOR LIVABLE PLANETS

NASA has a superpowerful orbiting telescope called "**TESS**" that is looking for evidence of other life on exoplanets in our Milky Way galaxy. Every star in our galaxy has one planet on average. By the springtime of 2020, astronomers have found and reported *4,025 planets beyond our solar system.* A few appear to have water and temperatures that might support organic life. TESS, the Transiting Exoplanet Survey Satellite, keeps finding more and more planets that could have life.

Elon Musk, founder of SpaceX and its reusable Starship rockets, tweeted in early 2020 that he plans to have a non-stop shuttle of Starships transporting enough people and cargo to Mars, beginning perhaps as early as 2024 to 2030, to create a new Mars city for a million people. Will it be underground?

A White Sands Missile Range scientist told me back in 1988 that he knew a Naval Research Lab physicist who had been to a Mars base half a dozen times. The physicist said that Martian lava tubes were strong and that grey extra-terrestrial biological entities had helped the United States seal off one of the tubes from the Martian atmosphere for a base in which "Earth air" was then pumped in for human breathing.

I first heard details about underground ETs inside Earth fighting with each other over territory, genetic harvesting, and clones from an American government intelligence analyst. We both traveled to meet in a place that he chose. There, the motor sounds of boats and yachts were almost as loud as the humans crowded onto the restaurant deck next to the water. It was lunchtime on a warm Sunday in early December 1999, at the Baltimore harbor in Maryland. I had driven from my home in Philadelphia to meet him, soon after he retired from twenty-three years of work for the Defense Intelligence Agency (DIA) in Washington, DC.

The invitation to meet had come a month earlier from a friend, Nikk, who did contract work for the World Bank. He had met me a few years before at a conference in San Francisco where the subjects included bloodless, trackless animal mutilations, human abductions, UFOs, other life-forms, and even the startling new astronomy debate: Is this a holographic universe that was projected by someone from a different dimension?

By the time of that Baltimore lunch, I had produced three large books out in the world that contained hundreds of color photographs, maps, illustrations, and documents from my investigations for TV documentaries (*An Alien Harvest: Further Evidence Linking Animal Mutilations and Human Abductions to Alien Life Forms* © 1989. *Glimpses of Other Realities: Vol. I: Facts & Eyewitnesses* © 1993. *Glimpses of Other Realities, Vol. II: High Strangeness* © 1998).

In our handshakes, I got the feeling that Nikk and DIA worked together—meaning the World Bank was Nikk's cover for intelligence work that involved monitoring humanoids on Earth who are not *Homo sapiens sapiens*. In fact, he said during that lunch, "Part of my work at DIA has been to monitor the worldwide barter system of Earth to keep track of extraterrestrial influence."

Lunch was a process of DIA getting a measure of me and deciding to go on with the sensitive content in yet another location. We left the deck restaurant and walked a few hundred feet down near the water that was churning with many Sunday boats coming and going. DIA guided us to a cement bench about six feet long built into a sidewalk not far from all the noisy engines. He said in a matter-of-fact tone, "I don't think our satellites can hear through all this white noise."

He extended his hand for me to sit on the cement bench. DIA went to my left and Nikk to my right. Sitting side by side felt awkward until DIA said, "My job has been to monitor and analyze the geopolitical and territorial conflict of three competing extraterrestrial biological civilizations that have been terraforming this planet and manipulating DNA in already-evolving primates for at least 270 million years. Our government has proof."

I asked, "What is the proof?"

"It's too dangerous to talk about—for you and for me. But, Linda, what do you think Earth would look like if you took away all the ocean waters?"

An image popped into my mind's eye, probably a memory from grade school. "Like an apple core?"

"What is the diameter of Earth?"

"Eight thousand miles."

"What is the deepest ocean?"

"The Mariana Trench, about seven miles down."

Instantly I realized that if I took seven miles off the 8,000-mile-wide Earth, it would not look like an apple core.

"Well, more like a nibbled apple."

"Which is bigger—the oceans or the continents?"

"Two-thirds of Earth is water, so the land under the oceans would cover more square miles than the continents."

"Right. And what I've learned at DIA is that for at least 270 million years three different alien intelligences have inhabited Earth below the surface."

"Do you mean that if I could go down to the seven-mile-deep Mariana Trench and drill through the bottom that I would come out into an ET world?"

"Yes. But that's not the only place. In my work for the DIA, I have monitored ET terraforming and genetic manipulation on this planet. Here's how their geopolitical territories break down.

"There are six- to seven-foot-tall, blond-haired, blue-eyed 'Nordic' types that are based mostly *below the ba-*

sins of the oceans and seas. There are many other types of shorter, large black-eyed Greys also known as extraterrestrial biological entities, or EBENs, that prefer to be inside mountains such as the Himalayas.

"And there are large, six- to eight-feet-tall reptilian humanoids that like hot temperatures, just like snakes do. The reptilians have lived beneath the Mesopotamian deserts for thousands of years.

"And, Linda, your *Glimpses, Vol. II* has many truths about the soul transfer technology into cloned bodies that I thought would never reach the light of day. When the praying-mantis beings call it 'Translation into the Light,' we have been trying to figure out exactly what happens and why."

THEY ARE US AND WE ARE THEY

In DIA's scenario, humanoid forms of insects, reptilians, grey-colored EBENs, and tall, blond "Nordics" live on different floors of hotel Earth, with oblivious humans on surface islands and continents. Humans have deliberately been kept from knowing this important truth because *we* are the focus of one, two, or three experiments in the Earth laboratory. First Contact was in the Garden of Eden where First Humans, Adam and Eve, met a serpent.

No matter what the original source and purpose of genetic manipulation were to create standing-up primates on this planet, one possible reason to help the new human creation survive might have been an experiment at the Divine Spirit level to insert very strong souls into the evolving-matter humanoids. The divine plan might have been to use Earth as a petri dish to test out a new hypostatic being with free will to choose good or evil. Those choices would determine the soul destinations at the moment of death. That hypostatic hypothesis might also explain why in some investigations of human abductions, other intelligences seem interested in what different dimensions human souls go after death. One abductee told me, "**The Grey seemed frustrated that some people can go to dimensions they can't enter.**" You reap what you sow, whether human, ET, or angel.

WHAT DO THE OTHER INTELLIGENCES WANT FROM *HOMO SAPIENS SAPIENS*?

According to government whistleblowers, humans have provided centuries of physical labor in the surface matter world of Earth to mine gold and other precious metals and jewels. Humans were also used to help build pyramids, ziggurats, and temples without knowing the structures were actually communication and energy "machines" for the alien power brokers. The non-humans also harvest genetic material from the slave-humans' strong bodies, minds, and souls to create clones that can be distributed for interstellar trade throughout the Milky Way galaxy and beyond—perhaps even for trade in different timelines and dimensions.

Then there is the concept of interdimensional conflict in which God versus devil and good versus evil emerge as the Big Box inside which the entire cosmic drama is taking place. In her 1998 book, *Voyagers, The Sleeping Abductees*, experiencer Anna Hayes writes: "**One group of advanced beings wish to see humans evolve into wholeness, equality, and co-creatorship, while another group of beings desires to stunt the evolution of humanity so it can continue to** utilize its Earth resources for self-serving purposes. The latter group has come to represent the 'dark' or 'evil' forces within the collective human unconscious while the former has emerged into your mythologies of the 'gods.'"

TWO MORE WHISTLEBLOWERS TALK ETS

Before DIA in December 1999, I had received in the 1980s valuable insights from two different retired intelligence analysts who had done work for the highly classified Operation Majestic-12 (MJ-12) organized by President Harry S. Truman in September 1947. Its goals were published in a TOP SECRET/MAJIC EYES ONLY SOM1-01 Majestic 12 group special operations manual titled "Extraterrestrial Entities and Technology, Recovery, and Disposal." It was stamped TOP SECRET/MAJIC EYES ONLY and dated April 1954. A retired government printing press manager at Kirtland Air Force Base confirmed to aerospace engineer Bob Wood, Ph.D., that the SOM1-01 manual had been printed under his supervision in 1954.

The manual was created in the Truman-to-Eisenhower administrations. Its purpose was to help the MJ-12 group **be able to more expertly deal with Unidentified Flying Objects, Extraterrestrial Technology and Entities, and increase the efficiency of future operations."**

The two MJ-12-related whistleblowers were from two different coasts of the United States, but their answers to my questions were similar. I especially wanted to know why there has long been a secret genetic harvest from humans and animals.

Both emphasized that there was a difference between the tall, grey-skinned EBEN types with pear-shaped heads versus grey-skinned entities that have triangular faces and pointed chins. The men thought the EBENs were our allies but also admitted the EBENs lie. Adding to the physical appearance and agenda confusions are biological androids made by the EBENs, Nordics and Reptilians that range widely in appearance from insects to humanoids designed by their makers for various planetary tasks in this and other solar systems.

Both men have given me information, which I have no way to prove, but offer now in the context of whistleblowers. To honor their requests for anonymity, I combined their information into one "voice" that I call "Sherman."

First, they both insist that MJ-12, or MAJESTIC 12, is real and was established by one of President Harry S. Truman's TOP SECRET Executive Orders in September 1947. MJ-12's mission was to study the UFO phenomenon, to oversee retrievals of crashed discs and alien bodies, to back-engineer extraterrestrial technology, and to study captured beings referred to as *extraterrestrial biological entities*" (EBENs). MJ-12 was also directed to keep the public and media ignorant of the extraterrestrial presence *"at all costs"* to prevent panic and to keep the aliens' advanced technologies hidden from Cold War enemies in the interests of national security.

I asked Sherman if he had personally seen non-human technology. He said he had held an EBEN device called the **"Yellow Book"** in which symbols glow yellow and three-dimensional images rise up like the Princess Leia hologram communications in *Star Wars*. Sherman said those three-dimensional images in the Yellow Book come from the EBENs' ability to *"capture time and play it back,"* as if the EBENs monitor and analyze the consequences of their genetic manipulations on Earth for whatever big agenda they have.

Sherman said he had been told that the EBENs experimented genetically in Bhutan, Tibet, and Nepal and then transplanted some of those altered human/ET hybrids to Central and South America. Specifically, he said the Mayan civilization was from an EBEN genetic experiment in Bhutan transferred to the Yucatan peninsula and surrounding region.

SHERMAN: The EBENs have been here since at least the time of the dinosaurs. And according to a classified report I read, the EBENs collected one of each species of dinosaur and placed them either on one big planetary zoo or on different planets—*before* the asteroid slammed into the Gulf of Mexico. And that was at least 65 million years ago. I guess they've experimented with other life-forms here ever since.

LINDA: What about the animal mutilations?

SHERMAN: The animal mutilations do occur and are performed by various aliens. We allowed them to conduct experiments using animals, not just cattle. I don't know if you are aware or not, but there were a lot of moose and caribou found mysteriously dead in the Arctic and Alaska. We think it was part of the EBEN experimentation, but we couldn't figure out what happened. The EBENs wanted to conduct experiments. Better animals than humans.

To complicate matters, in order to cover up the animal mutilations, our government launched a military program to test certain biological drugs on animals. This was to cover up the alien mutilation program.

LINDA: Do the EBENs themselves enter pastures and cut the tissues from animals in mutilations?

SHERMAN: After we had more communications with the EBENs, they explained to us: "You have to understand that for an advanced civilization, you have robots and androids to do these things." And we began to understand that the EBEN androids could be anything! The androids can be configured any way the EBENs want for whatever mission the EBENs want carried out. The EBENs are controlling a big part of an operation concerning Earth, and we can't control everything they do. But I can tell you the EBENs are big environmentalists. Huge! They would make the Sierra Club look like Brownie scouts. They were so worried about our nuclear tests and nuclear materials being exploded and contaminating not only the Earth, but the universe in general.

LINDA: Sherman, do you mean that our atomic bombs impacted other life-forms, or even other dimensions?

SHERMAN: Right. So that's one of the things the EBENs were very vocal about—they wanted above-ground atomic tests stopped and, boy, were they stopped!

LINDA: From your point of view, are EBENs the only non-humans that have experimented genetically on this planet?

SHERMAN: All I know is that the EBENs started an experiment, but they couldn't keep out other space travelers. Word got out that this planet was a strange place to visit and that different experiments were not going the way the EBENs wanted. Part of the EBENs' problems might be because there are "Bad Guys" doing experiments, too, that might harm us. That really confuses matters when it comes to telling who wants to help humans and who doesn't.

LINDA: In abduction reports, people describe creatures that look like praying mantis insects. What are those?

SHERMAN: As far as I've heard, they could be very advanced androids, which can oversee long-term solar system projects that last for thousands of years. But I'm not certain who they work with or for.

LINDA: What is the relationship between the Greys (pointed chins) and the EBENs (U-shaped chins)?

SHERMAN: They were enemies at one time. They are supposed to live without war today, but the EBENs have no control over the Greys. The Greys do their thing and the EBENs do theirs.

LINDA: Is there a pecking order among the alien types?

SHERMAN: To the best of our knowledge, no cooperation exists between the different alien groups. And I think there was a war about 6,000 years ago between the EBENs and the Blond "Nordics" over territorial rights to a planet somewhere. I don't know if it was out at Zeta Reticuli or around here or what.

LINDA: So do all groups—the EBENs, Greys, Reptilians, and Blond Humanoids—make android creatures do work for them on different planets?

SHERMAN: That's what I understand. Androids come in many different types—insects, reptilians, Greys, EBENs, humanoid Blonds, MIBs (Men in Black), and others. All the alien AI androids have an advanced implanted brain that can operate on its own—or by remote control. Ironically, we think some of these genetically engineered creatures have a higher intelligence than their creators. The EBENs and the Blond Humanoids know how to mix and match genomes in DNA easily. They can make robots or androids that can be anything they want them to be. Remember, the aliens are millions of years advanced beyond us.

Sherman said the EBENs even make Blond-looking and Reptilian-looking body containers that the EBENs control; and the Blonds make EBEN-looking and Reptilian-looking container bodies the Blonds control! And probably the Reptilians make EBEN-looking and Blond-looking container bodies they control!

LINDA: "The EBENs' genetic experimentation in Tibet and Bhutan—does that connect somehow to the Dalai Lama? I'm thinking about reincarnation through different body containers and different cycles of life. Would that concept relate to an EBEN supposedly telling an Air Force captain in 1949 that "**recycling of souls is the machinery of the universe**"?
SHERMAN: Exactly. There are only so many souls that just continuously recycle.

LINDA: Through any life-form bodies that can contain souls?

SHERMAN: Right, exactly.

LINDA: And if there are more container bodies than souls, what happens?

SHERMAN: I don't know. But souls are interconnected in some way. I think they told us that because the EBENs have been around so long, they have learned that there are only so many souls in this universe, which must be recycled.

LINDA: If there is a finite number of souls in the universe and the EBENs know that, then they also know that we humans are living on a planet in which there is an exponential increase in the number of bodies. Does that imply that not all bodies have souls?

SHERMAN: I guess you have a point there.

LINDA: And if not all body containers have souls, would the EBENs and Blond humanoids have some stake invested in souls—like souls could be the coin of the realm, so to speak?

SHERMAN: That's possible, I guess. I never thought of it that way before.

LINDA: Some abductee researchers, such as Dr. Leo Sprinkle, a Wyoming psychologist, and Harvard University psychiatrist Dr. John Mack, stumbled onto what appears to be a continuity of the same EBENs, or maybe other Grey types, present from human life to human life because the same alien being comes up in past life regressions at births and at deaths.

SHERMAN: I don't know. All I've been told is that

when the body container dies, the soul contains or maintains or keeps some thoughts or something from that life that was just lived. It said in the Yellow Book that the EBENs are concerned about human souls if our particular species continued on its course. They are afraid we would damage our container bodies and that could damage the souls.

LINDA: How would our body containers damage our souls?

SHERMAN: I don't know. I realize the containers are the human bodies. And that was why they were so concerned with what we have been doing—the wars and so forth. They are afraid that the souls will be damaged by *our* containers. One of the MJ-12 guys who had seen more of the Yellow Book talked to me about an analogy. He said that when you put something in a container and you pour it out, there's always some residue that remains. Something remains in that soul, so when you pass the soul on in different containers, it picks up the residues of all the different containers it has been in and a little of each remains and stays throughout. I guess there's an eternity; there's no end.

LINDA: Does the soul wear out after so many recycles?

SHERMAN: No, no—souls never wear out. The Supreme Being makes sure that doesn't happen.

While reviewing this dialogue from my *Volume II, Glimpses of Other Realities*, a research colleague and attorney, Michael Pill of Shutesbury, Massachusetts, wrote to me: "The notion of the 'soul picking up residues' may explain why we have memories of past lives.

"It may also explain why, after spending thousands of years and who knows how many wretched lifetimes trying to work out the karma from one or more evil incarnations, one can still feel the enticing charm of *the dark side.* Those seven deadly sins are like predators—they've got you before you realize they are there."

LINDA: Is there a Devil out there somewhere?

SHERMAN: There is an evil force. Even the EBENs talk about it. There is a Supreme Being and then there is the Evil One. The Evil Entity. The EBENs are as scared of that Evil Entity as we are of the Devil.

LINDA: Where is the Devil?

SHERMAN: I don't know. But what worries me is that if the EBENs are scared of him, I'm damned scared of him because the EBENs can control everything! They have been around this universe and done everything. And if they believe in the same Supreme Being that we call God, and they say there is an Evil One—then there really is a Devil.

LINDA: Would the Devil be equal to—and opposite of—the positive God? Are there two Gods?

SHERMAN: I don't know. You can think about that forever. There's another thing that puzzles me. The EBENs say that everything that occurs in our time span has occurred before. I guess it means we're just right in the middle of a huge, big circle and it just goes around and around again. And the way I see this is that Earth was created and one day 5 billion years from now, the sun is going to expand and Earth will be engulfed and destroyed and everything goes back into a Big Bang, and then everything starts over again.

LINDA: When the Yellow Book talked about the Supreme Being that created the universe, did it say anything about parallel dimensions, parallel time lines, or anything else like that?

SHERMAN: No, nothing. The aliens talked about the vastness of the universe, that there are life-forms all over. It talks about a Supreme Being creating the souls and creating the containers and distributing the souls to the containers. To the EBENs, it's just basic facts.

LINDA: If the EBENs made us and put us here, there has to be a reason. Are we a garden growing containers for souls to be harvested for some reason?

SHERMAN: It's another good question. All I can tell you is that one elderly man with MJ-12 told me, 'You don't want to know that' when I asked him about souls and why the EBENs made us.

LINDA: Some abductees also say that the main reason for the animal mutilations and human abductions has to do with the creation of a hybrid species. But no one knows whether the hybrids are supposed to replace the current *Homo sapiens sapiens* container model. There is a sense that whatever the non-humans are up to, it has something to do with survival—theirs and ours.

SHERMAN: Maybe. All I know is that the EBENs are supposed to have manipulated DNA in primates long before humans were created. So there must have been a series of experiments like Neanderthal before Cro-Magnon. And Neanderthal's gone! So who knows what's on the agenda for humans?

WHO ARE HUMANS REALLY?

Does "Someone Else" own—or battle to keep ownership of—Earth? Are humans unwitting pawns in a multi-level chess game?

If so, is there an alien ally—a Prometheus or Enki trying to help us advance more rapidly to better survive? Is there some kind of really hostile threat beyond the underground alien species already on Earth and in our solar system?

Our planet is now in the midst of its sixth mass extinction of plants and animals because of humanity's spread around the world, destroying and paving over so much ground that once sustained abundant Earth life. We're currently experiencing the worst period of die-offs since the loss of the dinosaurs 65 million years ago. Scientists estimate we're now losing animals, plants, and insects at 1,000 to 10,000 times the rate prior to the twentieth century, with dozens of species going extinct *every day*. That means by the end of the twenty-first century, as many as 30 to 50 percent of all Earth species could be gone!

Perhaps the non-human intelligences that watch this planet can see humanity's own future hanging in a balance, but will not allow humans to destroy the Earth. Perhaps that is why the aliens increased their interference at nuclear missile sites in the 1960s to 1970s and continue to conduct human abductions despite aggressive government efforts to keep everything about the alien presence a big secret.

One fact is certain: No matter who made humans or why, life on Earth is not guaranteed. But if the chokehold on the truth was released and the entire human family could know everything the governments and militaries are hiding about an alien presence on this planet that still manipulates DNA and harvests Earth life—perhaps human tribal warfare would slow down in the alien-concocted Garden of Eden where a reptile was the teacher!

There is a Secret War on Earth. One group of other intelligences wants to see humans evolve into oneness with the Divine Field responsible for all matter worlds. Another intelligence wants to stunt human evolution so it can continue to harvest us genetically for its own self-serving purposes. Thus, the confusion of contradictory literature and conflicting religions throughout human history. Religious inspirations have been used to homogenize various human groups to make them more controllable by the competing intelligences. But those have often been ET inspirations for manipulations—not honest guidance from the Divine Field.

That "political issue" about cloning for galactic trade or alien wars might explain why dramas of resurrected saviors from Osiris to Christ have been presented to humanity. Osiris and Christ were beings with human bodies and mysterious divinity who emphasized that death in the body does not end life for the soul and spirit. That concept underlies the Egyptian obsession with mummies and sacred rites to protect the soul at the moment of death from competing forces.

If there is a *finite number* of souls that are under a strictly regulated God force recycling program, then cloned bodies and androids might end up *outside*—excluded from that recycling process.

The full scope of the complex, multilayered chess game for souls, spirits, and bodies of humans, extraterrestrials, angels, and time travelers might be beyond human ability to understand.

One scientist in New England, who has also been abducted by grey beings who repaired his diseased heart, told me that he was shown holograms that depicted a series of universes in pairs—mirrored images, each the opposite of the other from the subatomic to the macro.

He said, **"Our universe is paired to another universe, which is completely opposite of this one. There, the skies are glowing white with dark suns. Colors are indescribable and iridescent. Like a conveyor belt, at the moment of death in our universe we move through a tunnel into the mirror-opposite universe where it is all light. There, time moves to the past and souls return back here to be born again in this universe."**

COULD STRAIGHTFORWARD CONTACT IN DECADE 2020 HELP ALL LIFE-FORMS?

The most comforting thought is that our alien creators don't want us to destroy us and Earth—their vested interests. So maybe by now, our Watchers and genetic manipulators are on the brink of finally revealing themselves more straightforwardly—not as gods, but as fellow life-forms in this universe that 13.8 billion light-years ago emerged on a razor's edge of equal parts antimatter and matter that could have suffered mutual destruction. But a tiny bit more positive atomic particles tilted the universe to matter that could sustain organic life. If this is truly a laboratory-constructed holographic universe projected from another dimension, then maybe the whole point of the experiment is to compare and monitor throbbing life consciousness in this matter cosmos versus cold, inanimate crystal consciousness in another lab-concocted universe.

If soon there is finally a **Mind-Cracking Contact**, my prayer is that other intelligences long involved with Earth will finally acknowledge humans as *fellow* sentient beings in the implicate order. If an upfront handshake is coming, it's also clear that "Someone" out there is trying to impress upon *Homo sapiens sapiens* that survival beyond petri-dish Earth may not be guaranteed if we continue to abuse Earth's environment with uncontrolled overpopulation that interferes with their various "harvests."

Maybe like political factions, the Dark Party and the Light Party are competing over legislation to legalize the production of cloned, android life outside the Force of Creation's reincarnation recycling program of a finite number of souls. Maybe alleged "captured" souls are put into cloned bodies, which is fouling up the Divine Field's infinite goal to see if all souls in all worlds, universes, dimensions, and timelines willfully choose light over dark.

Perhaps the unique isolation each human feels and the peculiar melancholy a dark sky filled with stars can evoke have something to do with knowledge buried in our genes and souls from recycled lives, a sensing of ancient intimacies with other beings and other worlds. Now, in this time of revolution when the whole world will know we are not alone in this universe, our greatest challenge as a species will be to stand up unafraid before the old "gods" and "Watchers." Ultimately, there is a common bond among all life forms ebbing and flowing on spirals of different frequencies supported by a singular force, an invisible matrix of energy from which everything emerges and to which everything returns.

5

STUDYING INTRUSIONS FROM THE SUBTLE REALM: HOW CAN WE DEEPEN OUR KNOWLEDGE?[1]

Dr. John E. Mack

I want to talk with you about what I have been finding in studying the alien abduction phenomenon. I wish to particularly talk about the ways that we know—how we actually know anything. What is the appropriate epistemology for a particular subject? It seems to me that all science—all knowledge, really—is about the discovery of patterns, and that includes patterns of meaning. But how we know, the approach that we use, depends on what the matter at hand happens to be.

For the sake of clarity, I would divide the realms that we are considering here between what has been called the gross material world on the one hand and the subtle realms on the other: in the language of psychiatrist Stanislav Grof, the hylotropic versus the holotropic world. In physicist David Bohm's terms, the explicate or manifest order or the implicate, or hidden, order, by which he means the structures, deeper reality, and meaning in the universe.

By and large science, as it is traditionally spoken of, has addressed, and its methodology has been appropriate to, the gross material, the physical or manifest world, and the approach to this world has been largely dualistic: An observer studies something from outside of or separate from that person or phenomenon.

We know that some of the best scientists do not think of their work in that way. Nevertheless, that is the standard that we often think we mean, or are told we mean, by the "scientific method." I might add that in the focus on the material realm to the exclusion of the subtle realms, we have virtually rid the cosmos of nature, rid nature of spirit, and, in a sense, denied the existence of all life other than that which is physically observable here on Earth.

What do I mean by the subtle realm? As I began to think about it more deeply, I realized this is not so easy to pin down. It has to do with phenomena that seem to come from another dimension: information obtained telepathically; clairvoyance and the whole psi realm; out-of-body experiences; near-death experiences; telekinesis; and the alien abduction phenomenon itself—that is, phenomena that may manifest in the physical world but seem to originate in another dimension, coming from a place unseen. We are speaking of matters that are not readily observable under ordinary "separatist," dualistic, scientific, or methodological conditions, but make their presence known more subtly through an opening of consciousness or more receptive perception.

One of the fundamental tenets of the mechanistic or dualistic approach is that consciousness is seen as an epiphenomenon of the human brain. This is one of the basic assumptions we have to challenge if we are going to be able to study the subtle realms, which not only involve consciousness itself but the relationship of consciousness to the material world. We have to consider the possibility that consciousness—spirit, self, soul—all have a life, an existence, separate from the physical body. That, for me, was once a very great leap, and I had to do my own self-exploration through work with Stanislav Grof, and a great deal of challenging of my own materialist scientific and clinical upbringing, to come to appreciate the fundamental parting of the ways required between the materialist scientific approach and one that can begin to allow us to study more profoundly these subtle realms.

The Western worldview, what Tulane philosopher Michael Zimmerman calls anthropomorphic humanism, has reduced reality largely to the manifest or physical world and puts the human mind or the human being at the top of the cosmic intellectual hierarchy, eliminating not only God but virtually all spirit from the cosmos. The phenomena that really shake up that worldview are those that seem to cross over from the unseen world and manifest in the physical world. That is why someone like Uri Geller may be hounded from pillar to post. That is why people like Brian O'Leary, who studies free energy, or people who study phenomena that seem to challenge the great divide we have created between the unseen realm and the physical world, are given such a hard time in this society.

By the seventeenth century theologians and other "spiritual people," perhaps even psychologists, were given a mandate over the subtle or unseen realm and scientists were given jurisdiction over the physical or material world. There was not a great problem as long as phenomena seemed to array themselves neatly on one side of the divide. But if a phenomenon appears to cross over, if it will not stay on one side or the other, this raises a big problem in our culture.

The matter that I am studying is just such a phenomenon. I think it is one that by its very nature seems to "grab" us where we live, because it crosses over and manifests in the form or language that we understand in this culture: spaceships, abductions, implants, instruments, surgery, hybrids, babies, reproduction, and so on. All that seems very physical and ought to be reducible, or at least be possible to study with the dualistic methods of traditional science. But the alien abduction phenomenon does not seem to yield its secrets to that approach. Not only that, but it commits a deeper crime, which is it challenges that very sacred divide that we have created between the unseen world and the material world, undermining the fundamental worldview of the Western mind.

I believe we need to consider another frontier, which I am only going to be able to touch upon briefly here, namely what makes us so attached to a particular worldview. Why do we cling so tightly to a worldview in general and the materialist paradigm in particular? What makes our worldview so fundamental to our existence?

I do not believe it is just the huge economic investments that derive from the materialist view. Indeed, the whole materialist marketplace mentality of technology and science as we know it is threatened by a worldview that tells us of vast realms unavailable to our direct observation. In fact, a result of the worldview in which we are embedded is ultimately the destruction of the material playground, the Earth itself as a living organism.

There is still more to it. A worldview organizes our sense

of self. It gives us the illusion that we have some control of ourselves and of nature—that we are in charge, that we are safe. Never mind that we all must die, and perhaps die more lonely deaths, for in this particular worldview we have rid the cosmos of all consciousness, of spirit, of God him- or herself. Thus, we can never come to grips with the notion of death except as a bleak end to everything. Therefore, there is a terrible loneliness in this worldview.

Nevertheless, the materialist worldview, like any paradigm, organizes our sense of self and constricts reality so that we have some illusion of control. When this or any worldview is challenged and shattered, it creates terror. I think that some of the resistance that I have encountered, and which, naïvely, I rather underestimated, derives from this threat.

One of the most powerful expressions of this resistance has been within my own university where I've undergone an investigation of my work. I had been doing this work for several years, talking for hundreds of hours with individuals who reported abductions, and I had not said anything publicly until I was pretty clear about what I was doing. The reaction surprised me, I must say. People have said to me, "*Well, didn't you know if you started saying that little green men or spirits or funny beings were taking men, women, and children away and doing things to them, didn't you realize that you would run into this resistance?*" But, like the frog who dies in gradually heating water, I think it kind of snuck up on me.

But now I appreciate that if an institution like Harvard Medical School or a church or any institution that is deeply connected with a worldview has that worldview fundamentally challenged—and I think contemporary medicine is based largely on a materialist, mechanistic worldview—then the empire will strike back.

Perhaps you have to be a little naïve to wander off into these insecure realms of knowledge or you will not go there at all. For if you know in advance the opposition you are going to encounter, you might not choose to take on the adventure of such exploration. If it's true what Bertrand Russell said about resistance being proportional to the square of the importance of what you are studying, I must be studying something very important indeed.

I've come to a kind of amicable agreement at Harvard. They don't necessarily buy what I'm finding or my methods, but there have not been any charges, really. I go about what I do as conscientiously as I can and there is a respect for the right to do that. We are at a sort of juncture of agreeing to differ. But I've committed no crime other than the ideological one of doing something that fundamentally challenges a worldview on which so much is invested.

In one sense I appreciate the criticism, even the attacks I have encountered, for it is, I believe, useful for all of us to know more deeply about what resistance our work is stirring up. For then if we can embrace the questions and polarities that the critiques represent, perhaps we can go to a deeper level of understanding instead of finding ourselves, as we tend to, in opposition to the people that will not take in what we are trying to communicate.

I would like to say one more thing about the challenge to our worldview that crossover phenomena like the alien abduction story represents. Consider all the blows to the collective egocentrism of humanity starting with Copernicus and

Galileo and going on to Darwin and then Freud, wherein little by little we had to face that not only were we not at the center in terms of the geography of the universe, we were not the only God-given ones among the Earth's creatures, and, with Freud, we were not even in charge of our own psyches. Now, finally, we are learning from the abduction phenomenon that we may not be the smartest guys in the universe after all.

In fact, we may not be in control of ourselves even in the most basic sense. Other beings—funny-looking ones at that, little creatures with big black eyes—can come, render us helpless, and do what they will with us. This is truly a fourth blow to our collective arrogance after what Copernicus, Darwin, and Freud had already done. (If only it were those magnificent Nordics we hear about, we might feel differently.) I must admit to being a bit perverse for, as a psychiatrist, I believe that anything that can be a big blow to the human ego can only be a good thing in terms of our collective development. Such shocks can perhaps help us to grow as a species.

Before speaking of my specific work, I want to say another word about how a worldview is maintained in a given culture. For this consideration, I suggest the idea of the "**politics of ontology.**" This has to do with how a society organizes itself, particularly through a certain elite group, to determine for the rest of that society what is real. It is a kind of governance of ideas. In this culture, there may be a very small group of scientific, governmental, religious, and corporate elite that determine the prevailing boundaries of reality. The forces that surround the determination of reality is an area of politics that we have not really thought about that much. We think about the politics of economics, the governing of communities, and the creation of a social order, but not much about how we are governed with respect to what we are supposed to think is real.

An interesting thing is happening, however, in this culture, that Michael Zimmerman has pointed out: With so much information available through the media, computer networks, and extensive public education, everybody is getting kind of smart. People know their own experiences, and know when they have undergone certain experiences that don't fit the prevailing mechanistic worldview. Whatever polling methods you may use, it is apparent that large percentages of people seem to know there is an unseen world or hidden dimensions of reality. They may not call it that, but they know that the subtle realms exist. They know their own experiences and trust them. They are not fooled by NBC or by *The New York Times* or *Time* or other official arbiters of the truth and reality. We have a kind of samizdat of reality going on here, an underground of popular knowledge, that the universe is not the one we are being officially told it is. It is really going to be interesting to see when the official mainstream, the small percentage of elites who determine what we are supposed to think is real, wake up to the fact that the consensus view of reality is gone. We are, I think, getting near that moment.

In 1974 Margaret Mead wrote in *Redbook* magazine (which I didn't know was such a radical journal in those days), "**People still ask each other, 'Do you believe in UFOs?' I think this is a silly question, born of confusion. Belief has to do with matters of faith. It has nothing to do with the kind of knowledge that is based on scientific**

inquiry . . . When we want to understand something strange, something previously unknown, we have to begin with an entirely different set of questions. What is it? How does it work? Are there recurrent regularities?"[2] I resonate with that, because I am always being accused of being a "believer," somebody who has gone over the edge from rationality to belief. My work has nothing to do with belief. It has to do with what I do as a clinician.

I began to see people in 1990 who seemed of sound mind but were describing experiences that simply did not fit into any kind of psychiatric category of which I could conceive. Child abuse, psychosis, neurosis, organic brain disease, fantasy-prone personality, you know the litany here. No diagnostic category came close to explaining what I was seeing. I often say this to audiences: There is not a single abduction case that does not fulfill my rather simple criteria for an authentic case; that is, the person reports, with or without hypnosis or a simple relaxation exercise, observing some sort of humanoid beings, being taken against their will into some kind of enclosure, and subjected to traumatic and sometimes enlightening procedures. There are now thousands of cases described in the literature that fulfill these criteria. These patterns are clear, down to quite specific details. But not one case has been shown to have a cause other than what the person says happened. No case has revealed that behind the reported experience is some kind of strange depression, or child abuse, or something else. Clinicians have made intense efforts to find this "something else," because the motivation is very strong to shoot this phenomenon down, to find another cause, what I call the *"anything but syndrome"*—anything but that we are being visited by some unusual intelligence that is entering our world.

The methodological issues are important. On what basis do I ask that these experiences be taken seriously? In some ways, it is easier for a psychological clinician, like a psychiatrist, to use these methods because, in a sense, that is the way we always work. We are not people who get anywhere by standing back from other people and observing them as specimens. The way we always work, to be helpful to our patients, is by entering into their worlds through a kind of intuitive use of our total self—using our intellect, inspiration, and intuition. We use the total psyche, our total consciousness. In effect, trained consciousness has been our instrument of knowing from the beginning of the discipline when we were doing it right and not trying to act like physicists or pharmacologists. Our true roots as psychological professionals come from the use of consciousness, including non-ordinary states. We learn by methods that are participatory and nondualistic. This is a "relational" way of knowing.

It is easy for people who use a dualistic approach to say, **"You're contaminating the field. You're influencing, you're leading."** In fact, you are joining with the other person in bringing forth experiences. But you cannot get away from the fact that in any exploration of human experience there are two consciousnesses, two energy fields interacting, connecting, and what emerges is out of that participation, out of the relationship.

Then, after you do that, you look at what you have found and apply rational judgment in analyzing the material. You ask, **"Was this person trying to please? Was this**

authentic? What was the emotional intensity that came with the communications? Was this emotion appropriate to what the person was talking about?" These are the yardsticks that psychological clinicians apply in assessing what a patient or client is reporting. It has nothing to do with belief. In my abduction cases, with few exceptions, I have felt people were describing as best they could what had occurred. In fact, they doubt as much as I do what they have undergone. They tend to come to me saying, "**Can you make this go away?**" Or they will report waking experiences as dreams if they occurred at night. They want the experiences to be found to be a product of their psyches, not to be "real." In case after case I have seen a person become stunned, the lips quiver or tears come down the cheeks, the moment in the session when he or she realizes they were not asleep and that what occurred was not a dream. I might then say, "**Yes, I'm sorry, but I know many people who have had experiences like yours.**" One woman who came to me a few days ago was eager to believe her experiences were dreams. She said to me, sobbing, "**But if it's real, then it can happen again. And I can't stop it and you can't stop it.**" These individuals prefer this be a clinical phenomenon that will go away, or that I might cure it by giving them a pill, or by talking them out of it, or by interpreting it in some dynamic sense, which of course is what many of my colleagues want to do as well.

So, the method I use here is to employ consciousness, my total self, my whole background or being, to be with a person to create a safe environment in which the individual can share and bring forth that which is the most sensitive, most troubling, most confusing, most extraordinary experiences that are imaginable, at least in the worldview of this culture.

I have worked intensively now with more than one hundred people and in about seventy cases I have done a modified hypnosis or relaxation exercise in which the person closes their eyes and just "goes inside." Contrary to what is said about hypnosis bringing distortions of memory, in such cases I often trust what comes out in the relaxation sessions more than in face-to-face interviews because the feelings are so intense and less acceptable. The person is able to bring forth more ignoble and more humiliating experiences than in conscious, more social kinds of interaction. For instance, a man may describe being on a ship and having a cup placed over his penis against his will, that kind of thing. Whereas when individuals tell what they have consciously recalled, they tend to organize their thoughts in a way that is more palatable and appropriate to their positive self-regard and worldview.

The basic phenomena associated with abductions seem to be consistent worldwide. At the same time, paradoxes abound, and it is difficult to make statements that apply in all cases. For example, I do not believe that in every abduction case the physical body is taken. Yet there are cases in which the person is witnessed to be not there. A child, for example, may go into the mother's room at night and the mother is gone, and the mother reports an abduction experience that occurred at that time. But there are also cases in which the person reports experiencing an abduction and other people have observed seeing the person still in place. But the basic phenomena: seeing a beam of light; the intrusion of humanoid beings into the person's life; the experience of being paralyzed and taken through walls into some kind of enclosure and subjected to a variety of intrusive procedures resulting in the creation of a "hybrid" species; the conveying of powerful information about threats to the planet such as nuclear war and vast ecological change; the evidences of an expansion of consciousness that occurs for the people that undergo these experiences, for people who work with them and for those who will attend to what this appears to be about—these all seem to be quite consistent findings.

Furthermore, the experiences seem also to be consistent worldwide. My colleague Dominique Callimanopulos and I have traveled to South Africa, Brazil, and a number of countries in Europe. We are also getting reports from all over the world and learning that the basic phenomenon appears to have a consistent core. I have worked with a South African medicine man, Credo Mutwa, a Zulu leader now seventy-four, who had a classic abduction experience when he was thirty-eight. This occurred during his training as a shaman. Mr. Mutwa was in the bush when suddenly he found himself in an enclosure surrounded by humanoid beings with large black eyes. He was terrified, and underwent the range of traumatic, educational, and transformational experiences described above. He believes the "**mandindas,**" as his people call these beings, are trying to teach us about the threat to the Earth that our mindless destructive actions are causing.

MEANING OF THE EXPERIENCE

I would like to turn now to what appears to be the basic pattern and meaning of the abduction phenomenon. First, abductees are being told over and over that this phenomenon is occurring in the context of the threat to the Earth as a living system, a response to the ecological devastation that our particular species has undertaken. (This doesn't mean that something relating to this phenomenon hasn't existed from before the early 1960s and the Betty-Barney Hill case.) Credo Mutwa told us that, according to African mythology, the Earth is one of what his people call "**mother planets.**" There are twenty-five mother planets in the cosmos, he said, and we may be destroying life on one of them. As one of the abductees I have worked with put it, the phenomenon is an effort to bring about "a cosmic correction." For the Earth, evidently, has a place in the larger fabric of meaning and significance in the cosmos, and this one species cannot be allowed to destroy it for its own exploitative purposes.

Second, this other intelligence appears to function as a kind of intermediary between the Source of creation and us, emissaries perhaps, of that correction. This does not mean that every kind of alien being is involved in that mission. But the beings are often perceived in this way.

Third, a message is coming through to us—I will shortly provide some clinical material related to this—that we have lost connection with what some aliens, and some humans who have had these experiences, call Source, or Home, the divine core of creativity, the light—different traditions have varying ways of talking about this realm. We are being told that we have grown too far from that Source and have lost our connection with it.

Fourth, these encounters are changing the consciousness of the people that are undergoing them, and, I believe, influencing consciousness on the planet as the power and implications of the abduction phenomenon are becoming more widely recognized. The phenomenon seems to hold the potential of reconnecting us with our divine Source.

Fifth, the hybrid "program," which can be deeply traumatic for the mothers and fathers (particularly when they are brought back to see and hold these odd children, especially as they cannot know when they will be able to see these creatures again), seems to be a kind of awkward insurance policy for the next step of evolution. We do not know in what reality these hybrids exist. It could be an intermediate realm between the material world and the unseen world. A number of abductees have been told that the hybrids represent a step in evolution that is being created for the time when we have destroyed ourselves, so that some aspect of our genetic structure or nature can be preserved.

Finally, the human–alien relationship, which is not simply good or bad, is, nevertheless, reciprocal. We do not know from what dimension or Source the whole connection is being orchestrated. Perhaps it serves them and us. It may emanate from another dimension, inviting us to explore its mysteries.

Now I will tell you about the case of Ifyani, a name derived from her alien encounters. She is a thirty-four-year-old mother of three children. Her oldest son was killed in an automobile accident several months ago, and her abduction encounters have been important in enabling her to integrate that terrible loss and to put it in a larger cosmic perspective. Ifyani has had a wide range of abduction experience, from being "used" for the breeding project to having a dual identity, seeming to serve the aliens, identifying with them and doing their work, while at the same time experiencing the trauma of her encounters. She has a complex religious background. She is a native of a Central American country, where she experienced Mayan-derived religious influences while also being raised as a Christian. She is an artist and writes poetry; these talents are utilized as a therapeutic outlet. We have been working toward enabling her to overcome the victimization aspect of her abduction experiences, and she has undergone profound personal growth in the context of her encounters.

The session from which I will quote occurred on July 31, 1995. Ifyani had been having ongoing encounters with the beings during the days before that and was struggling to change these encounters into more reciprocal exchanges. She sensed that the beings were struggling to connect with her at a soul level, even to take her soul, or to connect with her body and soul. She found that by emanating love toward them, the demonic or dark dimension of their being was affected. They seemed to pull back from the love she sent them and, at the same time, to thrive from it. Thus, a kind of loving connection seemed to grow out of that struggle. This was not a regression but a regular interview.

Ifyani, referring to love, says, "**I believe that love is the most powerful force in the whole universe, or in every other universe that might exist. I think it's what everything originated from. I think it's what created everything, and I think everything has love in it.**" Ifyani's beliefs seem to stem directly from her ongoing life experiences. She continues: "**I look at love as a cord that connects my**

soul to the main major Source, a sort of umbilical cord
that provides me with spiritual nourishment."

Speaking of the aliens, she says, "They seem very frail.
I think they feel a sort of envy toward us. Maybe they are
creating these half-and-half babies, using our bodies for
themselves, trying somehow to get enough human qualities to nurture themselves, to be mothered and reconnect
with the Source of love."

I hear this in a number of cases; that is, that the alien
beings envy our dense, physical embodiment and seem to
treasure our sexuality, our nurturance, our intense physi-
cality. This is something that they want from us, while they,
in turn, crack our barriers, breaking down the egoism that
distances us from Source.

In Ifyani's words: "They're like starving children who
are trying to sneak in with the other babies who are being
breastfed. I think that they remember what this felt like.
They know what it feels like, and I think they want to go
back to that. But for some reason, I don't know why, they
can't connect to the Source the way we can, and I think
they have to go through us to connect to the Source."

This is paradoxical, because in another sense they seem
to function like emissaries from Source. But what I think
she means here is that the beings do not have the kind of
deep, rich physical, emotional, and spiritual experience of
connection with Source for which we long. She continues:
"I would have to grant them permission to use my body
and give up soul willingly (which I don't intend to do), for
them to connect with the Source. To me, it's like they're
trying to use tricks and I don't know why. I don't con-

sider them evil in the way that we look at evil. I think that they're just interested in self-preservation. I do believe we all originated from the same Source. I believe if we look back on ancient myths and religious beliefs, many of the answers are there. But we've gotten to the point here where we consider ourselves so technologically advanced and educated, just 'up there,' that we don't even think it's necessary to remember where we came from. We've become educated fools.

"I feel religion has been made into a tool that keeps us blind and ignorant, keeping us from remembering where we came from. I think Source's purpose for allowing these encounters to take place—perhaps this is totally weird—was to let us remember things, to bring back to us the memory of Source so we can empower ourselves. It's not like Source is giving you this power now. It's always been there. It's self-realization. It's to open up our consciousness more. I think it's almost like a baby going from crawling to walking and realizing that *I am*. That's what I think was Source's reason. It was for this: I am . . .

"I think there's so much more to this body than we are aware of. We don't even know a lot about our DNA. I think we have the ability to restructure our DNA. We only need to remember how. I think we can become what the Bible said: 'in the last days people will have new bodies, indestructible bodies. They will be new beings.' And I think it's all inside of us. It's all here, this package, and I think the mind is the key. I feel that our minds will expand and open, and a percentage of the brain that we don't currently use will become accessible to us. Then we will be truly free, because I don't think humans are free now.

"We tend to look at everything as good and bad and say, 'Oh, how can God let this happen?' We look at things from our perspective only and think, 'Oh, my God, how horrible, how terrible,' but that's because we're looking at it through these eyes. We're not looking at the whole picture. I don't think there's ever an end to anything or a real beginning to anything—everything just is. Every action you look at, even sending a little kid to school for the first time, everything we do just mimics the way Source does things. If you take a good look at society and our individual lives you will notice that patterns are always being repeated—in the way we raise our children, and the way government treats us. Everything mimics over and over and over. Where is that pattern coming from? I think it comes from the main Source. I guess in a way we're like a small replica of what goes on everywhere else. I suppose we are baby Sources and we come here to mature . . .

"We're getting ready to graduate . . . A lot of us are starting to wake up and remember and realize. I think graduation time is coming up . . . Our Mother Earth has gone through a lot. She's gone through having to support a whole race of kindergarten kids and juvenile delinquents who've mauled, raped, and spray painted it, disfiguring and totally disgracing it. All of this was done in the name of technology and advancement.

"I think this class is gonna graduate, and I think the Earth will have to go through a cleansing period, and I think a whole new set of little Sources will come through,

and I think this has happened before. I think it's gonna
continue happening. I think it's basically what this is all
about . . .

"Poison in the water. Poison in the air. Poison in the
food. I keep having all these visions and dreams about
the water and other resources being deliberately poi-
soned. Just by being the way we are, here we are poisoning the planet. We are giving off negative energy, and
we're poisoning the planet by giving off these repelling
energies. We're killing our Mother Earth. Our thoughts
can destroy or create by the energies they produce. It affects the animals. It affects the insects. It affects everything. Everything—all of it, the trees and everything. If
we continue to give off this negative energy, after a while
the Earth will look at us as something like a harmful
bacteria and repel us. It will fight back. I think Mother
Earth is actually fighting back. These blue baldies"—
[that's what she calls the alien beings]—"I won't say they
own this Earth, but they see it as their home. I think they
were here before we were made. They are the true keepers
of this Earth. Whether they mean to or not, they're here
to help us with this growth period, to help us to mature."

This, I would remind you, is a person who has been
highly traumatized by her experiences, but with the trauma,
or perhaps as an outgrowth of it, she has demonstrated personal growth and knowledge.

"I would say we're getting to a point where we're becoming more aware, waking up, but I think these blue
baldies were put in charge of Mother Earth, and I think
they're the ones that are going to clean it up after we
have been dealt with. It seems to me that I'm becoming

more conscious of things around me. It feels like there's an actual chemical reaction happening in the lower back part of my brain; something is changing, and I am being changed by it."

In conclusion, I would begin by paraphrasing what the American Catholic bishops said in the early 1980s when they took a policy stand against nuclear deterrence: "We could destroy God's work." Also, the Dalai Lama, when a group of researchers met with him around the alien abduction phenomenon in 1992, suggested that, "These beings, these creatures, they are very upset. We are destroying their physical and spiritual homes." They have no choice, he added, but to become physical and come back and try to stop us.

Next, the alien abduction phenomenon appears to be a kind of outreach program from the cosmos for the spiritually impaired.

Third, we and the beings, evidently, come from a common Source, and that love is at the core of the cosmos as its essential creative power.

Fourth, to know in the domain of our relationship to the subtle realm, paradoxically (and this phenomenon is filled with paradox) requires an attitude of not knowing. What the Buddhists call "**empty mind**." Knowledge here seems to come like the creation of the universe itself. As the universe emerged from nothing, so knowledge in matters such as this seems to emerge from radical "**not knowing**." The new paradigm we have heard so much about has to do, I believe, with a different notion of our relationship to reality, one that is co-creative and evolutionary, as if we were co-creating with nature and with God.

Fifth, and finally, our job at this time, for all of us, appears to be to overcome the dualism, the separateness, that has characterized not only our worldview, but our scientific approaches to all the realms that have been studied up to this point. The task now is to integrate the polarities at every level. At the intrapsychic level, this means the darkness within us, as well as our transcendent, loving spiritual selves. At the interpersonal level, we have to overcome the polarized individual and collective human relationships that find expression, for example, in "ethnic cleansing," an instance of extreme polarization within the human community, what Erik Erikson called *pseudo-speciation*," feeling and behaving as if we were not even a single species.

Finally, we need to transcend the separateness that disconnects us from nature, which is the main characteristic of the Western worldview. If we could transcend this division, we might then explore, enjoy, and travel ecstatically, lovingly, materially and nonmaterially; and discover, among the unique particularities of our own being, our own natures within the cosmos, experiencing at the same time an essential unity and sacredness of creation. That possibility is, I think, what this extraordinary phenomenon has to teach us.

6

THE RETURN OF THE VISITORS

Whitley Strieber[1]

Deep one night in October of 2015, pain—severe—radiated through my left second toe. Anne had passed away just a few months before, and as I had every night since, I had spent my meditation session at 11 calling to her, **"Annie, Annie, if you hear me at all, please come, please come to me."**

I leaped out of bed and stood there gasping, then fumbled to turn on the lamp. But what was it, what just happened? There are no electrical outlets near the bed, no wiring or circuitry at all. I grabbed my phone and looked up symptoms of gout. Not a fit. I sat on the bedside, reached down, and rubbed my toes.

Everything in the apartment seemed normal. I looked at the clock: 3:25. Great, now my night's sleep was ruined. Next, I looked under the bed, but there was nothing there that could have shocked me. I lifted the foot of the mattress. Nothing there either. Finally, I turned out the light and lay back down. All was quiet, the bed was warm. I drifted into a sort of half-sleep.

During the day, I thought little about the mystery. I had no idea what happened. But somebody did. They were here in 2007, and now that my situation had changed, they had returned to start a new lesson in the course of study that is my life. Without any idea that this happened, I have crossed a threshold—or rather been zapped across it.

The next night I felt strong fingers grab my right nipple, pinch it painfully, and shake it. This time, I came roaring out of the bed. Once again, I fumbled for the light. I stalked through the small apartment. There was nobody here but me. All the doors and windows were locked. But that was a hand; those were fingers touching me.

You have every right to wonder, "Why is he being so dense?" The answer is that relationship with the visitors is both so improbable and so hard to grasp. They always seem to show up unexpectedly. But there's more to it than that. We may say we want to see them. We may even beg them to come. But actual contact is apocalyptic. It means tremendous, overturning change, and that is very threatening to the ego, and it is going to defend itself against what it sees as an unknown threat. This is why so many people can't take the close encounter experience. It is why we have been fighting the visitors for nearly a century on so many different levels. It's ego, defending its very existence—and all for nothing. There is no destruction of ego involved, and when you come to see that what you imagined was your "self"— the beginning and end of you—is actually just a social tool with a name attached to it, you realize that you're not really under any threat at all.

I sat down in the living room and tried to calm myself. I had finally realized that something extremely strange and yet very familiar was happening to me. There was no question in my mind but that somebody grabbed my nipple.

Given the life I have lived, there could be only one explanation: The visitors were back. They had been pretty much in the background ever since Anne's fatal illness began in 2013. She had been dead now for six weeks, and I was in a state of blackest grief.

I sensed that this wasn't just an anonymous "them," though, and here began a new level of my experience. I cannot say exactly why, but I knew that Anne was involved. Since her passing, I have learned more about how deeply true her insight about the relationship between the dead and our visitors was. We are not just having a close encounter with what appear to be non-human beings but also with ourselves.

If the mirror universe is where what appear to be aliens come from, then maybe it is, just as Homer thought, also where our dead go. After her near-death experience in 2004, Anne felt that there was a sort of breathing between this and another universe, and that when we died here, our consciousness was transferred to another version of ourselves there.

I sat on my bedside. The feeling that Anne was there was now very strong. It was as if I could almost touch her, and how I longed to! But there's more. A dissonant note, at least, dissonant to a man enveloped in deepest grief. I sensed that she was laughing at me. In life, she always saw me as entirely too serious.

I didn't sit on the bedside for long. My mind went back to the last time I was woken up by being jostled or otherwise disturbed in the wee hours. This happened back in the 1990s when seven people who indicated that they were from between lives kept trying to get me to meditate with them at this hour. I did it for a few weeks or months; I forget how long. Then we lost the cabin and moved to Texas, and I saw no more of them.

I recalled the weeks I spent meditating with them as being one of the best periods of contact of my life, a rich learning experience. (I've discussed it in more detail in my books *Solving the Communion Enigma* and *The Super Natural*.) After I entered the meditation room the first time, they called me; they came pounding down onto the roof, making seven loud thuds. Then they fell silent. A few seconds later, I had the impression that somebody was standing right in front of me. I explained that I couldn't meditate with invisible people present. I had to see them. When nobody materialized, I left the room and went to bed.

A few hours later, one of them, a man, human appearing, became visible for a few unforgettable moments while sitting on the foot of the bed.

Their ability to control their density might involve a natural process or technology, I cannot say. If they are coming and going from the mirror universe, then maybe they don't disappear at all but simply pass back into the other reality, perhaps using some form of mental process or, of course, technology. (How, I wish I knew!)

There is one thing that, if we could do it, we could control our own density. This would involve increasing and decreasing the space between atoms—in other words, controlling the gluons that mediate that space.

The physical world is a near-vacuum. For example, the atoms that make up most of the mass of a piece of steel are actually just 0.0000000000001 percent of its volume. Statistically, physical matter can hardly be said to exist. It is maintained by what is known as the strong nuclear force, which is the only reason that the world we live in is here.

Their ability to rearrange atoms has to mean that they can control the strong force and, thus, may be in possession of technology that can alter density. Of course, there are other possible reasons, too. This gets back to the mirror universe, which would necessarily occupy reality in a way that mirrors our own place in it. If this is true, the math of wormholes tells us that passing back and forth might be easier than would be using a wormhole to go to another part of our own universe. The amount of energy needed to bend space-time in order to bring two points in the same universe together is far greater than the amount needed to briefly open a hole in the membrane between mirror universes.

When the man materialized before my eyes, I took his hand. It was small and light, very light. But it had definite heft. It felt solid. But I wondered if he was actually, physically present. How could he be? No matter how real it appeared, it had to be in my mind.

So I held it to my nose and smelled the back of it. Once again, I was surprised. His skin was pungent. There was a sharpness to the odor that I associate with people who don't bathe. Frankly, the guy was ripe. There's no other way to put it.

I was so surprised that I dropped it—whereupon he winked out of existence. I sat there completely flabbergasted. Now, looking back to that event of more than twenty years ago, I would think that controlling the strong nuclear force may even be a natural ability, perhaps even one that can be found, with disciplined concentration, within ourselves. If so, then it must have something to do with control of attention. It really did seem, in that moment, that my dropping his hand had broken his concentration, which is what caused him to disappear.

Fast forward to 2015 and to the third night that I was called. The first night, I experienced a shock that was inexplicable to me. On the second night came a pinch that made me realize that I was once again in contact. And now came the third night and another awakening at three. No question now. I got up, went into the living room, took my seat, and began to move my attention from mind to body.

Since then, the early morning meditation has become part of my life, and with some of this unfolding so very close to physical reality. From October 2015 until April 2019, they woke me up every night by blowing on my face or the back of my hand, sometimes by kissing me.

It's easy to say, "He's just hallucinating," and ignore me. Many people don't even want to think about a life like mine, let alone entertain the idea of living with demanding invisible beings who refuse to allow you a full night's rest and who involve themselves in your inner life in ways that are often extremely challenging. But there's another, more fundamental reason they prefer to doubt me. It is that whoever or whatever is here doing this is obviously in possession of extraordinary capabilities, and that feels like a threat.

During the October–December period in 1985 in upstate New York when they were taking me physically, I felt captured, which was why I reacted like a wild animal that had been snared. And in fact, this is what I was. We are a social species, but that doesn't mean that we're not wild. We don't normally feel that wildness, but when one is face to face with an unknown being who is obviously in control of the situation and whose motives one cannot even guess at, it will come out.

This response is instinctual and is probably the underlying reason that we so generally reject this whole experience. The only way to overcome it is for both sides to keep trying to get used to one another.

There is a taming process necessary, and it isn't easy, not even when you know what is happening. I've been trying to get used to them for thirty years and have only just recently begun to think of my fear of them as something that has passed. Frankly, my wife's participation in the process from the other side has more than anything else been what has enabled me to make progress, and, to me, this is an indication that contact isn't going to succeed if we continue to deny the existence of our souls and thus also our dead, and they are not involved. We need to finally stop pretending to ourselves that they don't exist and get down to the business of enlisting their support as we go deeper into this new life.

Here are two examples of just how deep and powerful our fear of doing this is. In February 2017, I was at the Esalen Institute in Northern California at a conference with Jeff Kripal. We were sleeping in the same room, one in which I had briefly encountered the visitors on a previous visit. It's in a building called the Murphy House and is called the Sea View Room because it has a deck that overlooks the Pacific Ocean. When they are going to drop into a physical density, the visitors do tend to prefer spaces that offer a quick exit to an open area such as a large forest or the sea.

At 3 A.M. on the last morning of the conference, an

invisible presence blew on the back of my left hand. I was lying with my head turned to the right, which meant that I was facing toward the window that overlooks the sea. As the burst of air on my left hand caused me to open my eyes and turn toward the hand, I glimpsed a dark figure at the bedside on my right. I saw no detail except that it was short, and I assume that the fact that the left hand was involved was intended to cause me to turn away from it as I awoke. Even as recently as 2017, I would have reacted to face-to-face contact with a burst of fear.

The next moment, I recovered myself. I got up and, as usual, opened my inner self with the sensing exercise. Nothing further happened to me, and I completed the exercise, as I normally did in those days, after about fifteen minutes of inner work.

The next morning, Jeff remembered hearing a tremendous crashing sound and feeling an uncanny sense of dislocation. My experience had come around 3 A.M., and his about an hour later. He heard an inner voice that was at the same time his own say, "Oh my God." He told me later that he felt a sense of devastation, as if his entire world was collapsing.

This is because contact involves the breakdown of the barrier between the living and the dead and at least a partial drawing of the ego out of the time stream—a sort of death before dying. This threatens a fate that is horrifying in the extreme to the inner person, which is being plunged into the nonmeaning that accompanies knowledge of future and past.

The natural reaction is to think, "Oh, I'd love to know my future."

But what would that actually be like? In fact, you'd feel like you were riding on rails, or a marionette being manipulated by an unseen puppeteer. Your spontaneity would be lost. Life would entirely lose its meaning.

I think that this is why Jeff was so devastated in his moment of contact and why I and so many others have struggled with the ferocious, nameless fear that comes to us when the visitors approach.

The fear can be much worse than what Jeff experienced. It can be life threatening.

The previous summer, I had been at a country house where I've been encountering the visitors since boyhood. It has a sleeping porch upstairs, which a number of the bedrooms open onto. An individual who was in one of these rooms heard scraping footsteps outside her window and then a low, husky voice growl, "Why aren't you asleep?"

She called out and asked if it was me. I was in the living room and called back that I was downstairs reading. I had also heard those footsteps, though. When I was a boy, I heard them on that same porch many times.

In the morning, I asked her if she had been upset. She said no, but I knew from experience that an encounter like that, even one so small, can have powerful effects.

Sure enough, that afternoon she began to experience symptoms of what I suspected could be a silent heart attack. We called a doctor friend who lives nearby. He came over immediately, confirmed that a heart attack was in progress, called EMS, and got her to the hospital. She ended up with a pacemaker.

These are typical examples of the kind of stress close encounter produces. I was allowed on the night at Esalen only a glimpse of what was there. Any more than that, and my ego would have felt itself being drawn out of time, and the terror would have come.

Understand that this doesn't just happen when we have contact with non-human intelligences. The literature of ghostly encounters with dead human beings is a literature of fear. But although both types of event are among the most challenging experiences a person can have, both can also be not only endurable, but productive.

We can see a version of our own fear in the fear that wild animals have of us. In the distant past, I would think that they were no more wary of us than of other predators, and larger predators weren't afraid of us at all. That was, however, before we came to understand the inevitability of death. Because we know this, we are now different from all the other creatures on the Earth, and they know it because they can see it as a darkness in our eyes, exactly as we see in their terrible glances the visitors' knowledge of the future, not just that death is inevitable but the day and the hour.

The visitor who caused me to turn away from him did so out of kindness. If I had woken up while I was turned toward him, I would be looking right into his face. A moment or so of that, and the robotic existence I had experienced before could become my only life.

I knew a man who had something close to this happen. After looking into the eyes of a visitor, he spent the rest of his life in a state of permanent déjà vu.

Once you know the moment of your death, you also know everything that transpires between. We are not here to move through life on the grim rails of future knowledge but to experience events spontaneously. Even if they are preplanned, which for all I know they may be, our purpose here is to be surprised and to gain self-knowledge by observing the way we react to what life presents to us.

If the visitors, not to mention our own dead, are going to commune with us, they are going to have to hide very carefully, because if they slip up and cause us to lose the chance to react spontaneously, then they also lose what they are here to experience.

This is the primary, but deeply hidden, reason for all the secrecy that surrounds the contact experience. Contact—communion—involves not only a new kind of intimacy but also a new kind of mutual discipline. We have to open ourselves to them without seeking to know them, and they have to enter us without revealing their knowledge of our futures to us.

Without us having confidence that this won't happen, communion can only go so far, and it's not going to be far enough for either side.

The question remains, "If it's all predestined, why bother to do anything?" The answer has to do with the reason that history itself exists. Over the six or seven thousand years of the current cycle, in each generation, more complex lives have become possible. The number of alternative histories on offer to each soul has become larger and larger. Even though the end is always the same and the game remains the game, there are more possible moves in every generation, more twists and turns. Although the end is always the same, the paths of life become more and more forked, and the journey richer in discoveries.

Knowing all that, though, what practical means do we

have to work with the fear? Just as tame animals don't fear us, we can learn not to fear the visitors. That's a great part of what my 2019 book *A New World* is about.

In February 2017 at Esalen, I dared not look into their eyes. Now, in Santa Monica in August 2019, I understand why I shouldn't and, therefore, have no fear of this. I'm not going to ruin the spontaneity of my life when I'm with them because I know how to avoid doing it.

I get knowledge from them. My life becomes richer. They get relief from me. Yes, it's a game, and just as Shakespeare said, this is a theater and we are the players. He didn't think about the audience, though. They are the audience, and when they have a seat in the theater of our lives, they enjoy the great pleasure of being alive again.

It's an illusion, of course, but it must be a satisfying one because they do come back to me for it very often indeed, and they are clamoring for more opportunities with more people. If we can do a good job for them on the little stage that is this Earth, they are going to help us keep the theater open—that is, help us rebalance nature.

It's going to be hard to make the relationship work, though. Probably a goodly number of my readers are recoiling in horror right now, thinking to themselves, "My God, he lets himself be possessed!"

No, shared. If they controlled me, they would bring the knowledge they want to leave behind with them. A lot of close encounter witnesses intuit this. It's why they are so often called "The Watchers."

Communion is a new state for us. From experience, once one relaxes into it, the idea of living in the old way becomes the real terror. This is especially true because of the alternative, which is upheaval, incredible human suffering on an unimaginable scale, and possibly even extinction.

They hunger to share our sense of newness. I think the reason for this is explained by an insight that was published in the April 1977 issue of the magazine *Science*. T. B. H. Kuiper and Mark Morris make the observation that any intelligent entity appearing here from another world would have essentially nothing to gain from us except the results of our own independent thought. They would be after newness and they would therefore be concerned about our state of preparedness to engage with them. As Kuiper and Morris speculate, "**We believe that there is a critical phase to this. Before a certain threshold is reached, complete contact with a superior civilization (in which their store of knowledge is made available to us) would abort further development through a 'culture shock' effect. If we were contacted before we reached this threshold, instead of enriching the galactic store of knowledge would merely absorb it.**" They continue, "**By intervening in our natural progress, members of an extraterrestrial society could easily extinguish the only resource on this that could be of any value to them.**"

If they are going to emerge we're going to have to accept certain basic realities. They are: that we don't know what they are, that we don't know the degree of danger involved, and that we are going to have to take a gamble. But it is an informed bet. If they were an invading force, we'd be slaves by now, or dead. While not all of them may have motives that are to our liking or in our interest, some of them do, or I and others like me would not be having positive experiences with them. When I reacted to them, trying to overcome my fear, they responded in a deeply positive and persistent way. They have demonstrated to some scientists and with me what is available in terms of a richer and more true inner life and understanding of the world.

Still, it is going to be a very hard job for us to do this.

How can entities with different biology, different histories, different perceptual systems, and a different relationship to reality possibly hope to make any sense to government officials or scientists who cannot conceive of any form of communication other than the spoken or written word, which is, in fact, not adequate to the situation? There is simply no way we can tell what is actually happening when we attempt ordinary conversation with them. They may choose words that they have learned will be a fitting response to some question or comment, but how can we know what they think they mean?

Contact will bring rewards, but it is also dangerous. As it unfolds, we have to be very careful to stand by our own beliefs and expectations for life and to treasure ourselves and our civilization. We need to present our visitors with an open mind but also a careful one. Otherwise, the warning is clear: Things are not going to go well. Spiritual and mental contact are real and deeply shocking. But physical contact is going to be more intense. It will offer with it rapid cultural change, confusion, and all sorts of unanticipated consequences.

We might encounter entities whose culture will overwhelm ours. So we must keep our own counsel, make sure our society remains intact, and stand up for the values of our minds and the cultures we have created. Unless we take responsibility for ourselves and our part in contact, we cannot succeed. To me, successful contact means three things: first, clear communication; second, enrichment for both sides; third, life shared in the new way of communion.

Not only must we be careful not to become supplicants when faced with breathtakingly advanced skills and technology that we long to possess, we must also be aware that the entities that possess them, and the extraordinary power that accompanies them, are not necessarily going to be ethically more advanced than us.

When people placing their trust in certain beliefs are confronted with what to them appears to be a greater power, they lose faith in all of it: their gods, their beliefs, their sense of self-worth. The cargo cults of Melanesia are an example of an attempt by a less powerful culture to acquire the desirable qualities of a more powerful one but without understanding anything about the skills that are actually involved. There is a level of humanization and loss of self-worth that leads to the degeneration not only of secular society, but also of the spiritual culture, even when it is actually superior to that of the more powerful technological culture.

It is time for a new conversation with the visitors to begin. The challenge goes both ways. They have to take the risk that we won't be able to bear their presence, and we have to take the risk that they might be dangerous to us in irrecoverable ways.

There is such a promise for us: the knowledge that the energetic body is real and that it exists to serve the soul that is also very real, the knowledge that you can leave your physical body and travel far, the promise of learning to accomplish reliable communication between physical and nonphysical mankind. Most of all, gaining real communication with the visitors and from there entering a state of communion with them that enriches them with newness and us with knowledge.

Only if we can open ourselves to the possibilities and dare the dangers are we going to succeed in the endeavor of contact. Because they are here to share our surprises and our discoveries, we are never going to be sure of anything about them, not even when they are more engaged with us than we can ever be with each other. This will be more intimate than that. It will be the most intimate thing that can happen. Can we get used to it, in the end, and make it our own? In other words, can we bear it?

That is the fundamental question, I feel rather sure, of human life. Can we?

We know that there are trillions of stars, in trillions of galaxies, and that this is probably only one of an effective infinity of universes . . . which all probably have an infinity of mirror universes breathing neutrons back and forth between their realities like great, enigmatic hearts. And then there is this band here on this tiny speck of dust, touched with intelligence and struggling to find our magic as we sail through infinity on the coattails of a wandering star.

EXTRAORDINARY ACTUALITY: MY JOURNEY TO THE STARS

Alan Steinfeld

PART 1: THE JOURNEY OUT

Simply let wonder fill your being until it takes you out of yourself and into the staggering mystery that is the existence of the world. A mystery that facts alone can never begin to fill. If spirit does exist, it will lay in that direction, the direction of wonder, a direction that intersects the very heart of science itself . . . in the search for an ultimate ground.

—Ken Wilber, *The Marriage of Sense and Soul*

I have always been a person of wonder and imagination. As a child I looked up at the stars and just knew they must be the porch lights of other people's homes, just like the lights in the distance I saw riding in the back of my father's car at night as we approached our neighborhood after holiday visits. The stars fascinated me, because they seemed so odd to be just hanging there in the night sky. Yet when I asked the grown-ups about them, no one seemed interested. They just nodded in my direction, semi-amused with my fascination. But I wanted to know what made these points of white specks twinkle out of the unfathomable blackness that held them in place. I wrote a poem, "**Stars**," for the elementary school paper about the light of those distant suns. My parents said, "**Isn't that nice.**" But no one knew what I meant. I didn't know what I meant either, but I was compelled to call out to our neighbors in the infinite blackness, to say, "**I see you. I know you are out there. Thanks for keeping your light on so that we know that you're home.**" None of this seemed to matter to anyone. No one I knew ever looked up to wonder what was out there. They kept their head to the ground, occupied with the toils of the everyday world, doing what they had to do to get by.

I never did find any satisfaction in my childhood's quest to understand what the stars really were out there in space, until fourth grade. Somehow, I discovered my first science fiction book. Maybe it was Madeleine L'Engle's *A Wrinkle in Time*, with the mind-bending idea of tesseract or a hypercube of fourth-dimensional space that allowed the characters in the book to travel inter-dimensionally to any point in the universe by folding space and time. From there I became fixated on all sorts of sci-fi possibilities. I was particularly obsessed with the Dig Allen Space Explorer series by Joseph Greene. I read all six books in the series religiously, as they were teaching what I would now call spiritual principles, such as the ability of human consciousness to be transferred into robotic bodies: "**Once transferred, the person can see**

**through the robot's eyes, move the robot's body, and has
the robot's invulnerability, which is critical to carrying
out any mining expeditions."**[1]

I didn't care for Isaac Asimov too much, but I loved
Ray Bradbury. One of his stories that I still think about
today was **"Dark They Were, and Golden-Eyed,"** about
Earth pioneers who settled on Mars. By growing food in
the planet's soil, they physically turn into Martians. I was
fortunate to grow up in a time when television, in some
way, stimulated my young imagination. I enjoyed *My Favorite Martian* with Bill Bixby, just because of what the
name suggested. Not a very deep show, in retrospect. Neither was *Lost in Space*, which I also had to watch, because
the idea of traveling to other planets was something I knew
was possible. Of course, the mother of all sci-fi programs
in the late 1960s was *Star Trek*: **"These are the voyages of
the starship *Enterprise*, to search out new life and new
civilizations. To boldly go where no one has gone before."**
I would miss dinner, ball games, cub scouts, and whatever
else might have been going on in suburban Long Island to
absorb every single word of every single episode of the original series.

The sci-fi books together with the space shows filled my
mind with wonder and learning. They helped me be creative in learning to imagine new ideas and think in different ways that would not have been possible without them.
Those years were fun and exciting until I reached sixth
grade. It was there that I was in for a shock. In the first few
months of the school year of fall 1967, I was still absorbed
in the panorama of other worlds. While other kids were
studying math and history, I was journeying with these in-

genious writers to distant planets, parallel universes, finding humanoid creatures that were different from us but still
could communicate with their minds. I was moving deeper
into more abstract realms of thinking and understanding . . . until my teacher said he didn't want me reading any
more sci-fi. I said, "**What!?**" He told my mother I was not
to read any more of those books, because it was limiting my
studies on other subjects (little did he know).

Now, I don't know if he did this or I just felt like he did
it—he either took my books away from me or threw them
away. Whatever it was—he killed it. This narrow-minded
view of what reality was supposed to be led to a traumatiz-
ing incident for me. It was like I lost a best friend. Granted,
my obsession may have been an escape from the harsh realities of the world, but it was an educational excursion into
mind expansion and possibility. For a while I felt empty. I
think the urge to conform to the grown-ups made me not
even want to take a sneak peek at the emerging classic liter
ature of Robert Heinlein and Arthur C. Clarke until much
later. I never fully rejected the ideas from science fiction,
but the taste had been soured. I still watched *Star Trek*, of
course, just not as enthusiastically. The shock of the loss
made me disconnect from some of its more fascinating
concepts.

I still looked up at the stars and wondered. I turned to
science with the hopes of being an astronaut. I loved the big
yellow moon as it rose on the first night of Passover, and
I wondered: What was the moon, really? How could it be
so arbitrarily the same size as the sun as seen from Earth?
Science said it was a coincidence, but I knew there had to
be more to it.

In high school, with science fiction gone, and the likelihood that I was not going to be part of the Apollo team to the moon, my curiosity turned toward the science of human behavior. Entering college in 1974, I began by studying psychology. But one English class on D. H. Lawrence showed me the vastness of human creativity and activated my imagination again. I discovered the genius of Shakespeare: **"There are more things in heaven and earth, Horatio, than are dreamt of in your philosophy."** I wish I could have thrown that line in the face of my sixth-grade teacher. I realized literature was not about words as much as it was about understanding the intricacies of human emotions. Writers knew more about psychology and behavior than all the statistics and analytical studies that I was forced to read for a psychology degree. In my senior year, I took a course on James Joyce for the two semesters and saw how his stream-of-consciousness style made me understand reality as a flow of endless thoughts through our minds. When Joyce wrote at the end of *A Portrait of the Artist as a Young Man*, **"Welcome, O life! I go to encounter for the millionth time the reality of experience and to forge in the smithy of my soul the uncreated conscience of my race,"** that sentence sent a lightning bolt through my body. It set the course of my destiny. I knew my mission was somehow connected to bringing *"the reality of experience to the uncreated conscious of my race."*

To be honest, at the time I didn't really know what that meant or how one would go about doing it. All I knew was that I couldn't think of anything more exciting than discovering the unknown and bringing that awareness to others. I started by taking multilayered photos of the East

Village in the 1980s and making short films. Later on, I wrote and created television programs about strange new ideas and streams-of-consciousness art displays. Since the mid-1990s I have been producing an interview program on cable TV and YouTube called *New Realities* with the subtitle *Making Known the Unknown*. But I don't want to get ahead of myself, because all that came after my first voyage into the unknown.

The adventure began quite innocently, as most meaningful adventures do, on a cross-country trip in a van that I bought in New York City from the money I made working in film production. I had already become aware of the emerging trends of a new spirituality that were beginning to percolate in the mid-1980s. On Easter morning 1987, I took off in my van, like a starship, "**to discover strange new worlds and seek out new life and new civilizations.**" As I left the city cruising westward, the sun was shining and the church bells were ringing. I set my course for its destination: Sedona. That coming summer was to be a worldwide celebration of what was called **the Harmonic Convergence**. It would be the first New Age holiday, a global meditation for peace and prayer. Spiritually minded people everywhere would gather around the planet at different sacred sites for a vibrational shift.

One of the reasons for my road trip was to find the best place to be on that auspicious date, when as the ancient Mayans predicted **the Nine Hells** would end. According to the originator of the Convergence, José Argüelles, "the hell cycles" began precisely on the day that Hernán Cortéz landed in Mexico, April 22, 1519. This coincided with the first day of the year of the Aztec/Mayan calendar, "1 Reed," a day sacred to the mythic hero Quetzalcoatl.[2] Nine cycles of fifty-two years each (468 years) brought us to 1987, where Argüelles and others like Terence McKenna prophesied that this would lead to a countdown of twenty-five years in a final reevaluation of humanity. In 2012, the Mayans, through their precise astronomical calculations, predicted an exact alignment of the Earth, the sun, and the center of the galaxy, which would begin a next phase of planetary awakening.

From that time, I knew that 2012 would never be the end of time, only the end of time as we knew it. Furthermore, I realized, after it came and went, that the Mayan legend helped expand our view of the cosmos. Their astronomy was based on not just the family of planets in our solar system, something that has been the central concern of the Western mind since ancient Egypt and Babylonia. The Mesoamerican cultures were aware that we lived in a greater neighborhood, beyond the celestial domain of our yellow sun, we were part of galaxy. Of course, this is well known, but in school the main focus has always been on our local family of planets, not the fact that we are part of a greater galactic environment. The Mayan time keepers gave us the galaxy to contemplate. Whether it was connected to their ancient prophecies or not, in early 2013 *National Geographic* published the article "**2012: A Banner Year in the Hunt for Exoplanets**," which called forth the awareness of what they called "alien worlds." *National Geographic* wrote: "**In 2012 astronomers came closer than ever to zeroing in on an earthly doppelganger—or at the very least a planet considered potentially habitable . . . In October of 2012,** a detection of an Earth-size planet orbiting Alpha Centauri B, only 4.3 light-years from Earth, makes this the closest exoplanet to our solar system."[3]

Back in 1987, I had an inkling of alien worlds from my science-fiction days, but I had no idea what that meant for me until after my journey. All I knew was that the *Harmonic Convergence* was going to be a celebration of planetary unity. It was like the Woodstock moment of "**the New Age**," as it was called then. This brought us the crystal craze, the explosion of Reiki energy healing, and the start of the channeling phenomenon. Unfortunately, I guess every Woodstock has its Altamont. In just a few short years, **the New Age** would go from being a time of hope to being labeled in the media as a superficial trend laden with the denials of harsh realities. *Time* magazine summed up their criticism of the trends with crystals as flashy rocks, and channeling as "*a ventriloquist act with one partner missing.*"

Despite the mass media's disapproval of the momentous occasion, it did not deter thousands of seekers from gathering on August 16 and 17, 1987, at what is called geo-activated power spots around the planet; places that also see a lot of UFO activity. This included the Inca site of Machu Picchu, the Australian aboriginal home Uluru, the Anasazis' Chaco Canyon, and hundreds of ancient temples and sacred sites on every continent. After looking at a few of the sacred sites from the southwest to the northwest, I decided to return east and celebrate at the home where the counterculture festivals were born, legendary Woodstock, New York. In the hills above the town in the **Magic Meadow** across from where the Karmapa's Tibetan monastery now stands, about

a thousand of us gathered, danced, and sang around camp-
fires all night awaiting the dawning of what was supposed
to be a new epoch.

However, before I decided to go to upstate New York,
one of the strangest events that I ever experienced trans-
pired for me and my starship as I was scouting out the
perfect destination for the sacred Mayan activation. After
a brief stop in Mount Ida, Arkansas, digging for what was
at that time the emblem of the New Age: quartz crystals,
I picked up my New York friend Tony in Albuquerque to
join me on this portion of the trip to the promised land.
This was, and still is, the Mecca for spiritual seekers and
UFO enthusiasts: Sedona, Arizona, also known to some as
the *"Crystal City in the sky."* I felt an immediate connection to the spectacular red rocks. Legend has it that energy
vortexes enrich the land there, because iron gives the earth
its red color. This does two things: It attracts more oxygen
to the place the way iron in the blood does, and it creates
a huge magnetic field. I felt it immediately once we passed
what felt like the gateway rock formation of Bell Rock. Suddenly we were tangibly immersed in a heightened vibratory
field, like entering a warm bath.

Since this was the epicenter of the New Age, as soon as
we arrived we went to a channeling gathering called *Laughing Your Way to Ascension*. It was not a great channeling,
but there were two women who entered the room after the
session began. As they walked by, I distinctly felt a sweep
of energy go past me. I wondered which of those women
was the one I felt vibrating. After the event, I said hello to
both of them, and I knew that Jane was the person I had
felt. I visited her the next day where she worked at the *Food*

Among the Flowers, the town's only health food restaurant at the time. We hit it off, and when I left Sedona a few days later, we knew we would see each other again.

Eve Lorgen says in her book *The Love Bite* that sometimes two people are drawn together inexplicably, so their behavior could be observed by alien beings of other realms to survey us. She calls it "**a set-up into bonding dramas by alien beings**." Whatever it was at the time, something definitely seemed to draw Jane and me together.

When I arrived in Oregon at the country fair, Jane called to say she wanted to fly out to see me. We could drive together back East. We left the fairgrounds of Eugene, stopping at the serene Cougar Hot Springs for a night to wash the dust off us. Then we headed over the Three Sisters Pass, picking up I-80 somewhere in Wyoming, driving as far as we could in a day. Exhausted, we pulled off the interstate onto the farmlands of western Nebraska to find a place to sleep. The sign at the front of a quiet dirt road said "Enter at your own risk." I thought that must be for the irrigation ditches and that we would be safe for the night. We parked by a low water canal, passing out in the back of the van. It was a strange sleep, and we woke up in the morning itching to get out of there. We both felt as if we were unusually inactive throughout the night; normally we would roll around during sleep. It was not just that we were tired, but we both remembered getting up in the same position in which we went to sleep. It was a strange sensation. Why would such a thing be noticed anyway? Thirty years later, after not seeing each other for a few decades, I asked Jane, "Do you remember that night after we left Oregon?" She said, "Yes, when we were frozen."

When I dropped her off at her parents' house in Michigan a few days later, before we parted, we could feel that there was something electrifying about our physical connection. When I returned home, I thought nothing about that odd night out west until I was at the family swimming pool and my mother said to me, **"What is that mark on the back of your leg?"** I said, **"It is probably just a spider bite."** But upon closer inspection I could see it was an evenly placed four-pronged puncture mark that formed a square on the back of my left knee joint. I thought that was weird, but I put it out of my mind. However, later that month I was filming a video for a dancer who wanted to choreograph her alien abduction. While curious about her experience, I didn't have a feeling for it one way or another. But I did happen to mention that I had this mark on the back of my leg. She said casually, **"Oh, that's an abduction scar."**

I then went into a panic. Not knowing how that could have happened, the only thing I could connect it to was the night in Nebraska. But the consideration of an alien abduction was simultaneously both repulsive and fascinating. The dancer, Christina, was a member of Budd Hopkins's Intruder group. I went to a meeting where everyone was so open about the fact that they had met aliens, while I was still freaked out.

Nonetheless I couldn't stop looking into the subject, even though I was quite resistant to the idea that aliens could have captured me. This inner conflict between acceptance and rejection of alien contact was somehow linked to my sixth-grade trauma. Being told that all those sci-fi books were pure nonsense walled off a section of my mind, but this newfound occupation was starting to break that down. On the other side of that wall was an eleven-year-old child who still clung to the feelings that those stories were absolutely true.

In meeting Budd and the people of the Intruders Foundation, I had to reach back to that moment of disconnect and find a way to trust my childhood feelings. Hearing experiences about little grey and reptilian beings traveling here from the stars was right out of the sci-fi literature. Twenty years after my childhood trauma, I struggled to resurrect my curiosity and reengage a part of my mind that had locked away the imagination of other worlds. There is still a slight disconnect in me to this day, because sometimes I wonder, how can aliens really be part of a greater reality? I think that distancing gives me a healthy skepticism, but conversely, I have no intention of discounting my own contact experiences. Confronting new realities demanded an updating of what I thought was actually real. Years later my inner struggle to affirm the truth about science fiction was appeased when the Disclosure article in *The New York Times* appeared on December 17, 2017, which publicly stated that the government had secretly been studying UFOs: **"A 2009 Pentagon briefing summary of the program [Advanced Aerospace Threat Identification Program] prepared by its director at the time asserted that 'what was considered science fiction is now science fact.'"**[4]

Around Christmastime, Jane flew out to see me in New York. We went to Budd's holiday party and were both overwhelmed by the people, not with shock but with a higher energy that seemed to be present. It was like a general feeling of love permeated the gathering. I think, for us, it was like coming into a field of expanded vibration because of the openness of the group mind.

Meeting Budd, then John Mack, and later Whitley Strieber, showed me people who were sane, sober, and, above all, highly intelligent. These sincere and honest people helped pry open the doors for me to realize a greater actuality. Being in this company, going to lectures and conferences any chance I could, helped reactivate an awareness of other embedded experiences. I started to remember as a child seeing faces outside the window of our second-floor apartment. Also, I had horrific flashbacks of my bedroom turning red and the feeling of something trying to pull me out of my body by the back of my neck while I was sleeping.

Another odd thing I remembered was that in 1966 my family received biweekly editions of **Look** magazine. It wasn't a seductive Elizabeth Taylor on the cover of the October 4 issue that inspired this prepubescent boy to browse through its pages. No, it was the equally outstanding headline, right below the Look logo, stating "ABOARD A FLYING SAUCER," that made me eagerly read the article. This was during my science-fiction phase, and I was eager to find legitimacy to a reality that I felt had to be true. There in black and white was the story of a young New Hampshire couple who claimed to have been taken by aliens in 1961 while driving home from Montreal to Portsmouth. What was strange about finding the article was that I don't think anyone in my family ever looked at any of the magazines that arrived every two weeks. Plus, I don't know why we ordered **Look** in the first place, when everyone's magazine of choice back then was **Life**. Second, I was never interested much in reading a mainstream journal about Hollywood socialites, but I remember anxiously waiting fourteen days for the final edition of the Betty and Barney Hill tale.

I knew this was not a hoax. I knew what happened to this interracial New England couple actually happened. Still, my adolescent mind concluded that if this was true, then why wasn't everyone talking about this startling news? I put that question in the unanswered box of my youth that also included: *"What is the Vietnam war about? Who killed JFK? And why does everybody get so excited about their favorite sports team winning a game?"* Reading the troubling story of the Hills left me with an odd sensation—much eerier than those other mysteries. It felt like a slight warp of reality that stayed with me for quite a while due to the vivid descriptions of the aliens and the scope of the encounter.

While hearing the experiences of other abductees at conferences, I started to remember odd stories from my family. One was how my mother as a child lived with her mother, my maternal grandmother, for a year in Tucson, because the dry air would help her childhood asthma. What I thought was not just a coincidence was hearing about the times they would get lost in the mountains above the city. This was during the same pivotal summer of the Roswell crash of 1947, in the neighboring state. It was around that time my mother developed a phobia of cats, which she has to this day. I asked her what was it about them that was scary, and she said it was their eyes. I happened to like cats myself, but I remembered something about strange eyes that totally freaked me out as a child. ***Children of the Damned*** (1964) was the scariest movie ever. These zombie-like children had wide, white pupils that made me run screaming out of the room. Even seeing a commercial for the film was too much.

To this day just looking at the poster of the film sends chills through me.

Still, the strangest of all things happened in 1988, a year after my cross-country venture. That summer in a dream I felt as if sperm had been extracted from me. A few weeks later I was awakened out of a dream state by what felt like a furry creature brushing along the inside of my thigh. When I sat up, somebody or something placed a little being in my arms, more animal-looking than human. It looked like a little deer with big black eyes. I felt no fear, neither did I feel love. There was no connection at all; I just remember thinking this is weird to be holding this creature. I had the sense of other beings around observing, but I didn't see who they were. Some investigators say that egg and sperm are taken from people to develop a hybrid race of aliens and humans, bringing out the best of both species. It has also been reported in many cases that the human donors are often asked to hold their genetic offspring as a sort of bonding exercise. I have to say that I did not feel any bonding in my case. This whole scenario was somewhat confirmed in a reading I had with the entity named Bashar. He is a being, as Darryl Anka explains in this collection, who comes through him from the future and claims to be the result of hybrid experiments between the grey aliens and the humans.

Thinking of the possible abductions of my mother and grandmother, I conducted the following interview with Bashar:

ALAN: I feel like there is a part of me that has already been genetically altered for the last, maybe, three generations in my family.

BASHAR: Ten generations.

ALAN: They do this so each succeeding generation can be modified so that the genetic samples will eventually match the frequency the greys need to integrate the DNA into their cellular structure, right?

BASHAR: This is by agreement whether your physical mind remembers it or not.

ALAN: Actually, I don't really remember all of it, although I do have vague memories of this little being placed in my hands. Was that one of my . . .

BASHAR: . . . early hybrids in a sense. Different degrees of genetic material will wind up in different hybrid children.

ALAN: So basically, I've had a lifetime of abductions, would you say?

BASHAR: If you want to look at it that way, or you could say you have a lifetime of co-participation in a very large-scale program that will benefit your world immensely. It depends on how you wish to look at it.

ALAN: No, I'm actually very honored to be the father of an alien race.

BASHAR: We thank you for your participation, without which we would not be great, great, great, great, great, great, grandfather.

ALAN: You mean we're related?

BASHAR: Distantly.

ALAN: You mean some of my genetics went into Bashar?

BASHAR: Not directly, but into the lines.

ALAN: I love that. Thank you.

Before this all gets too sci-fi, I must say that in 1985, two years before my fateful cross-country tour, I wrote about a dream that never really made sense to me. I recently found it again in a journal, and only now does some of its mystery seem to be resolved.

I am on a cruise ship. I am watching a dance show. There is a blond woman watching too and I see that her face keeps changing. It changes three times, or maybe she becomes three different women, not sure. We somehow connect and become more intimate. Then I am in a dormitory room, like they have at colleges. The woman asks me to watch her baby. The baby is about one year old and cute like babies are. I take it for a car ride and David Letterman is driving. We go down an exit ramp near the ship. Now I am holding the baby, who seems very content. We ride around a little bit and we get back on the ship. I give the baby back to its mother. The baby starts to talk to me, saying he is very happy for the car ride, and there is a feeling of connection.

People have these sorts of indecipherable dreams, but I think this dream indicated that perhaps Bashar was right: I may have had a lifetime of contact long before I suspected it. Was that why I always felt different from the rest of my family? They were very good people, but I always felt that I was part of a different realm. Maybe my fascination with science fiction was a way of accessing those parts of myself.

I like going to every UFO conference I can find. There is always a sense of security in being around other people who think outside the box, where science fiction has become fact. Sometimes at the large gatherings such as **Contact in the Desert** with thousands of people seeking new information, I get the same feeling I had at Budd's Christmas party, a wave of opening and upliftment. For me these gatherings are less about the idea of aliens, and more about bringing out a greater truth of human existence. People like Whitley Strieber, Linda Moulton Howe, J. J. and Desiree Hurtak, and frankly everyone who has contributed to this volume are on a personal mission to *"forge in the smithy of their souls the uncreated conscience of our race,"* and to be in the company of that quality of dedicated souls is quite satisfying.

Nonetheless, even after all the people I met and all the conferences I had absorbed, reassuring me that indeed people were having alien contact, after all the books I accumulated on the subject and talking to the most well-versed authorities and explorers in the field, I never felt compelled to find out what happened during my possible UFO contact in the summer of 1987. My reluctance was brought home during a conversation I had with one of the witnesses at Stephen Bassett's **Citizen Hearing on Disclosure**. In 2013, I was present at the National Press Club in Washington, DC, for all five days of mock hearings in front of former members of Congress. One outstanding testimony came from former sergeant James Penniston, who witnessed a UFO landing while stationed at RAF Woodbridge in the Rendlesham Forest in the United Kingdom in 1980. Touching a triangular-shaped craft that landed with blue and yellow lights swirling around the exterior, he said, "**It was**

warm and felt like metal . . . Part of the surface and the air around us was electrically charged. We could feel it on our clothes, skin, and hair. Nothing in my training prepared me for what we were witnessing."[5] Talk about sci-fi? Later, feeling the intensity of the incident, he received a mental download of twelve pages of binary code that has been interpreted as locations of various sacred sites around the planet. The key for me, however, was what he said after the testimony in a private conversation. Wanting to hear more, I went over to him during a break and asked him what it was like to touch the landed craft. He said the whole experience completely freaked him out. He added that the anxiety of the event has kept him on edge since. Every night he has had to take a sleeping pill to sleep. I asked **"Still? That was 1980 and this is thirty-plus years later?"** He said, **"*Yes!*"** In this way I felt relieved that I never indulged in deciphering what had happened to me in western Nebraska. Whatever it was seemed to be safely tucked away in the deeper corners of my subconscious. I knew something probably did occur, not just because of the mark on my leg, but because ever since that time I have had an irresistible urge to find out whatever I could about the UFO phenomenon. It is what Grant Cameron calls **"being sucked down the rabbit hole."**

PART 2: THE JOURNEY BACK

In the presence of extraordinary actuality, consciousness takes the place of imagination.[6]

—Wallace Stevens

Like Jim Penniston, my hesitation to journey back to the likely abduction had to do with the trauma to my sense of self and my attachment to the worldview, as John Mack mentions in his essay. Cathy Caruth, in her book *Unclaimed Experience*, says that severe trauma occurs when "**truth** [the reality we live in] **in its delayed appearance . . . cannot be linked only to what is known, but also to what remains unknown in our very actions and our language.**"[7] She proposes that PTSD comes about from the bewildering attempt to understand fragment memories of overwhelming events that have interrupted our linear "straightforward history."[8] What integrates the experiences is to move the hidden implicit memories into an explicit awareness, to gain control over the reactive associations so that they can be used in a continuum by the conscious mind.[9] "Memories that are transferred to explicit awareness cease to acutely and constantly disturb the subject."[10]

Since 1987 I hesitated to be hypnotized, a hesitation that lasted thirty-two years. Jane had already found out long ago what had happened during our frozen night along a deserted canal. She had been regressed just months after our return. What she saw was a kind of electrical connection between her ankle and the back of my knee. But I felt there was more to it.

Finally, in 2019, I found a hypnotherapist I could trust, who seemed open to the idea of alien abductions. I needed at least two sessions before I could drop into a place of peace and start to journey back to July 1987.

Although I have thought about the incident many times over the years, the following is the first time I have attempted to piece together the ordeal into a narrative allowing me to gain greater insight into the personal effects of the phenomenon. The regression took me to a deeper place until I saw myself sleeping in the back of the van. I have to say that I never heard anyone talk about hypnotic regressions in the way I experienced them. Most people say they had a regression and remembered this or that event. But for me it was not like that at all. On one hand, the images that came to me during the session were not memories, like I remember what I did yesterday or last week. Because I had no conscious recall of an experience, I could not say I remembered them. On the other hand, it didn't feel to me like it was an imaginary fabrication either. What appeared to me as experience was from another place of mind.

Under a gentle, relaxing meditation, I opened up and trusted that some kind of extraordinary actuality, beyond imagination, emerged out of my deeper consciousness. A collage of impressions floated through my mind and I found myself sleeping in the back of the van next to Jane. A bright light started to shine through the window at the back doors. Then the doors flung open. I was not scared. I didn't quite see anything out there, but I had a sense of a non-human, almost a nonphysical, presence standing outside. Then the forms solidified into focus. I saw Them. They were not the classic grey beings. They were taller, with faceless heads without features—no eyes, nose, or mouth. They were just a translucent head on a translucent body.

As they were going to lift or levitate us out of the van, they put what I later apprehended was a sort of "time mold" to hold the exact position we were in when we were taken. This way they could put us back in the exact same place upon return. It was like a film strip that is spliced in the middle of a scene, and a whole other scene was added. When the scene is finished, the original sequence is edited back in place as if nothing happened. No movement can be seen between frames. It was like a freeze frame covered the moments of missing time, however long that lasted. The being who seemed like the leader had energy that appeared kinder and more compassionate than the others who were two feet shorter and were just following orders. We were floated out of the back doors. All I could see was a bright light. I got the impression that my partner and I were separated, but still connected. At the same time I also felt like I was still sleeping in the van. I didn't remember any visuals about intrusive procedures or when the imprint of a mark was made on my leg, but I did get a feeling of peace coupled with a total body buzzing sensation. A high-frequency tune-up is the only way I can describe it. During the abduction, if I want to call it that, I had a sense of being uplifted. As we were put back into the time mold, and normal awareness came over me, the ordinary motions of the world returned.

After the regression, I was curious about this idea of a time mold, because it was something I never heard of before and I thought maybe I just made the whole thing up. In searching online, I came across a talk by Linda Moulton Howe from a 2017 Conscious Life Expo. She was describing her interview with Bob Lazar, the man who first revealed the truth about alien craft at Area 51. Linda reported that one of the most fascinating things Bob saw was how the military was learning to control time. Lazar talked about how one of the scientists at the base gave him a demonstration: **"He lit a candle and put it on a table. Then he took an extraterrestrial device and aimed it at the candle. The flame went from a flicker to a flame that did not move, the fire was suspended . . . like in a suspended animation, as a flame . . ."**[11] However, the difference between my experience and the suspended animation of a flame is that it felt like it was not just us who were suspended, but all of time was stopped in that moment. The idea of frozen time may also be another reason for a lack of memory to occur. This idea was first developed in Budd Hopkins's book *Missing Time*.[12] Given the fact that our minds are connected to the ongoing flow of time/space, even in dream states—if there is no time flow for the conscious mind to exist in, there is nothing that can be remembered in an ordinary state of recall.

Either way, it is clear that we don't understand the complexity of time or space, and have been conditioned to think of reality in a linear, simplistic form.

Overall, my actual regression to the encounter was less frightening than I thought it would be, maybe because I needed thirty years to integrate the experience. In the book *Abduction*, John Mack calls this **"pushing through."** He says that when we **"fully experience the terror and rage association with the helplessness and intrusions of instruments on the ship . . . acknowledgment and acceptance of the reality of the beings becomes possible and a more reciprocal relationship follows in which personal growth and learning can take place."**[13] If I hadn't *pushed* *through* I am not sure I would be writing and editing this book.

Strangely enough, the dream I had the night after my regression was of a group of large, rather friendly birds looking down on me as I slept. One of them looked like a large owl, which most people know is a classic screen memory for grey aliens with the big wraparound eyes. But the flock of beings around me was quite harmonious, not wanting anything at all. However, I must confess that even though Bob Lazar apparently confirmed my "time mold" revelation about feeling frozen, I was not sure if I was just making up all the regression images. Maybe the doubt came from having to divorce the possibility of a sci-fi reality when I was a child, or is it just that alien visitations have no place in our reality? It was only recently, in May 2020, actually while writing this essay, that I heard something that helped me understand the recesses of my mind and what I thought I had made up, imagined, or perhaps misremembered: On Whitley Strieber's *Dreamland* podcast was an interview with the remote viewer Simeon Hein. Talking about how he used his mind to see objects nonlocally, he said that when he started, "**I thought I was just making this up, just inventing . . . It turned out none of it was made up, because it was quite accurate.**" What really got my attention was when Hein said that the process happens "*in a slightly relaxed . . . semidreamlike alpha state.*" Very similar to the light trance that I was in under hypnosis. Hein continued:

> *It is about moving into a kind of daydreaming.*
> *Maybe daydreaming is more than just daydreaming.*
> *You start listening to another part of your mind . . .*

*that we are not used to paying attention to. The bias
in the West is that the stronger something seems to
our senses the more real we think it is. This is just the
opposite . . . The hesitancy to believe in the images
coming to you is a sign of good contact with the
target. The made-up feelings are there because the
awareness comes from another part of our minds,
which many of us are taught to believe is just a realm
of the imagination.*[14]

The problem is that we are educated, trained, and conditioned to believe that only the logical science of a linear explicit reality is valid. Nothing else is real, or can be real. Science is based on facts that are verified by our senses. There is no room for a reality not defined by the substantive validation of our five senses and the technologies that modify them. This kind of thinking reminded me of one of my favorite quotes from a former professor of psychiatry at Harvard, John Mack. His credentials validated the experiential reality of people's alien abductions. He said, **"We are dealing with a phenomenon which violates our sense of reality. This will not yield its secrets until we discover other ways of knowing."**[15]

One other significant dream that I put in the category with these other experiences occurred sometime after the 1987 abduction. Suddenly I found myself in the presence of something, or someone, I call **the Ancient One**. It appeared to be female, but she was very, very old and wrinkled, with yellowish folds to her skin. She was showing me the way grey ETs are genetically cloned to be workers. In my brief exchange with her, she felt as primordial as time and full of wisdom that was unfathomable. Whitley Strieber has referred to a similar being in some of his writings. Perhaps I met the same female ET type that he presented on the now classic cover of **Communion**. To me she was less robotic-looking and more compassionate, emanating a force of presence. I cannot remember why, but for some reason she was showing me a DNA cloning scene. Maybe the knowledge has been encoded into my psyche.

DREAM REALITIES

Is all that we see or seem
but a dream within a dream?
—Edgar Allan Poe, "A Dream Within a Dream," 1849

Hein's notions that a shift in mental activity is what is needed to perceive objects at a distance corroborates two observations I have about my ET-occupied dreams: First, it seems that these were not regular dreams that fade upon waking, like vanishing footprints on the beach, as most night dreams do. Instead these nocturnal visions stay lodged in a place of conscious memory, which is to say they are probably not dreams at all. According to Grant Cameron, ETs use the dream state to visit us, because they are not part of our third-dimensional existence, because our reality is held in place by our rational mind. Since they are not of this world, to interact with us they have to bypass our logical mental concepts of the world. This is why they come to us in our dreams or in dreamlike states. In the book *Tuned-In: The Paranormal World of Music*, Grant Cameron refers to hundreds of popular rock songs written by what seem like downloads coming to musicians in their dreams. In particular he points to

Neil Young's *After the Gold Rush*, which reinforces the idea of dreams and their UFO association. He starts off the well-known third verse of the song by saying that he "*dreamed I saw the silver space ships flying,*" and he repeats in the next line "*all in a dream, all in a dream . . .*"[16]

Second, my own contact interactions, such as watching gene splicing and being given a hybrid creature to hold, came in a half-awake state, and even in my regression the sense of reality I experienced had a distinct quality of disorientation in space, time, and awareness. The only way I can describe the physical sensation of interacting with ETs is that it felt like being in the emanations of echoed moments, almost like the effects of drugs or alcohol, but more pervasive. In other words, it feels as if encounters are not happening in a normal waking state. The echoing sound of this disorientation comes through in one of John Lennon's own favorite songs, "#9 Dream."[17] The words and the melody came to him around the same time he had a UFO encounter in **New York City** near the East River. On the *Walls and Bridges* album, he writes: "**On the 23rd of Aug. 1974 at 9 o'clock [pm] I saw a U.F.O.**" I can't say for sure that the song was a direct reference to his UFO experience, but John didn't know where it came from either. He claims it just "*churned out*" with "*no inspiration.*"[18] In a 1980 interview he says that "*it was a bit of a throwaway. It was based on some dream I had.*"[19] Like most UFO-related dreams he starts the song by asking, "*Was it in a dream? . . . It seemed so real to me.*" Then, as in a vision he sings, "*two spirits dancing so strange.*"[20] He ends with a nonsensical phrase "**Ah! Bowakawa, pousse pousse**" that he repeats twelve times, like many Hindu mantras, until it fades out. He says that *"it doesn't mean anything . . . it is just a phrase that came to him in a dream and he decided to base a song around it."*[21] It is interesting that the phrase has nine syllables and the song is called "Dream #9."

Could this be rock and roll's first attempt at what Mary Rodwell calls in her essay "**light language**" (see page 246)? The utterance of meaningless sounds is something contactees have made to communicate messages in the form of vibration and not in the meaning of words. I am not saying that Lennon consciously knew this, but these sounds came to him around the time of his UFO sighting in New York. This is a demonstration that we are possibly part of other realms besides this one, which shows up in lucid dreams, premonitions, déjà vu, or flashes of a multidimensional existence that most people tend to ignore.

WHY THE SHIFT

The question is, why does it seem that making contact, or being in the presence of extraterrestrial or higher conscious beings, so severely shifts our awareness into a dreamlike state? For starters, just seeing a UFO can cause cognitive dissonance. Psychological disassociation occurs when we see an object that is not supposed to do the things it does: hover in midair with no sound, zoom off at incredible speeds, or pop in and out of space. That alone shatters our sense of what we think is real and actual. It is hard to stay present when the unbearable shock of uncertainty appears in circumstances that are not supposed to exist. This is because we are so conditioned to form our identity around a world that is predictable. In other words, reality must be more solid than the ground under our feet or our sense of self is threatened. Merely being in the presence of an even so-called friendly or nonthreatening ET seems to likewise distort our ego awareness. The essay by Darryl Anka in this collection explains this feeling (page 223) in his dream of meeting the extraterrestrial known as Bashar. Anka writes that when Bashar approached him, **"the energy is so much more overwhelming at this higher frequency that it can overpower your sense of identity."**

Then again, it seems like it is more than just their energy that disturbs our consciousness. It is the very nature of their mind-field emanations that can knock us out. My guess is that these beings are attuned to a whole different vibration of mental formulation. For instance, the resonance of our normal waking state is at a certain rate, but when we come in contact with a more expanded realm it is like trying to get Wi-Fi on an AM radio, not the same level of wavelength. One of the possibilities that occurs to me is that our consciousness in general is calibrated by the particular solar output of our native star. This is why dogs, cats, and other Earth animals can connect with us, but when they sense some sort of other eerie presence or mind field set by another star resonance, they go running.

Staying present in the face of an onslaught of overwhelming input is part of the initiation of making contact. Again, from the Citizen Hearing on Disclosure, part of Linda Moulton Howe's testimony concerned what one military whistleblower told her about being ordered by his commanding officer to look into the eyes of a captive EBEN (extra biological entity): **"He said, 'Linda, imagine having seven feature films with sound, touch, heat, with every sensation that we know and over all of the**

films running in your mind are gold three-dimensional symbols. I remember that my knees began to shake and buckled. I knew that I was fainting . . . They put me on a cot and they left me there for three hours. When I woke up if God himself had asked me what had been communicated in those seven films I would not know.'"[22] This supports the idea of cognitive distortion that humans have such difficulty in making sustained contact with other beings. Their awareness is not linear or definitive in the three-dimensional sense as it is for us. Their perceptions seem to exist in a fluid and multilayered flow of reality. The **"many worlds theory"** of creation postulates that super-positions hold many timelines of actuality existing all at once. A similar multiplicity of realities could exist for us if we were not confined by our cultural restrictions of concretizing the world into a definitive form, what quantum physics calls "collapsing of the wave function," in perceiving existence in only one possible way. The poet/painter/mystic William Blake explained it this way: **"If the doors of perception were cleansed everything would appear to man as it is, Infinite. For man has closed himself up, till he sees all things thro' narrow chinks of his cavern."**[23] We remain controlled and out of touch with the subtle realms, because if we were educated to perceive more we might realize that there is more to us as human beings. No wonder science fiction was taken away from me, because it started to widen my view into a more infinite possibility.

In considering my and others' interactions with these **"beings,"** a hypothesis has come to me. It seems that these beings live in and germinate around a property of their state of consciousness I define as a **"cognitive field."** The same is true for humans; it is just not as strong or tangible as the ETs'. These fields are an attribute, such as density and body shape, of all life-forms. However, in this case the frequency of a particular field is paramount, because it seems to generate a gravity of its own within a time/space matrix. It seems to me that it is the force of cognition that propels these "beings" through space/time, allowing them to maintain an existence in a separate realm qualified by the frequency of their awareness. It seems to me that this creates a *"gravity of presence"* that can affect and distort our perceptions and state of consciousness. A quote from the Tibetan Lama Govinda describes the condition: **"Lower consciousness is unable to experience the life of the higher worlds and is even unaware of their existence, although it is interpenetrated by them. But if the beings of a lower world can raise their consciousness to a higher level then that higher world becomes manifest to them."**[24] Confirmation of my *"cognitive field theory"* came when I saw a video claiming that Christopher Mellon, former deputy assistant secretary of defense for intelligence in the Clinton and George W. Bush administrations, produced copies of slides on his website dealing with the AATIP program, mentioned earlier (also detailed in Nick Pope's essay on page 33 and Grant Cameron's on page 58). These reproductions mention the **"cognitive environments"** and **"unique cognitive human interface experiences"** in dealing with UAPs.[25] This verification convinced me that **"making conscious contact"** requires an aptitude of cognition to orient ourselves to the vibrational domains of ETs and their craft. This can only happen when we shift to higher frequencies beyond the navigation of an ego-based reality identification. If we don't learn to do this individually and collectively, we will be stuck in an ordinary field of awareness, separated from the mysteries of the cosmos that continue to elude our perceptions.

OLD HUMANITY

Making contact will have to be a "**push through**" our old humanity, because as veteran UFO researcher Stanton Friedman used to say, *"Who wants to hang out with a bunch of apes, whose favorite pastime is tribal warfare?"* It has been going on way too long. The author of the first book about an alien invasion, H. G. Wells, decades later shifted his message from aggression to compassion and wrote: "**A time will come when men will sit with history before them or with some old newspaper before them and ask incredulously, 'Was there ever such a world?'**"[26] Was there ever such a world that we still inhabit in the present timeline perspective of climate change denial, gun violence, racism, corporate greed, and human indifference? I think one reason for their presence of comings and goings is to break us out of that narrow vision into seeing a more expansive view.

THE KEY IS LUCIDITY

By most accounts, as well as my own, I conclude that the ETs (or whatever they are) do not belong to our physical world. When they appear here, their emanations drastically impact the shape of our reality. If we were more finely evolved, we would realize that the dreaming sense of encounters was not like dreams at all, but rather of a whole other extraordinary actuality. Although actuality is not quite the right word, because it implies a crystallization of perception we think is actual. More to the point: "They" are not of this world. They may enter this plane and leave traces of presence in crop circles, genetic manipulations, and scars on the body. But they seem to be of another realm altogether. Therefore, I feel that making contact has to be a practice in the art of lucidity. We have to start to be conscious of other forms of awareness. Using language as an example, if English was more attuned to other ways of expression, we could be more sensitive to the distinctions between dreaming and dreamlike states, as it is in Spanish. For instance, the word for dreaming while sleeping is *sueño,* but in referring to daydreams or dreams appearing more consciously, the word that is used is *ensueño.* William James was a professor of psychiatry at John Mack's institution (Harvard). He wrote in *The Varieties of Religious Experience*: "**Our normal waking consciousness . . . is but one special type of consciousness, whilst all about it, parted from it by the filmiest of screens, there lie potential forms of consciousness entirely different . . . No account of the universe in its totality can be final which leaves these other forms of consciousness quite disregarded.**"[27]

For that reason, if we really care about making contact on an even playing field, we have to practice lucidity, *ensueño.* We need to investigate our own minds where an "implicate order" of David Bohm's exists, as both John Mack and Linda Moulton Howe indicate in their essays. It is in these subtler realms of awareness that I feel learning to be lucid will bring us closer to "making contact."

The problem for us modern folks is that while psychology has done us a great service in understanding human behavior, it has also made us afraid of our own intuitive knowing, of opening up telepathically to others' thoughts. Perhaps (for most of us) hearing voices in our heads is not a sign of mania, but a calling card from beings reaching out to make contact. If we allow a greater awareness to open, we might feel these beings all around us. It is like they have been knocking on our door for a long time, and we say, *"Go away; I am waiting for someone to knock on our door."* I think it is time to answer the call.

As I see it, the way of contact is to exercise a multi-layered sensibility to cope with the expanded perception at increased vibrational rates. Our identification with the personality gives us a very limited range of reflection we call self. When Whitley Strieber talks about the nightly practice of his **Gurdjieff sensing exercise**, he seems to be practicing lucid awareness. He calls it in his essay on page 154 "**control of attention**." Since this has been an ongoing discipline for fifty years, I consider him one of the most lucid contactees in the field. Some people might think that drugs or, as it is referred to these days, "plant medicine" is an easier road to altered states, but drugs will only disturb a baseline sense of well-being. Drug use lacks the focus that comes from a daily practice, which excavates a deeper level of a multi-faceted awareness to grant us access to other realms. A call for digging into our greater nature was sent out two thousand years ago in a book that was banned from the New Testament by the church. **The Gospel of Thomas** says, *"If you bring forth what is within you, what you bring forth*

will save you. If you do not bring forth what is within you,
what you do not bring forth will destroy you."

ALIENS MAKE US MORE HUMAN

To graduate from the current cosmic and dimensional isolation we are going to have to stretch beyond our addictions to fossil fuels, corporate greed, and abuse and degradation of the planet itself. We need to become the "**Mind at Large**," as Aldous Huxley named it, and bring forth our capabilities for lucidity. Only then might we be able to meet the "others" on an even playing field. The expansion of our mind beyond our limited personality will bring in a sense of super-conscious awareness of the implicate order, as Linda Moulton Howe and John Mack claim in this collection. In this way, meeting the others will make us more human and more humane. Additionally, as others in this collection—the Hurtaks, Mary Rodwell, and Caroline Cory—indicate, becoming multidimensional is becoming more of ourselves as human beings. Only then will we have what it takes to truly make contact.

CONCLUSION

A friend of mine, Darin Stevenson, made a startling suggestion: "**Perhaps human consciousness is alien**." This would certainly explain why our lives based on creative expression are markedly different from all the other inhabitants of this beautiful planet. If we do have this alien conscious inside of an apelike animal body with a very emotional human ego and a divine soul, no wonder most people are confused and don't know who they are. It seems to me that

EXTRAORDINARY ACTUALITY . . .

the smooth integration of all these parts—the divine, the alien, the human, and the animal—is the purpose of the incarnational sentience. To be the oneness that can be alchemized with an open and curious nature, with an inner journey of the mind and an outward communication of creative expression, is the Universes of being. Then the implicate order becomes the explicate.

A key for me came from an Australian aboriginal elder who said, **"We humans are not of this world. Dreamtime is the true nature of our existence."**[28] The reason this might be true is that there is a craving in us to return every night to that non-human realm in the hope of refreshing the vitality of life here. There are many examples that point beyond the scientific labeling of us as merely biological machines. The chronicled stories of various non-physical experiences attest to greater realities. These such events as NDEs (near-death experiences), OBEs (out-of-body experiences, otherwise known as astral projections), remote viewing, and signs of telepathy—all demonstrate aspects of our consciousness that are alien to our physical containers. Conceivably beyond these Earth suits there are no divisions of us and "them," living or not, dreaming or waking. Somewhere in my research I came across the phrase that **"we are always dreaming, but our conscious mind makes such a loud sound that we don't notice it."** One of the best examples is about the neurosurgeon Eben Alexander. After coming out of a near-death coma with brain function nearly null, he said that he was perceiving phenomena that would have seemed inconceivable to his scientifically based understanding before the experience. He reckoned that the human brain was more than an organ to create thoughts. It was a filter to slow down the infinite awareness that is always flooding into us. Alexander surmises in his book *Proof of Heaven* that rather than asking how much of our consciousness survives the loss of the body, a better question is how much of the grand expanded being that he witnessed in his NDE survives the birth of the body. Our job is to ground the embodiment of this vast alien mind into a multi-level experience to make us fully human. By merging the implicit with the explicate, the one with the many, the light and the dark, and not dividing contact into us and them, but us as them. This means that the subtle awareness must be upgraded from the old humanity to knowing that we are part of and not separate from the cosmos. Only then can we arrive at a place of evolution, required to bring in a new level of sentience. Linda Moulton Howe expresses her hope in her essay on page 107 that "**other Intelligences long involved with Earth will finally acknowledge humans as fellow sentient beings in the implicate order.**" My feeling is we have to work to earn that acknowledgment. Only now after reviewing the sweep of events that I personally encountered do I realize that we don't need to journey to the stars. In other words, "**There is no out there out there.**" Only with wonderment do the stars shine through us. The cosmos twinkles from our eyes when we embrace as equals the presence of extraordinary actuality. This is neither science as we have been taught, nor fiction as we have thought. Consciousness is the way to bend, twist, warp, and wrap reality, but we must never undermine the vastness of the self that is more than alien—it is destiny.

The universe is wider than our views of it.[29]
Direct your eye inward, and you'll find a thousand re-
gions in your mind yet undiscovered. Travel them, and
be expert in home cosmography.[30]

—Henry David Thoreau, *Walden* (1854)

8

SOMETHING MOVING

Henrietta Weekes

A new world is a world that DOES NOT YET EXIST.
                                    —Sri Aurobindo

Whatever moves, within us or without us, when humans are
undergoing what has commonly come to be called "the alien
abduction experience," is still unknown. Just as a dream or
a mystical experience cannot be translated into language,
poetry and metaphor are my tools of investigation. For words
can hardly convey the experience of a kiss. If one chooses to
see this strange but undeniable experience with poetic insight, in whispered, not yet known hints of reality—that has
been my "way in," thus far. And I would never have looked
at it this way, had it not been for John Mack and a series of
personal experiences that forced me there. So I offer this, as
it might open doors for a multitude of minds.

> *Who is visits me? White beings, white feathers, white*
>   *shapes. Lately, scorpions.*
> *Life crawls, seethes, pulsates. A majestic ceaseless*
>   *spiraling dance.*

Formation in-formation . . . What is being birthed,
   over and over?
The white beings come at night. Sometimes in the
   day. Are they my friends?
What do they receive, and what do they take?
They imbue me with stars.
Beware the scorpion; symbol of the ego.
Two nights ago, I killed one.

How might we become more intimate with visions or dreams? There are thousands of gradations of experience within our minds. I think we shy away from investigation when it comes to any talk of the strange white beings, being taken aboard spaceships, and the cold, frightening sexual happenings often described.

What if we were truly open to exploring, together? Pooling our data. What if the cool hand of science would aid us, and the adventure of psychoanalysis and hypnosis turned up a collective "syndrome" that we might see as evidence of something really far out, a part of ourselves that cries out to be known?

It is up to us to hitch a ride with *something moving*. This was how Einstein answered when asked what his investigations had revealed about the secret of life: "**Something moves.**" Or rather the whole quote is: "**Nothing happens until something moves. When something vibrates, the electrons of the entire universe resonate with it. Everything is connected.**"[1]

Yet it seems that we know very little about what we are most connected to—this fantastic, mysterious organ: our brain. What is moving? What is the source of this great force that drags all of life along with it?

WHITE BEINGS . . .

Who, or what is it that visits us? Vague white shapes with a surety of presence. Odd life forms communicating not with language, but through feeling—telepathy decoded through the mind. Beings that seem to prod or probe our bodies, or appear in dreams or out of the corners of our eyes in daylight. Who or what? A force that makes love to people violently, causing the entire body and mind orgasms to ripple like cascading waves. My recent experience of this was twofold: It was a feeling of possession, not unpleasant but rather intense and ecstatic. And a physical feeling of electricity, *"something vibrating,"* as if I was a conductor *"resonating with the electrons of the entire universe."* Some kind of potent proof, like a key to an unopened door.

Do we know the rhythms of our world? What is a sigh of wind? Is it the breath of the dead? Are we visitors here on Earth? Have these white beings pierced this dimension? Those vehicles that we see in the sky—flying cigars, saucers, balls of light—do they slip in and out of our reality frames, time frames? Their motion is un-cognizable to us; they seem to slide, defying gravity as we understand it. There is no "thrust." Imagine their huge and perilous adventure: What have they had to invent to get here? My mind chatters on . . . the intellect gabbles: *"This stuff is nonsense. It doesn't make sense."*

In my dreams I saw them, peeking around a corner. I lay in a Mexican field with vast clouds overhead, surrounded by mammalian bones and teeth, the hot desert sun beating down. The clouds shape-shifted into tigers, laughing old hags, exotic birds, dragon-like creatures with fierce eyes, coy

Disney-like maidens. Then they came vaguely into view: blank faces, black almond eyes, childlike innocence, wisdom that we have yet to touch. Is there something they can give to us? And yet we resist, preferring our battles, our outcries, our hungry desires . . . Our sensorial system is our antennae, a navigation system when it comes to meeting "them"—*white beings*—we call them *aliens* in our culture. I think they want to meet us more intimately. I feel there is a purpose we can't ignore:

Involve-evolve: *They are here to aid us in that endeavor as a species.*

Sri Aurobindo's *Mother or the Divine Materialism* seems relevant to these explorations:

> *Our language is misleading, because it is entirely made up of "high," "low," "future," "past." It is a three-dimensional language used to describe a world that has never been three-dimensional, any more than the sun "rises" anywhere.*
>
> *We are the ones who revel, who journey in our consciousness. And one day we will find ourselves naturally in the middle of a completely mapped-out Supermind, the way today we are in a well-ordered Mind . . . Indeed, it is the strangest experience to discover suddenly, stupidly, that our body knows better than we do and that it has a fantastic vision and maybe a very simple and fantastic power, only veiled by our mental habits . . . At the end of the circle one finds the origin of things again. True liberation is in the body.*[2]

I have seen white shapes in the sky, as thousands of other people have the world over. My story goes thus: I am seventeen on a beautiful, clear summer's day in England. I am walking the dogs high up on the Sussex Downs. A fleet of five white disks swings into view, gliding and zipping above me, making no sound. Moving with such ease and grace, it is not a motion I recognize. The feel of them is like they weren't built here; they do not appear to obey the physical laws of motion or gravity.

From the time of a recurring childhood dream, between the ages of six and ten, there were entirely new experiences frequently erupting around me and in me. Perhaps this is so for many children unpolluted by cultural and familial contexts. There were peculiar little happenings that felt more rich, more meaningful than what presented itself in the popular culture, or in adult conversation. I wondered why the adults weren't passionately discussing this vast and magical world—or had they forgotten? During that time, a string of strange experiences occurred: A large painting once crashed violently onto my bed in a thunderstorm in a friend's house. I had been staring at it. It filled me with a sense of unidentifiable foreboding, about fifteen minutes prior its fall . . . A white horse appeared, abruptly, out of the bushes on my walk home from school one evening. Like the white disks in the sky, it felt out of place. It seemed slightly luminous, and made no sound, but peacefully stood there, staring at me—and then in a flash, disappeared back into the tiny bush. It didn't reappear on the other side when I looked . . . One extraordinary night after learning about the ice age in school, my body went into paroxysms of shivers. I felt on the brink of extinction. I felt I was initiated into the terror of death. And always asking my mother about death.

* * *

"Something moves" us, if we know how to look, if we know how to use our mind correctly and navigate the entire system of our multiple senses. Imagine if we could, en masse, an approach to the abduction/visitation experience with the investigative coolness of a scientist. I think there is much to gain from this sort of approach to the so-called mystical experience. We are at a juncture, where the twain shall meet, where dualities are collapsing, diffusing piece by piece, and melting into a Oneness. Something entirely new awaits us around the corner, where we can know **"everything is connected."** Are our night dreams weirder and richer since the virus of 2020? Are our daydreams full of a feeling of warped, accelerated, extended time? Is now the time to . . . call them up, dial them in—these so-called aliens? Are they in outer space or inner space, or both?

I have a clairvoyant friend who is rather undercover about her gifts, but she recently told me that "**they**" are from the other realms, and they need to know things from, and about us. They also have things to give to us if we can give them information in turn. "**I'm asking you to attempt to do this,**" she said to me. "**They want to understand humanity's sadness. I can't tell you why.**" The very next day, I received the unexpected opportunity to say hello and report in on this exact thing. Taking the smallest amount of a psychoactive substance rocketed me into what felt like a field of never-ending sadness. In fact, I embodied and performed grief, from my depths, for a chorus line of mollusks along with enormous golden insect-like creatures with vast, fanning wings. Humanity's grief is also the Earth's, I was told by the creatures. They returned to me the opportunity to develop gifts of feeling and knowing that can best simply and quietly be used . . .

Back to abductions, relationships, our physical, cellular matter, and electricity. A recurring childhood dream goes thus: I wake up in my top bunk bed. Everything is in place, normal. I want to switch the bedside light on so that I can read my favorite book. But it won't turn on. This becomes the signal in each dream that I am not awake, but somewhere else. I rush to my parents' room. Their bed is empty, neatly made. As if they had never slept in it. A sense of no one in the house. I run into other rooms. Empty. Footsteps, outside, bear down, gaining momentum and sound, toward the house. The front door opens. They come inside. Doors bang as they go from room to room, searching for me. Terror. I hide in cupboards, then make a dash to my room. I'm chilly, only dressed in a thin cotton nightdress. Goosebumps. Someone enters; their presence, or their energy field, overwhelms me. They kneel down and see me hiding under the bed, my face to the wall. Breath on my skin. They move closer to me and lay a finger at the base of my neck and run it slowly, steadily, down my spine to the bottom vertebrae. Skin on skin. Not aggressive, frantic, or pressured. A systematic nonfeeling "act." Always at this moment, I wake up, as if **"electrified."** I turn on the bedside lamp, and light emanates. I am safe, but what was that? I dreamed this scene over and over again, for a period of five years.

There is a writer I admire, Darin Stevenson, whose words rang bells for me with a hint of discovery about these strange experiences and dreams. His words: "**I believe that our species was originally an intimate symbiont of another form of intelligence that we are presently both unaware of and largely unavailable to. The nature of the relationship was a form of 'traveling' . . . We're** not a single thing, or a thing within a single dimension. Sometimes I think that nonhuman intelligence is actually what human intelligence is."[3] This "exchange of information" that I have had with beings from other places echoes what Darin suggests. I feel he is on to something in relation to my recent discoveries.

IS THIS COMMUNION, OR IS THIS REUNION?

I instantly became friends with Alan Steinfeld upon meeting three years ago. He would slip the idea of ETs into our conversations. By nature, I am avidly curious, but I was skeptical. I rejected giving any serious attention to this subject due to movies and the fake sensationalism of YouTube videos. I had to find my own way. "**Read this,**" he said, producing a well-worn paperback of Whitley Strieber's *Communion*. He gave it to me with the perplexing words: "**Whitley will give you a key to a world that you won't recognize, yet in a way you have already. There is no map, no language to speak about it. But try it.**" And I did recognize the world of which Whitley spoke.

As I devoured *Communion* in twenty-four hours, a cascade of memories flooded through me. *Are these encounters with such beings a communion—or a reunion?* I had an extraordinary certainty of being somewhere I know I had been before, a lost city within my inner world, regained. Every detail simultaneously unsettled and energized me. A vivid flashback occurs: *I'm by the side of the road, in England, and a group of uniformed policemen get out of a car, walking toward me, shining flashlights. They are coming to get me, but I have no idea what for.* Then the memory is over. Is this meeting with these other beings a communion as Whitley wrote,

or is it a reunion, an initiation? Whichever, there is no going
back . . .

Then I went on to John Mack, the prestigious Harvard psychiatrist, who in the early 1990s risked his credibility pro-
nouncing that the abductees he had interviewed at length
were not experiencing psychosis. Like Jung, he felt the
meetings with so-called ETs and UFO sightings were part
of our consciousness we have yet to understand. **"Something is going on here,"** Mack proclaimed, **"but I haven't
a clue what it is."**

I began to bask in the mysteries, feeling released from
my mind, and in reverie. The literature I was schooled in
echoed back to me: The English bard came to mind, and
that odd confirmation of Hippolyta, the Athenian Queen
from *A Midsummer Night's Dream*. She muses on the tale
of the two couples lost (and found) in the realm of the
fairies:

> But all the story of the night told over,
> And all their minds transfigured so together,
> More witnesseth than fancy's images
> And grows to something of great constancy;
> But, howsoever, strange and admirable.[4]

Are we being "dragged"—as in **"something moves"**—by
a great force? As Sri Aurobindo describes, **"Yes, the well
of honey beneath the rock, the Life that has yet to be."**
Moved by a great force, to commune with these so-called

aliens? Is it for our own good, and how can we know that? Through fearless, intrepid, scientific investigation, but are we the experiment of someone else? Or are they a part of us? The *"everything is connected"* refrain comes, but I wonder, *"is this a suspected intimacy as the way forward?"*

Sri Aurobindo again: **"We have the body—the key is in the matter."** They seem to long for our sensual body and our extraordinary range of sensibilities and sensitivities. The key for us could be gaining intelligence and skills to which thousands of reports can testify. Is it a trade-off, and a merger? Like a great duality playing out in our cosmos, unfolding into One; **"the new being,"** Aurobindo said. And Rilke warned: *"Every angel is terrifying."* I suspect I know what he means. So would you if you've met them. He also wrote these beautiful words that evoke the feelings I have about these odd little white ones: *"You are the bird whose wings came when I wakened in the night and called."*[5]

Since my initiation of sorts, the little neuroses that buzzed around me like irritating gnats have diminished, as if a field of protective warmth enveloped me. Slowly I feel in possession of a sharper navigation system, which continues to expand, but only if I engage, relate, listen, and have the courage to actually take the phenomenon seriously, without knowing what it is.

I revisited that recurring childhood dream one night in New York City last summer: *I lie as an adult in my childhood bed, staring out of the curtainless window. Silently, a robust, round craft glides down and hovers in front of it, flashing garish blue and red lights enwrap its girth, an object out of a* Doctor Who *episode in the 1980s. I whisper to myself matter of factly:* **"It's a UFO."** *I keep staring at it and* *it doesn't move. Nothing else happens.* I woke up. I felt like I had seen that many times before. I had a strange feeling of "home." Funny how that line *"ET phone home"* has perforated the collective cultural consciousness since the '80s. It has more meaning to me now.

My father died two months ago as I write this. Something hints to me that when our ancestors depart this earthly realm, they are close at hand and want the relationship to continue. Just like the golden mollusks that ask to be talked to in psychedelic reveries, or the beings that knocked on my door when they entered my body, or ran their finger down my spine, the central conduit of our entire nervous system, in my childhood dream.

In my experience, we can *"conduct"* between these realms. In the realms of departed souls, my father has appeared to me countless times as white feathers. Blatantly, almost "impossibly," one small feather on my car's passenger seat, for instance—how did it get there? One feather that instantaneously wafted in front of my face when I asked him for help. It went on. I think Dad could relay information. I have a niggling feeling that perhaps he is a conductor, a middle-man between myself and these strange beings that want something with us. Whitley talks about this with regards to his departed wife, Anne. She helps him find his way with the odd and unsettling relationship he has with "the visitors."

"Dad, the dream I had when I was with you. I was thirty years old." We were in next-door rooms in a seaside hotel in Devon, England. I spent childhood summers there, and years later we made a nostalgic return. I awoke from the dream and felt darkness, a dense kind of energy engulfing me. In the dream I had been examined, like a specimen. I had been treated like a lifeless object. Just how doctors examine cadavers or scientists experiment on animals. The dream: *I am in a large building, like a parking lot, and I step into an elevator. There are no signs of vitality here. No people. The elevator drops with sudden speed, and hurtles downward as if voyaging to the center of the Earth. I step out into a vast grey room with low ceilings and no windows. Stifling. Small groups of people are pushing around trolleys, robotically and silently. They wear white suits, gloves, and masks and are busy with purpose. Long metal work surfaces are dotted around the place with metal implements laid out. They don't notice me as I skulk around like an intruding observer, and I wish I could get out, but there is no exit. Then I find myself in a cot, like the one I had as a baby. Except it is metal and there are no blankets. A group of these masked "people" loom over me, scrutinizing me. I feel claustrophobic, trapped. I look down at my body to see I am a baby, but I have my adult mind. I sense that I know one of the examiners. They poke me and prod me with instruments. It's as if I'm anesthetized and they are cutting me up. I feel upset, but they're not aware of, or interested in, my feelings. They seem to communicate with each other, but silently.*

I woke sweating, breathless. I grabbed a pen to scribble the important details: "**I know one of those beings. I know something about what is going on. I won't forget this!**" But that piece of paper disappeared. I looked for it for days around the hotel room, in my bags. I asked the cleaner. No sign of it. I remember looking out of the hotel window and watching the sea rhythmically coming to shore as the wind breathed gentle sighs. Something is moving in our world, but there are other worlds too.

"The day after that dream, Dad, I walked up and down on the miles-long beach, alone, speaking continually, as if in a fevered state, a hallucination. I wanted you to protect me from who I had encountered in my dream. Now that you are not here, Dad, I do feel your protection. A powerful and pure love, a guard. I want to become more and more intimate with you, like I am learning to with the incredible golden-winged insects and mollusks, or these white beings with strange almond-shaped eyes and gelatinous, fragile bodies that I have glimpsed, and so many others I have seen. I feel that together with them we could be creating a symphony, an epic unfolding of the great creation."

Something moves—at a terrific pace.

"To dear Sri Aurobindo and The Mother, I offer this reflection as a tribute to your work. May we carry it on." I suspect we "conduct" all kinds of spirits or energies in this matter that we are encased in. And which is encased in the matter of all things on Earth, and beyond into the galaxies. It is with a scientific eye and spirit that I venture into the mystery, the conversation, the intimacy of relationship. *How far are we willing to go collectively, is my desire to know?* A great team is better than a single person, and the space between our intimacies births explosive insights and creations.

Perhaps the third point that lies between "these beings"

and us is the new creation—an entirely new species. Perhaps, if we can become it, we'd do a better job of inhabiting Earth. Or will we travel somewhere else? Anything is possible, but it is up to us.

> *We will not understand unless we understand that a man is a summary of the world. Everything is interconnected. We will never realize it enough. From this point of view our little colony here is a sort of seed plot, a laboratory. The things I work out in it are then extended outside. Indeed, the greatest obstacle of all is our own idea of things. We raise instantaneous walls about us.*
>
> *The best part of our development occurs when we do not understand anything, when we grope in the dark, stumbling here and there and floundering in the unknown. The minute we have "understood" we are defined by our comprehension. It takes a sledgehammer to get rid of our saintly ideas—they are more resilient than our devilish ones. The devilish ideas are at least humble enough to know they are stupid.*[6]

I understand Sri Aurobindo's conclusion when he says: **"The power that I am developing, if it reaches consummation, will be able to accomplish its effects automatically *by any method chosen.*"** I feel that when an expanded sense of mind, and the heightened empathy and vitality that also resulted for me, gained from meeting with these beings is fully integrated into our conscious awareness, then perhaps we can know and become that something which is moving. And I desire to be closer to them. Is it with language or the space between words? Is there poetry in contact?

Either way we may find ourselves occupying "*a new world*," as Whitley Strieber says in his book of the same name. "*If we can take it*" is also connected to that phrase.[7] Yet it seems they are us. Us, them—reunited. Together we become an entirely new being, if we choose . . .

9

TELEPATHIC CONTACT WITH EXTRATERRESTRIAL INTELLIGENCE

Darryl Anka

Contact with extraterrestrials has been depicted in science fiction books and movies in scenarios that range from the scary to the sublime. Scientists who work at SETI (Search for Extraterrestrial Intelligence) Institute have scanned the skies for decades with radio telescopes, listening for messages from interstellar civilizations. Aside from a few anomalous signals that could be the result of natural phenomena, the project has so far recorded nothing but silence.

There's an interesting paradox here: Many scientists have stated that a communication from an extraterrestrial would likely be in a form that would be alien to us and yet, many scientists still assume that a message from an ET would utilize everyday radio waves to signal other civilizations. The question is, does the latter assumption prevent them from recognizing more unusual forms of communication should they occur?

Much has been made in recent years about the possibility that extraterrestrial beings might use a form of telepathy to reach out to other worlds, since it's possible that distance and time may not be inhibiting factors in the way they are for mundane forms of communication, like radio waves that can only travel at the speed of light.

Quantum principles like entanglement, or something similar, might play a role in an ET's ability to "*link minds*" with another being. With quantum entanglement, a change made to one particle in a pair of "bonded" particles—for example, causing it to spin left (change its angular momentum)—immediately causes the complementary particle to spin in the opposite direction, no matter how far away it might be in normal space, thus making it appear as if information traveled faster than the speed of light between the two particles.

Einstein referred to this phenomenon as "*spooky action at a distance*" since it seemed to violate the laws of physics where the speed of light is concerned. However, if quantum entanglement does not display action at a distance, but instead displays that distance (space-time) is an illusion, then the effect can be understood because the two particles are not, despite appearances, separated by any distance at all. While many physicists doubt entanglement can be used for communication, an advanced ET civilization may have found a way around that obstacle.

Which brings us to the concept known as channeling. It's been assumed for hundreds of years that mediumship, an early label for the channeling experience, was a matter of the "*possession*" of a human "*host*" by some spiritual entity, be it malevolent or benign. This is, in my experience as a channel for nearly forty years, an old-fashioned, outdated, and erroneous definition. A more modern interpretation would be to think of channeling simply as an altered state of consciousness that, whether another entity is involved or not, allows a person to perceive concepts in a more holistic manner, from a higher, all-encompassing point of view.

Neuroscientists have labeled this altered state "Gamma." While in the Gamma state, the brain operates between 40 hertz (cycles per second) and 100 hertz. This state is often called being "in the zone," and any expression of passion, creativity, focus, or deep meditation will push the brain into Gamma from its everyday state of Beta (ordinary waking awareness), which is below 40 hertz.

Therefore, the Gamma state is the channeling state, where information is processed at faster speeds and new, more creative associations are made within a person's consciousness, thus generating information from a higher state of awareness.

However, from my personal experience, the channeling state is also capable of allowing a person to connect, not only to one's own higher levels of consciousness, but also to other independent beings whose consciousness operates at those higher levels, much in the same way that one tuning fork will cause a second tuning fork to vibrate in harmonic resonance if they are tuned to the same frequency. Thus, like quantum entanglement, two minds, no matter how far apart they appear in space or time, might be able to connect by matching frequencies.

I believe this principle of "*harmonic resonance*," rather than the medieval concept of "*possession*," is the physical basis that allows a trained medium or channel to act as a "*biological translation device*," if you will, for non-physical or extra-dimensional entities who routinely use telepathy to communicate.

If so, this leads to the understanding that telepathy (or perhaps *tel-empathy* would be a more accurate label), far from being an ability to read other people's minds, is simply what happens when two or more individuals are "on the same wavelength." In other words, no one is actually reading someone else's mind. It's just that, if two or more conscious entities are operating at a similar frequency, then they will manifest the same thoughts at the same time as one another. Technically, they're not reading someone else's mind; they're reading their own mind, which happens to simultaneously be thinking the same thoughts as the other beings on that frequency.

In my opinion, this is why people who are in love often know exactly what each other is thinking, without having to say much. We see this in strong emotional bonds, be it lovers, close siblings, or a parent and a child.

My journey with making contact began in 1973, when I had two very close, broad-daylight sightings one week apart of a black, triangular UFO over Los Angeles, where I live. The sightings were not distant lights, but a solid vehicle about thirty feet on each side and no more than one hundred fifty feet away and seventy feet away, respectively.

This inciting incident prompted a lifelong investigation into all manner of paranormal phenomena, including channeling, and, ten years after the sightings, this path led me to a channeling class. The exercises and meditation techniques taught by the entity that came through the teacher induced a state that allowed me to receive a telepathic communication from the being that allegedly occupied the UFO I had witnessed ten years earlier.

At first, I passed off the experience as either a figment

of my imagination, a hallucination, or some strange "*side effect*" of the meditation. However, the instant the message popped into my head, the entity coming through the teacher stopped talking to the class and addressed me directly. Without having said out loud what I was experiencing, he nevertheless said, "**There's an entity here for you now if you're ready to begin.**" Startling as that was, I happened to glance to one side and noticed that one of my classmates was drawing a sketch of the alien being I'd seen in my mind because she'd caught a glimpse of him in her own meditation.

Needless to say, I was stunned. However, having two immediate validations that the being wasn't simply in my imagination encouraged me to explore the experience further. Over time and with a lot of practice, I was able to hone in on the brain-wave frequency that allowed the telepathic contact to grow stronger and the ET's messages to become clearer: the Gamma state.

The alien entity referred to himself as "**Bashar,**" a word that I eventually learned wasn't his name, but an Arabic word that means "*messenger*" or "*bringer of good news.*" Although I don't speak Arabic, it's part of my ethnic background on my father's side. Bashar later explained that the word was chosen for a variety of reasons that are personal to me and, thus, aren't relevant to this writing, but also because his people, being telepathic, don't have personal names like Earth humans do. Instead, they recognize each other by their distinct energy frequencies. Still, he knew that we would need to call him something in one of our human languages, so the word was chosen to represent his purpose, which is to deliver messages that lay the groundwork for eventual open contact between his civilization and ours.

In Bashar's culture, called the Sassani in their ancient and obsolete language, he's one of several **First Contact Specialists**. As the title implies, he's experienced in the art of initiating first contact with other planetary civilizations when they realize they may not be alone in the universe.

According to Bashar, Earth is now in the initial phase of contact, which involves establishing a telepathic connection with a member of the society (in this case, myself) and disseminating new perspectives and information. How the society chooses to react to the messages—positively, negatively, or indifferently—provides an indication of whether or not the civilization is ready for the additional phases of contact. This process can last for years, and, as of this writing, I've been channeling Bashar for nearly four decades, since 1983.

The thing I appreciate most about the messages Bashar delivers is that, while he might refer to paranormal and spiritual concepts, like the importance of acting on one's passion in life, or psychic phenomena, or reincarnation, the way that he explains them has more in common with physics than metaphysics. Bashar delivers a practical, down-to-Earth toolkit of why such experiences are possible and how they work according to *the "mechanics" of physical reality*. In many cases, his explanations are very different than the labels our society has attached to such phenomena. The processes he describes allow a person to apply the metaphysical principles in a grounded way that produces a physical result. Thus, while the information doesn't prove the existence of Bashar himself, the results that many people have experienced by applying Bashar's suggestions in their daily lives are proof that the information works.

This is an important point: It's not necessary for anyone to believe that Bashar is real to benefit from the information that comes through from the channeling state. For all I know, Bashar could simply be an aspect of my own higher state of consciousness. In the long run, it doesn't matter because the experience has taught me that we all have the ability to shift into Gamma, the channeling state, and, from within that state, process information in a manner that generates new perspectives and new solutions to challenges that appear unsolvable from a less holistic state of being.

In 2016, along with my production partners at Zia Films and Bashar Communications, I made a documentary called *First Contact* about my experience in becoming a channel for Bashar. One of the reasons for making the documentary was to demystify the process of channeling. One of the ways we accomplished this goal was to wire my head to a brain-wave analysis device (an EEG machine) to determine if there were any significant changes in my brain-wave activity while in the channeling state (Gamma) in contrast to my ordinary waking state (Beta).

Aside from the obvious shift from Beta to Gamma, the EEG technician observed some profound differences between the two states. Without going into technical detail, we discovered three major changes:

First, my brain's processing speed increases significantly, becomes more coherent overall, and recognizes more connections and associations between seemingly unrelated data.

Second, according to current brain science, my brain's *"set point"* (the rate at which the brain perceives the world) is not supposed to change over the course of my lifetime, yet when in the channeling state, it changes in seconds to a higher rate, especially when listening to another person, thus perceiving and analyzing more data.

Third, while certain sections of my brain become more active, other sections switch off, including the area of the brain responsible for processing my personality. Therefore, the question is, if my personality is suppressed during the channeling, then who's delivering the information that comes through?

While these and other effects are fascinating attributes of the channeling state, they are achievable by anyone who raises their brain waves to the Gamma frequency, either by being in a state of passion, slipping into a deep meditation, or training themselves to shift to that state at will. It's about being "in the zone."

Decades ago, achieving Gamma took longer than it does for me now, and it came with a flood of odd sensations. An hour or two before I was scheduled to channel, I often felt like I was coming down with the flu. I would feel feverish, my body would ache, pain would grip the base of my skull, and my neck muscles would spasm and lock, sometimes for over an hour. However, as soon as I started channeling, all the symptoms would melt away.

Then, as my brain shifted from Beta to Gamma, I experienced a spectrum of emotions, from anger, through sadness, and, finally, to joy, like I was letting go of, and rising above, human concerns to a higher, spiritual perspective. Once I reached the Gamma state, I was infused with a sense of peace, balance, and focus. At that moment, the telepathic link was established with Bashar and I felt my mind taking a *"back seat,"* so to speak, while his consciousness slid into the driver's seat of my brain.

I knew I was always in control and could stop the channeling any time I wanted, but the energy that poured through me was so soul-stirring that the last thing I wanted to do was leave that state. Over time, as I let go of any resistance to the high-frequency energy that was the hallmark of Bashar's consciousness, it flowed through my body with more ease, and the uncomfortable *"symptoms"* I experienced before each channeling faded after about two years. From that point on, the energy uplifted me, like the way a gentle wave lifts your feet off the sand when you wade in the shallows of the ocean.

When a person initiates a conversation with Bashar by asking a question, I feel his telepathic response blossom like a flower in my mind. The entire answer is there in a heartbeat, although it may take several minutes to "unspool" and get translated into language. The words are faint and far away to me, like a muffled conversation in another room. I experience feelings, mental images, and abstract symbols that represent what the conversation is about, but the words are secondary, like when a person is lost in thought or caught up in a daydream and someone has to repeatedly call their name before they realize they're being spoken to.

One analogy I often use is that the state feels similar to standing under a pounding waterfall, while the person receiving Bashar's response is merely getting the spray.

I mention all of this because, in discussing these things with other channels, I've found that these symptoms and sensations are common to many of them as they learn to let go of their fear and begin to trust the process. In addition, while not experienced by all channels, these sensations form a sort of general road map that can guide those who desire to channel and provide a few markers for where they are on their journey.

In addition to what I see and feel while in the channeling state, the questioners who engage in conversation with Bashar have their own experiences. When Bashar connects with me and comes through, people often report that they feel an expansion of energy, or they might suddenly feel dizzy or drowsy, or they might feel electrified.

My theory is that these sensations happen because we all have biomagnetic energy fields that extend from, and encompass, our bodies. While these fields are relatively weak and hard to detect without ultrasensitive superconducting sensors, it appears from people's physical reactions to the channeling that humans are able to sense the field emanating from my body, possibly using their own biomagnetic fields as detectors.

Bashar's energy changes the frequency of my field and, if nearby people allow their own fields to synchronize with that higher frequency, they would then feel a shift in the frequency of their own biomagnetic fields that could manifest the physical sensations described above.

Bashar has said that, in addition to his telepathic thoughts being translated into language, there is additional information embedded in the biomagnetic and infrared energy patterns that radiate from my body. He has stated that the purpose of this is twofold:

First, the technique allows his communications to

reach parts of the listener's brain that process information in ways other than language, and, second, it allows people who are willing to synchronize with his frequency to see things from his perspective, as well as understand and process higher-level concepts more easily.

While all of the above may explain Bashar's unique style of delivering messages, the questions many people really want answers to are: What if Bashar isn't just an aspect of my consciousness? What if he's actually a telepathic, extraterrestrial entity? What if his messages are the first phase of contact between Earth and an alien civilization? What would that mean for our society?

If Bashar isn't real, then if nothing else, the information generated while in the channeling state has still improved the lives of hundreds, if not thousands, of people over the years. Perhaps the reason that the channeling has presented Bashar as an autonomous individual is somehow in service to my subconscious desire to draw people to the messages in a novel way. I honestly can't dismiss that possibility out of hand.

But let's suppose for the moment that Bashar is a real entity from another world. If so, then, as a **First Contact Specialist**, he's acting as an ambassador for his people. Can humanity afford to discount and dismiss the possibility that he is who he says he is, just because the communication comes in an unusual form?

Would an alien entity really choose to contact humans by radio? Would ETs actually attempt to make contact by landing on the White House lawn? Or would they take a subtle approach—one that would focus us on their messages instead of on the messengers?

Bashar has explained that there's an important purpose for remaining in the background, even to the point of allowing us to believe he's not real. It boils down to a familiar science-fiction concept: **"a noninterference directive."**

Undeniable physical proof that advanced ETs exist could be extremely disruptive to our society. A civilization that operates on a completely different level from humanity could undermine us technologically, socially, mentally, and spiritually if they introduce their way of life to our world too quickly. Sharing their information in bite-sized chunks over a period of time gives us a chance to adapt to new concepts at a comfortable pace, ensuring a smooth process of change.

In essence, if we choose to become more like them, then open contact won't be such a shock to our system, if or when it finally happens. I say "if" because, despite Bashar's willingness to make open contact with Earth, it's still our decision and, should we decide we're not ready for such a sweeping change, a benign ET civilization such as Bashar's will not force their presence upon us. His people respect that Earth is our world and that contact is ultimately our choice.

Speaking from personal experience, I believe that contact with other civilizations in the universe would be a good thing for humanity. Channeling Bashar's powerful messages for this long has had a profound and positive impact on me, as well as on those who've also applied his principles in their lives. The information he delivers is based on a deep understanding of how reality is structured and how it works, summed up in his **"instruction manual"**—a four-step formula for living:

TELEPATHIC CONTACT WITH EXTRATERRESTRIAL . . . 239

1. Act on your passion every moment that you can.
2. Act on it to the best you can until you can act on it no further.
3. Act on it with no assumption or insistence on the outcome.
4. Stay in a positive state no matter what results from that action.

These are just a few of the amazing changes that can occur using this formula:

- The understanding that we create our reality.
- An observable increase in positive synchronicity.
- Greater clarity and discernment of what is or isn't the best path to take in life. A perception of time and space as an illusion.
- Increased mental, emotional, and spiritual balance.
- A more effortless, passionate, and creative life.

Bashar's concepts shine a light on how our deepest beliefs can either hold us back or propel us forward and how physical reality acts like a reflective mirror to help guide our choices. Bashar has even discussed quantum mechanics with several physicists, who left those conversations with new insights into the nature of existence.

In my opinion, these types of exchanges are mere previews of the benefits available to humanity if we can learn to open our minds and engage with highly evolved, extraterrestrial intelligences in a way that allows us to adapt to the information and expand our understanding at a comfortable pace that serves the greatest number of people.

Of course, not everyone will accept this approach or even believe this is possible. That's okay. We must all make our own choices and allow others to do the same. Each of us has a unique path, and it's important to be true to ourselves. At the same time, it's crucial that we don't nullify our vast potential by holding on to irrational, fear-based beliefs.

Granted, building a relationship with an ET civilization that's very different from our own will be one of the greatest challenges humanity has ever faced. But I believe that with willingness and patience, it can be done. It will not only require that we expand our knowledge of the universe, or at least consider radically different points of view, but it will also require a deeper understanding of ourselves and a drive to integrate the fragmented aspects of our individual and collective personalities into a more balanced and holistic expression of humanity. Please don't misunderstand—this will not be achieved by homogenizing humankind, but by validating each individual's unique skills, talents, and perspectives in a way that allows our differences to work together in a more harmonious manner.

Some might question what humans would have to offer an advanced ET society in exchange for the knowledge they impart to us. There's an anecdotal story involving Benjamin Franklin that illustrates at least one aspect of humanity's potential value to our extraterrestrial neighbors:

In 1783, tens of thousands of spectators went to Versailles, near Paris, to see the Montgolfiers' hot air balloon set off on one of the world's first untethered, manned-balloon flights.[1] People gasped to see them rise high into the air. When a man saw Dr. Franklin watching the event from his carriage, he asked the aged inventor, "**It's a wonder to be sure, but of what *practical* use is it?**" Smiling, Franklin answered, "**Of what practical use is a newborn baby?**"

A civilization thousands of years more advanced than ours couldn't be blamed for viewing humanity as a group of toddlers just learning to walk. However, as with most children who will eventually mature, they might also perceive our potential to run. Regardless of our status, we have unique experiences and perspectives that an ET might find illuminating, since we would be as alien to them as they would be to us.

Aside from the diversity of our philosophies, our myriad cultures, and our customs, there are also practical considerations for such an interaction, such as trading goods and art, or piquing an ET's interest in the vast diversity of our planet's climate zones, ecosystems, plants, animals, and minerals. It could be to their civilization's benefit, whether in the near or far future, to help guide and integrate Earth into their interstellar community.

Bashar's descriptions of the life-forms he's encountered on other planets, and even in other dimensions, can stoke our imaginations and open our minds to the variety of ways that life can be expressed in the universe, long before we develop the technology to travel to the stars and encounter those civilizations ourselves. Three of these cultures are:

- A society that has the ability to telepathically make you forget you encountered them.
- Interdimensional life-forms that can siphon information about the universe from the event horizon of a black hole.

- A culture that inhabits an "inside-out universe" where, instead of living on the outer surface of a planet that floats in the void of space, they live on the interior surface of enormous hollow bubbles in a realm filled with a gravitational "fluid."

He's also hinted at the prospect that humans could eventually be guided to observe and make first contact with other planetary cultures that are at a stage of evolution similar to where we are now. In effect, our future spaceships would become the UFOs of those alien societies.

What does all of this add up to? Whether or not Bashar is real and transmitting this information, or whether it's simply an exercise in altered states and imagination, it speaks to our place on the evolutionary scale that we've awakened to the possibility that we're not alone in the universe. We've sent probes into space that carry invitations for ETs to contact us. We've catalogued thousands of exoplanets, some of which might harbor life. We're beginning to realize that some denizens of Earth, such as dolphins, exhibit intelligence equal to or surpassing our own, and we are exploring ways to communicate with them as we would with an alien species.

Though mankind has pondered its place in the universe for thousands of years, only recently, historically speaking, have we begun to discover a few answers to our questions. While science is responsible for providing most of those answers (while, of course, creating many more questions as well), it might be time to consider that the science of an extraterrestrial society may look nothing like our version of it. As Arthur C. Clarke, the author of *2001: A Space Od-*

yssey, once remarked, "**Any sufficiently advanced technology is indistinguishable from magic.**"

To illustrate how differently an ET might express a physics principle as compared to our approach, Bashar has provided the following example of Heisenberg's Uncertainty Principle, which states that it's impossible to determine simultaneously both the position and the velocity of a particle.

Figure 1 is the principle expressed in human mathematics. Figure 2 is the principle expressed in Sassani geometrics.

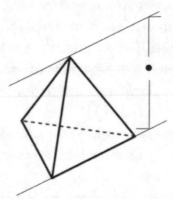

FIGURE 1

$$\Delta x \Delta p \geq \frac{\hbar}{2}$$

FIGURE 2

The Sassani geometric describes the potential position of a particle relative to the base of the tetrahedron (the *x, y, z* positions of three-dimensional space) while the top apex of the tetrahedron represents time. Thus, any measurement within any one of the triangular planes that make up the figure cannot include all four points (apexes) at once, and so the position in space and velocity in time cannot be measured simultaneously.

As is evident, the two approaches are so different that the Sassani symbol is unrecognizable as the Uncertainty Principle when compared with our physics notation. So, too, might a telepathic contact be unrecognized as a legitimate communication from an extraterrestrial source compared with an audio message from the stars delivered by radio.

So why not make it easy on us and just deliver messages via radio? After all, if an ET prefers to be cautious and not physically land on Earth, what's the advantage of choosing telepathy over radio waves when hardly any humans are telepathic?

There are a few reasons why telepathy may be preferred. First, it may simply be the natural way some ETs communicate.

Second, an alien civilization may have outgrown radio technology so long ago that choosing it as a mode of communication may not even occur to them. An amusing illustration of this point is a video that appeared on social media in which two teenaged boys are trying to use an old rotary-dial telephone. It takes them quite a while to figure out how to place a call, and that technology is only a few decades out of date. Imagine a society that hasn't used radio for a thousand years.

Third, a person willing to be trained to act as a "biological translator" comes fully equipped with the vocabulary and body language of that person's respective culture. No muss, no fuss, no awkward misinterpretations. Or at least, not many. The fact that humans often misunderstand each other's text messages, even when we're using the same language and cultural references, might prompt an alien to include the physical, mental, and emotional components by involving a human who can deliver a fully nuanced message.

In the *First Contact* documentary I mentioned earlier, we used the following examples to illustrate how differently a message might be interpreted, even if the only difference is punctuation:

1. A woman without her man is nothing.
2. A woman: without her, man is nothing.

The misunderstanding that could ensue from one interpretation over the other could easily ignite heated arguments if the intention behind the message isn't crystal clear or in keeping with the perspective of the one receiving the message. How many personal vendettas throughout our history were started by some innocent remark taken the wrong way?

In various science-fiction films and internet articles, much is also made of the concept that advanced civilizations tend to overpower and replace less advanced ones. The films and articles often refer to the European conquest of the Americas to underscore the point. However, setting aside for the moment the question of what it means to be "advanced," examples like that are from *human* history.

Extraterrestrial history could be very different and, if a civilization is truly, well, civilized, it seems more likely that they would go to great lengths to make sure no damage is done to the planetary society with which they're observing or interacting.

Not only might a truly advanced star-faring culture adopt some type of noninterference directive, as mentioned earlier, but, in my opinion, higher intelligences would be prone to view the universe as *a whole system* rather than as merely a collection of unrelated components. In other words, what happens to us happens to them. The loss of one is potentially a loss to all, which is why an advanced, interstellar civilization would never attack, plunder, or destroy a planet-bound one.

A lot of people wonder, if benevolent ETs are observing us, why they don't land? Why don't they just reveal themselves? Bashar explained that a lot of civilizations more advanced than ours operate on a very high-frequency level of energy. Because we tend to compartmentalize things in our consciousness and give in to negative and fear-based definitions, our energy is of a lower frequency more often than not. He has likened the idea to gears. A high-frequency race will operate like a fast-spinning gear, while a lower-frequency race will be like a slowly turning gear. If you jam those two gears together too quickly, you will strip the gears. They have to be more synchronized before you can bring them together.

The way Bashar showed me this was in a dream. I saw his ship land, and I saw him get out and walk toward me. As soon as he got about ten or twenty feet away, I suddenly lost my identity and saw my body through his eyes as if I became him, as if I was absorbed by him. He said, **"You see, our energy is so much more overwhelming at this higher frequency than yours, it can overpower your sense of identity. You are not fully integrated enough to hold your own. So, by delivering information to you in the way that we are, you can then absorb it and change at your own rate. When you have upgraded your frequency enough and meet us halfway, then our energies will be harmonized and synchronized. You won't experience this loss of identity or give your power over to us. If we do it too soon, too prematurely, we are not really doing you any favors. It would be disruptive, not only to your society, but to you as an individual. The more you change and grow and become more of yourself, the more you will be like us, the more compatible we will be, and the more we can interact physically, and that is when contact will occur."**

The fact that many humans appear hell-bent on destroying their own planet is why ETs may prefer to communicate from a safe distance. In addition, our civilization's almost desperate denial of the existence of UFOs sends a clear message that we're far from ready for open contact.

In 1997, a mile-wide, boomerang-shaped UFO passed very low and very slowly over Arizona from north to south. The incident was dubbed *"The Phoenix Lights."* Despite having been witnessed by more than ten thousand people, including the governor of the state, the sighting was dismissed by most news stations as either *"small planes flying in close formation"* or *"military flares."*

More recently, around 2017, the Department of Defense declassified and publicly released videos of **"Unidentified Aerial Phenomena"** that were captured by the cameras on the F/A-18 Super Hornet fighter jets that pursued the forty-foot-long unknown crafts. Military officials at the Pentagon verified that the videos were authentic. Despite the veracity of the officials and the Navy pilots, some newspaper articles chose to add a counterclaim by anonymous "experts" that the pilots probably mistook a weather balloon for a technologically advanced craft, even though their jets were unable to catch up to one UFO, which was reported to travel sixty miles in under a minute.

Dismissive comments like this are, in my opinion, an insult, not only to the experienced pilots our country relies on to protect us from aerial attack, but to everyone's intelligence as well. If we're ever going to have any chance to experience contact with ETs, we need to start taking these reports seriously, investigate them thoroughly, and not legitimize the debunkers who cynically, and falsely, pass themselves off to the media as "experts."

Ever since my two UFO sightings, my life has definitely taken "*the road less traveled*." Prior to 1983, if someone had predicted I'd be channeling an alleged extraterrestrial to thousands of people around the globe for the next forty years, I'd have thought they were crazy. But here I am. If I've learned nothing else from this experience it's that you never know where life is going to take you.

Because of the channeling, I've traveled to cities and countries I may never have visited otherwise. I've made close friends with people I probably never would have met. I've learned a lot about a wide variety of topics, from astronomy to psychology, from business to biology, from metaphysics to quantum physics, and so much more. Most importantly, I met Erica, my loving wife of thirty-seven years, directly because I took this path. To say that my life changed for the better because of the channeling would be a profound understatement.

I am often approached by people who tell me that they experience less struggle, more abundance, more creativity, better relationships, and more joy because of the information that Bashar delivers. I deeply appreciate the gift I've been given to touch so many lives in positive and profound ways.

I feel Bashar represents what we could all become. We often say we are only human, but maybe we are not—not yet. Maybe we don't know what it means to be fully human. Perhaps Bashar is showing us how to express our humanity more fully. He has said, "**Contact is an ongoing experience and part of the natural evolution of you as a species from what you may loosely call *Homo sapiens* to *Homo galacticus*.**"

Channeling Bashar's information may not be the only path that leads to contact with other worlds, but I believe that, by expanding our awareness, by knowing ourselves more deeply, and by actively living our best lives, we will uplift our individual and collective consciousness, make ourselves more compatible with advanced civilizations, and increase the probability that, one day, we will have open contact with beings from the stars.

10

AWAKENING TO OUR COSMIC HERITAGE

Mary Rodwell

Making contact with a non-human cosmic race occurred since before I was born. These beings were my family before I came to the Earth domain, and I had a close relationship with them which continued after my birth.

—Tracey Taylor

Since the founding of the Australian Close Encounter Resource Network (ACERN) in 1997, I have worked with more than 3,000 individuals and their families who feel they have had some sort of "anomalous" paranormal experience. The main aspect of my work has been to support people encountering beings of Non-Human Intelligences (NHI). I have been particularly drawn to highly intuitive individuals, who feel a strange connection to the stars and other galaxies. All this research has led me to discover major changes in an emerging generation of children. Their common feature is the demonstration of increased psychospiritual awareness, which appears to be resulting in an overall transformation of human consciousness. The following are extracts from my interviews, research, and conclusions about the awakening star seeds I call the "**New Human.**"

HOMO SAPIENS SAPIENS, A HYBRID SPECIES?

My work with the New Human has led me to ask an initial question: "**What will humanity look like when we realize we are part of a larger cosmos?**" Many people who have had contacts with non-human intelligences have conveyed to me the information that humanity is a hybrid species and that non-human intelligences are the genetic ancestors to *Homo sapiens sapiens*. If this is correct, where is the evidence? **Who exactly are humanity's genetic ancestors? Why is it so important for us to understand our genetic origins and what does this ultimately mean for our species?** In this essay I will explore the evidence through testimony from both adults and children regarding their contact with NHIs, their awareness of their hybrid status, and why this is vital at this present time.

The public, for the most part, now understands that it is illogical to believe we are the only intelligent life in the universe, given we have two trillion galaxies in the observable universe and considering the number of stars that could potentially support life. The plethora of footage captured by the public of Unidentified Aerial Phenomena (UAP) and disclosure from military sources of such craft make it increasingly difficult to deny non-human intelligences are not only "out there" but have visited Earth throughout human history.

The modern perspective of "visitors" from the stars indicated by indigenous peoples is that these intelligences are the gods of mythology and religions who came down from the stars and had been visiting our planet for millennia. Another modern perspective indicates the creators of *Homo sapiens sapiens*, the gods of religion, were in fact extraterrestrials. Therefore, if we explore these perspectives not as supernatural events but as visits by real extraterrestrial beings with advanced technologies, it is logical to conclude there has been genetic engineering in our past. Numerous indigenous peoples across the globe have told these "gods" were responsible for creating us. This certainly explains many of our anthropological, archaeological, and theological mysteries. The late biblical scholar Zecharia Sitchin, in his translation of ancient Sumerian tablets in his book series Earth Chronicles, wrote that "**the 'Gods' i.e. Annunaki, came to Earth and modified human DNA.**"[1] The Christian bible also suggests we were intelligently designed: "**Then God said: 'And now we will make human beings; they will be like us and resemble us.'**"[2]

The question arises, just *who* was "us"?

Tracey Taylor is a contactee/experiencer who has received a "*download*" of information that also confirms the mythologies of indigenous accounts: "**One night, I had this intense feeling before sleep. I wrote in a process that I had little control over; something beyond my present understanding. It was contrary to everything I had been taught. The human race had been created by extraterrestrials—and it contained information about genetic manipulation and the use of human and extraterrestrial DNA to create another species.**"[3]

The molecular biologist Dr. Francis Crick, winner of the Nobel Prize in medicine for working with James Watson in proposing the double helix structure of the DNA molecule, also hypothesized we are a "created" species of intelligent design. *Homo sapiens sapiens* emerged after what is termed "a missing link" in evolution, after earlier species of human, that is, Cro-Magnon and Neanderthal, disappeared. This new species *Homo sapiens sapiens* emerged with twice the brain size and 223 extra genes related to higher psychological functioning. How did such a dramatic change with new genetic material of such specificity get added to the human genome? In Crick's book *Life Itself: Its Origin and Nature* he attributes the anomaly to humanity's design by non-human intelligences:

> *The DNA molecule is the most efficient information storage system in the entire universe. The immensity of complex, coded and precisely sequenced information is absolutely staggering. The DNA evidence speaks of intelligent, information bearing design. They (extraterrestrials) programmed the molecules so . . . they could therefore teach us about ourselves and how to progress. For life to form by chance is mathematically virtually impossible.*[4]

Dr. Crick's work has been followed by other scientists who concur with this hypothesis. For instance, the molecular biologist Dr. William Brown stated: **"The possibility is that human DNA is a combination of indigenous and ET DNA. There are many indicators of genetic manipulation showing advanced technology has been used to remodel the genomes in humans."**[5]

I had to ask: **Is this evidence that not only are we a hybrid species, but that we may have DNA from numerous non-human intelligences in our DNA?**

Former command sergeant Robert Dean, the late Ufologist and contactee, stated from his research and information from secret military sources **"that *Homo sapiens* is a hybrid species."** Dean was informed of extraterrestrial reality in the military, where he had access to top-secret documents that revealed the US military already knew of extraterrestrial visits, and that at least four different species of extraterrestrial were known to have interacted with government forces. In recent years, Dean revealed he personally had been taken aboard spacecraft and told by these "intelligences" about the non-human genetic origins of our species.

In another case from my second book *The New Human,* Dr. Maree Batchelor shared that after a series of life-changing events she began to have interactions with NHIs, downloading information and specific frequencies that she was able to use in healing and activating dormant human DNA. Dr Batchelor said: **"People don't realize the matrix is Galactic . . . the 'gods' of the old religions . . . are really multidimensional galactic beings."**[6]

Jo Sheval Iskra, another contactee/experiencer, recalled encounters with NHI praying mantis–looking beings who communicated to her that they were **"Master Geneticists."** She wrote to me the following:

> *In 2018 I was with a tall Mantis being and
> benevolent Reptilians. They took me to a massive
> laboratory inside a cave-like structure. There were*

thousands of incubators with hybrids in them. The
Mantis told me "they" the Mantis were the "keepers
of the Universe." They have blueprints and DNA for
every species that has ever existed including extinct
species on our planet. They populate planets with
life-forms throughout the universe. They said they
were proficient at genetically modifying humans.[7]

If we accept the reality that *Homo sapiens* is a hybrid
species with the addition of DNA from a number of extraterrestrial species, it makes sense that our genetic links are
sufficient reason for their interest in monitoring and communicating with us. But what contactees and experiencers
are conveying is that this interest in humanity and its evolution as a hybrid species is not yet complete. Humanity has
not yet realized its full potential and is in the process of being upgraded, activated to awaken and to evolve to our full
potential as a species. Dr. Francis Crick hypothesized that
there was more to our hybrid DNA than we had realized.

HYBRID HUMAN, EXTRATERRESTRIAL DNA, AND MORE?

Crick also believed not only are we a created species, but
additional "information" may have been programmed
into human DNA. He stated that he believed at some future point we will access this programmed data **"and this**
would therefore teach us about ourselves." Was he referring to humanity reaching a certain level of "technological
evolution" where we would discover human hybridization,
or did he mean something even more profound? I believe it
may have been both.

My next question was: **If we are a hybrid species as**

Crick and others suggest, is there more to be revealed to us? I found that scientists Vladimir I. shCherbak from the al-Farabi Kazakh National University and Maxim A. Makukov of the Fesenkov Astrophysical Institute suggested we are a hybrid species and that there could be a "message" hidden in human DNA: **"The genetic code suggests it was invented outside the solar system several billion years ago. It appears there is an intelligent signal embedded in our genetic code. A mathematical and semantic message, a 'biological SETI.' This method would have greater longevity and chance of detecting ETs than a transient extraterrestrial radio transmission. There are recognizable hallmarks of artificiality, patterns essentially irreducible to any natural origin."** [8] In this regard, DNA has already been found to be a truly amazing storage device. One gram of DNA can store 215 million gigabytes (215 petabytes) of information.[9] **Does human DNA have information encoded from our makers, a "biological SETI" or "signal"? And could it be that some DNA has functions not yet understood?**

DORMANT DNA: WHAT DOES IT CONTAIN?

Geneticists confirm that we only utilize 5 percent of our DNA, the remaining 95 percent is considered "junk" DNA because of its "unknown" function. However, contactees have stated there are enhanced abilities encoded in this so-called junk or dormant DNA. **Is it possible this dormant DNA holds new abilities and encoded information or signals to assist humanity in an evolutionary shift?** Astrophysicist Dr. Rudy Schild has said: **"I have long understood that the DNA does more than chemistry, and is in res-**

onance with the quantum hologram to bring emotional and spiritual content into our being. The mathematics of how this works in human consciousness involves the soul, and has been described by me 'with hints of mathematics.'"[10]

Dr. Lena Ohlson, another molecular biologist and contactee, said:

> *The information of the donors [to our DNA] and their background is there; a hidden key, like PC programmers hide their work. This key can be activated and these "programmers" know the person is ready to be "contacted." The activated ones spread a signal to wake others up . . .*
>
> *If my information . . . is correct, there will be twelve different main groups of new DNA people. It corresponds to the twelve different main groups of ET/alien DNA-donors; so nine more to go. Their/ our DNA is activated mainly via remote control and frequencies, so it is like putting a virus in a software (computer program). They will give off energy patterns that spread to their surroundings.*[11]

More insights about the genetic manipulation of our DNA came from the most wide-ranging study ever undertaken of people claiming to have contact with UFOs/ETs. **The Edgar Mitchell Foundation for Research into Extraterrestrial and Extraordinary Encounters (FREE)** conducted the world's first comprehensive and international academic research study with more than 4,200 individuals from more than 100 countries who have had UFO/UAP

(Unidentified Aerial Phenomenon) and related contact
with Non-Human Intelligence (NHI). One of their results
found that **25.58 percent of respondents received messages
about upgrading human DNA.**

DORMANT DNA: THE NEXT STEP IN HUMAN EVOLUTION?

Visionary and scientist Nikola Tesla said in 1942, *"If you
want to find the secrets of the universe, think in terms of
energy, frequency, and vibration."*[12]

Another insight from Dr. Lena Ohlson is that "**the
'energy container' controls the process i.e. soul, in combination of the soul choosing how and what time the
frequencies will activate the bio container (body).**"[13] The
question comes: **Are we being primed for some grand activation to come at some time in the near future?**

"**Awakening to contact**" or "**Activation,**" as it has been
called, was an extremely profound process for Dr. Maree
Batchelor. This occurred spontaneously on a spiritual journey visiting a temple in India. Dr. Batchelor told me that at
the time she felt she received some sort of download that
instantly expanded her conscious awareness and ultimately
changed her life. She reports that "**Previously I was living
as a GP married to a surgeon with four amazing children.
In 2014, I experienced this download of what I would call
now 'Cosmic' frequencies. And boom—suddenly I am in
Cosmic Consciousness. This event propelled me into the
realms of energy medicine and the holographic field.**"[14]

Dr. Batchelor believes her downloading to her patients
can activate their dormant DNA and she has seen profound
"awakening" in her population. She feels she operates more
as a "shamanic healer" than a doctor. She calls herself a

"**DNA galactic re-wirer**" upgrading humans through her galactic connection. She writes:

> *I use embodied "light frequencies" to remove*
> *behavioral triggers and energetic blocks down to*
> *DNA level. This activates the individual to their*
> *full potential. I believe I have become a modern*
> *Shaman, better than one trained in 3D. When my*
> *patients come into the room, I sometimes need to say*
> *to them "Your brain is not going to comprehend this*
> *but you will feel it." They get the vibration and that is*
> *enough . . . My understanding with DNA is that we*
> *have all been shut down. This can be changed with the*
> *frequencies I bring this through with my hands, voice*
> *and mantras as in the "light" language I speak—the*
> *vibrations create an upgrade [in their DNA].*

Dr. Batchelor states her mission is to "awaken" individuals by helping to activate their dormant DNA in the people she works with. She says the new DNA looks golden with codes and symbols that create the transformation. She adds that, "**When someone says to me, 'I hear you have gone spiritual,' I respond, 'Actually this is reality. It is a quantum reality, it's science. I feel intuitively we are changing from carbon based to crystalline. I believe the "new children" [coming onto the planet] are already activated.'**"[15]

Over and over again I have met experiencers who feel that they have been "turned on" or activated by their encounters with NHI. Some liken this to a spiritual expansion, like the bestowing of a multidimensional awareness. They feel as if they have been asleep their whole lives and now they have awakened to a much greater reality. As Dr. Batchelor says, **"I wake people up . . . this is reality."** These experiencers feel that this new consciousness offers access to knowledge about their own non-human genetic origins as well.

More results of the FREE survey show that after someone has had an encounter with an NHI, **85.38 percent of respondents felt that they had awareness of knowledge and information not consciously learned. While 25.58 percent received information about the upgrading of DNA, 24.84 percent were shown how to heal and practice energy work.** And *86.42 percent believe they have a purpose or Earth mission.* It is this last piece that I am very interested in.

It is significant that both Drs. Batchelor and Ohlson state certain vibrational frequencies can activate DNA. I find that experiencers often use frequency as part of healing or energy work that some of them discover after their encounters. Many are inspired to create music and vocalize unusual, apparently nonsensical sounds—which is referred to as "star language" or "light language." It only seems nonsensical because it is not from a language that we know, but the vocalization carries frequency of sounds that perhaps have more meaning and intent than any words we could use. I also find that some experiencers develop complex and detailed artwork, often placing visual "activators" such as written script or symbols in their art. Again, it seems like another form of coded energetic frequencies that can activate other individuals. Furthermore, it appears that such "activated" people often "shift" toward a more holistic perspective, a more balanced lifestyle, and alternate beliefs about the nature of reality. I have documented some of these activating frequencies along with people's profound reactions to the encoded scripts and light languages on the DVDs *Expressions of ET Contact: A Visual Blueprint* and *Expressions of ET Contact: A Communication and Healing Blueprint.*

My research indicates "**awakening**" or "**activation**" can also occur through a sighting of a UFO and/or a close encounter with NHIs. This occurs in the same way as other non-ordinary experiences. As we have seen in people who have had transformations from Near-Death Experience (NDE), Out of Body Experience (OBE), Shamanic experience, Kundalini activations, meditation, and energy work and/or healing, these states of altered consciousness can be catalysts for the awareness of our multidimensional abilities and an understanding of galactic origins.

THE NEW GENERATIONS OF HUMAN

The awareness of the "new children" can override the dominant conditioning and programming which occurs from birth. Superior mental and analytical capabilities link directly to the subconscious, superconscious, with an innate connection to the universe, balanced by spiritual understanding.

—Tracey Taylor

The further research I have done with more than 3,500 families and children has indicated to me that each successive generation follows a pattern of greater shifting that included heightened dimensional attunement as well as expanded physical senses. Children who displayed these abilities have been called in metaphysical terms "**Indigos,**" "**Crystal Children,**" "**Children of Light,**" and so on. However, other less positive labels such as ADHD (attention-deficit hyperactivity disorder) along with forms of autism such as Asperger's syndrome and dyslexia have been placed on these new children. **Could some of these misunderstood symptoms really be the indicators of evolutionary capabilities not yet understood and currently underused?**

Molecular biologist Dr. William Brown certainly believes this is the case. He feels that we are witnessing a program of upgrading, indicating a more multidimensional mind. Brown feels "**genetic modification is occurring right now in utero, and is actually producing a New Human. This is shown by the exponential increase in autism, ADD, and Indigo children. The new genetic architecture allows them to see the world in a multidimensional fashion. Their brains work faster and they have access to more information. In the classroom, their learning is much faster than normal, [because] I believe they already 'KNOW' what is being taught . . . I believe research would show dormant genetic regions are being integrated into the biological systems and occurring in all of us to produce expanded awareness . . . The modification of the DNA is more the remodeling of the genome to make dormant regions accessible again . . . and can be accessed with greater efficiency to produce savant-like characteristics.**"[16]

This hypothesis was backed up by Tracey Taylor, who wrote about her own understanding of genetic modification:

"The DNA of a Star Kid contains tenfold the amount of information as compared to that of an ordinary human body. Things such as telepathy, manipulation of time and space . . . are all very much conscious abilities for these children . . . They are children with a higher percentage of extraterrestrial DNA."[17]

Neil Gould is a contactee, researcher, and author of *Close Encounters of the ADHD Kind.* He shared with me that he didn't know he had ADHD until he was in his middle years. He then realized that the label of ADHD indicated that he had an expanded awareness others didn't have. Neil refers to ADHD as "**Always Dialed into Higher Dimensions.**" In his book he writes that in meeting "**beings of light**" he realized that "**being symptomatic of ADHD I am not limited to the squarer template of the universe; my personal internet browser can browse into chaos be it on Earth or the multiverse. I can perceive hidden layers of order and make sense of it all. Most folk without this supercharged browser cannot do this, they are focused towards conventional reality.**"

In 2013 I was approached by scientist and molecular biologist Dr. Lena Ohlson, who personally experienced a profound NDE (Near-Death Experience) that included encounters with many different forms of "otherworldly" intelligences and an instant healing from green luminescent beings she called "Cone Heads." She describes herself as a "letter person" (ADHD, Asperger's) and acknowledges the intergenerational progressive pattern of these experiences, which was evident to her from her parents and subsequently her children. Dr. Ohlson states, "**Individuals with ADHD, Asperger's, and autism do not have 'faulty' genes, but are**

a human upgrade." She adds that "**it is not so simple as foreign DNA. It's a combination of genetically improved bodies, in combination with souls from different places in our universe, incarnating in these improved bodies. The souls have different frequencies/vibrations, depending on their evolutionary status and that plays a role in activation of the DNA in that particular body. I believe we also have to consider the collective soul of *Homo sapiens*.**"[18]

Dr. Ohlson further claims a similar understanding about the number of non-human species that have been added to the human genome: "**If my information, which was downloaded to me, is correct, there will be twelve different main groups of new DNA people. It corresponds to the twelve different main groups of ET/alien DNA donors; so, nine more to go. Their/our DNA is activated mainly via remote control and frequencies. It is like putting a virus in software (computer program). When they are using their DNA, as long as they are alive, they will give off energy patterns that spread to their surroundings. Almost like the flu or GMO genes, which can contaminate via frequency patterns.**"[19]

This idea about the variety of genetic combinations was likewise affirmed by Robert Dean, who stated: "**We are a combination of at least twelve different species of extraterrestrial mixed with the human genome.**"[20]

HOMO SAPIENS SAPIENS UPGRADES

Zac lives in the United States, and at just sixteen he shared with me that he understood himself to be a hybrid human. He explained to me an overall hybridization of humanity:

I like the term "The New Human." I think that title fits very well because we are going into something that is new for us. Crystal, Indigo, or Rainbow child does not describe the person, only the person's expression of self. The Indigo child has the warrior personality, to break down a system that is wrong and needs to change. The Crystalline child has the aura of love and peace; the healer, the medium bringing in the "sight." The Rainbow child has the energy of the creator, leader, kingship personality. They are all vibrationally different . . . Those who call themselves these labels are just resonating to the frequency of those attributes, and not staying with the status quo. Animals are changing too, personality-wise; animals are evolving as we are.[21]

Hybrids also are part of that New Human archetype we are evolving into . . . there are scalar imprinted memories of all the other beings our DNA has passed through, and because we contain that information, we can express it in the New Human template. We can express it in the hybrid form, or Indigo, etc. . . . They are all interconnected, but you can perceive them as different as you wish to.[22]

When I found Marina, just sixteen, living in Spain, she shared that she woke up to her hybrid nature when she was thirteen years old. She stated that she was aware of different grades of human hybrids she calls "Star Seeds." She explained to me: "**There are two levels to human DNA in the Star Seed, i.e. the DNA from human parents and [the]**

metaphysical (soul genetics) blended together expresses the ET higher frequency . . . A Star Seed is awakened to their multidimensional self or true essence of unconditional love, and reconnects to its star origins. They have extra ET genetics, as when my mother was pregnant, they genetically altered me with their DNA so I connect more to my star origins."[23]

Amanda, a former air hostess from Brazil, also shared her deep connection to a wonderfully supportive non-human feline species. She acknowledged they have been with her and supporting her all through her life. She also encountered her hybrid feline daughters on spacecraft and felt her six-year-old human daughter was also a hybrid: **"Strangely my husband a few days later woke me up one morning and told me he knew our daughter was a hybrid; he saw her in an out of body state as a Mantis being. My husband said he just KNEW it was her. My daughter has six toes on her right foot and seems immune to viruses and disease, she never had colds or fever. [If she] shows symptoms and she recovers quickly. And can do healing, sometimes she places her hands where it hurts and the pain stops."**[24]

Another child, Eli, nine years old, explained to me that his past life origin was on the planet Orion. He worked as a "light physicist" on "time travel technologies." He said, **"I know [a] totally different math. Before I came here, I was doing light physics and I changed light, used light, [and] made things out of light . . . I need to go to a different school, because even in my special group I am more different. I am supposed to be different because I learn more, I learn differently than they do. I know I am from** a different star, a different planet, different Universe. I KNOW I am a Star Child. I know more science and math than we have here. I know how to build a portal. I know how to teleport."[25]

THE NEW HUMAN AND INNATE CONNECTION TO SOURCE OF CONSCIOUSNESS

It has been so compelling to hear how many of the new generations of human children are born with conscious access to past life origins and knowledge, similar to those of Eli. What is also fascinating are the pre-birth recalls. Hayden at seven years old told me about the pivotal moment he incarnated into human form: **"Before I came to Earth, I was just a 'willo-wisp' spirit angel form. I programmed my life on Earth and decided on my star mission. Then I found myself in mummy's tummy. My home/star planet is Elba. I have traveled to the moon in another life. I can go to the ninth dimension."**[26]

These children's connection to the NHIs and their frequent references to their "special friends" assist them with downloads of information and higher frequencies. Like ten-year-old Matthew, who was a musical child. In sharing an experience with a **"non-human being"** who, he told me, assisted him to channel music frequencies, with a specific purpose to alter or activate DNA. He also described an experience onboard a spacecraft where he felt his own DNA shifted: **"They seemed to be good, he (the Being) was short, light grey, a big head, small slit for a mouth and big black eyes. I was lifted up to the ceiling and blacked out. I woke in a dome-shaped ship to see the beings around a control panel type desk where they were communicating in** another language, telepathically, which I could hear. I focused in on the control panel, hearing sounds, which I felt was altering my DNA."

Following this experience Matthew had the urge to play on the piano what he called "songs," one of which he told his mother was to be called "**Decoding the Human DNA**." Four more of these songs were completed within three days. The last song, song six, was named "**Arrival**," and was recorded two weeks prior to his onboard contact experience. Matthew's mother stated at no time did Matthew practice the songs; he just knew what they were and spontaneously produced them. It is remarkable to note that when these songs are heard by others, they can have a profound effect.

Another example that these children are so connected to their "star" lineages comes from hearing some of them speak in their curious "**light**" or "**star languages**." Nine-year-old John from Australia speaks in these non-word frequencies to his mother. What is more amazing is that his mother responds back with the same "light language" that sounds as if it is the same "tongue." She said that she doesn't understand what she is saying to him. However, her son does know what he is conveying to her. John also speaks of his soul origins: "**How do I connect to my REAL home? I use my spiritual mind. Some people in my spiritual home do not exist anymore. But I can still connect through spirit, so I talk to them through spirit. I do not talk through 'human' as I do to another person, like 'Hello, how are you?' I speak through my mind. I speak my spiritual language [light language]. I say it through MY SOUL. It's through my mind and soul mixed together. I can talk to other souls exactly like mine. That is** how I connect to my real home . . . Earth is not my home. I do have a home here but I also have a HOME where I really belong, that's how I connect to my home. I can see with my eyes closed. I can see through other people." [27]

NON-HUMAN INTELLIGENCES ASSIST WITH "SOULS" FROM OTHER DIMENSIONS

All dimensions and souls are linked together.

— Kaza (from Australia)

The Cosmic agenda from multiple species of non-human intelligences appears to be complex and all encompassing. Although some souls have come directly from other planetary origins, some adults along with children recall their "soul" origins may be from other dimensions. Not all of these individuals incarnate at birth. There are what is called "Walk-in Souls," sometimes referred to as a "soul swap." This is a phenomenon where a "Walk-in Soul" has incarnated in a human body previously inhabited by a different soul from birth. They understand the first soul of that human body/container agreed at soul level to vacate at some point in their human life and allow another soul to take over the human biological container. This is usually because they believe it is part of their soul mission to help with the awakening of human consciousness.

This scenario occurred in the case of Kaza, a mother of four. She understands that she is a "Walk-in Soul," which occurred after multiple NDEs (Near-Death Experiences). She feels her soul is from the thirteenth dimension and believes that the previous soul relinquished the body and "allowed her soul" to inhabit it. This occurred to allow her consciousness to assist with the "evolutionary" shift in humanity. Kaza explained to me that as a thirteenth-dimensional intelligence she was just a "light form" without name or physical body. She stated that the place of thirteenth dimension is full of compassion. She has chosen **to come into human form to help teach and heal humanity and coming in as a "Walk-in Soul" she can help more efficiently.** I figured this was because she can skip over all those years of childhood development where we have to learn the rules of society.

HOMO NOVIS: UPGRADES GUIDING HUMANITY

Walk-ins are one of the many ways humanity is being assisted in evolving a greater human potential. Lea Kapiteli describes herself as a **Homo Novis** (a new human). I met Lea when she was just nineteen years old; she told me she had numerous contacts with non-human intelligences. As a talented artist, she draws portraits of many of these beings, as they appear totally real to her. Likewise, Lea wrote about her many past lives on different planets in a book called *A Soul Remembers* (2019). In this incarnation her mission is to help with the awakening of humanity: **"Homo Novis is here so humanity survives, we (as a species) are being upgraded to Homo Noeticus. The Homo Novis is trying to wake humanity up through drawings, music, sacred sites. All [those] born after 2002–2010 are Homo Noeticus; they are literally the next step and will be able to do things that Homo Sapiens never dreamed of."**[28]

AWAKENING TO CONTACT AND COMMUNICATION WITH INTERDIMENSIONAL LIGHT CONSCIOUSNESS

Awakening to who and what we truly are as an evolving conscious species seems to be supported by incarnating souls from many levels of existence. Their mandate is to help with humanity's transition to another level of being. Some souls have chosen to awaken to this prior to their birth. Another ten-year-old boy told me this was his first Earth life and he is a "center seed." He has come to Earth to help clean up the pollution on the planet.

Others choose to "wake up" during this life at a critical point for them, such as Marina at just thirteen and Dr. Batchelor's wake-up activation on her spiritual journey. For others it may come through just sighting a UAP/UFO. However, there are other forms of making contact that are not with physical biological beings, but are with a consciousness in light form, such as an orb of blue light. This is what happened in the case of former military pilot Jimmy Jones. His encounter with a sentient blue orb of light was so profound it changed his perceptions of reality from that moment onward. Jimmy relayed his experience to me:

> When I asked the Blue orb, "Are you all light?"
> The ORB communicated "Yes" . . . [Then] the light
> poured into my mind and I understood we are now
> in the Aquarian age. I understood Hindu cycles of
> time are correct. I understood God is literally light
> and has appeared in all cultures throughout endless
> cycles of time. I understood the world is eternal and
> has always existed. I understood why all ancient
> cultures worshipped the sun and oriented their

*temple complexes with Orion. I understood what
we see on Earth is the remnants of countless cycles.
LIGHT IS CONSCIOUSNESS. The world is a fractal
of light. DNA upgrades are via light. I now know
what Tesla knew. It felt like someone had saturated
every molecule of my being with pure love. As if I
could not hold any more love within my vessel (body
and mind). Absolute ecstasy, nirvana, no words can
do it justice. Even to this day I cry tears of joy when
I think about it. It told me that I go to the highest
heaven. Imagine it left me in a state of residue where
I am always connected; where I see light everywhere,
even when my eyes are closed in a state of a waking
dream. Strange things have continually occurred
since this event such as: lights flickering, bells
ringing, a tornado of physical orbs appearing in our
home.*[29]

Hence, the assistance from our "cosmic cousins" is both physical and interdimensional. A cosmic agenda suggests multidimensional strategies in preparing the human race for a global shift. Each soul contract has decided when they will "wake up" to their greater Earth mission. Every person has their own unique awakening process. Some may involve DNA manipulation, frequencies via art, music, and symbols, star languages, downloads, or direct contact. Whatever is needed to assist in the soul mission and their role as planetary agent can also involve visits to spacecraft and/or out-of-body travel. Sometimes this can bring in levels of multidimensional education onboard craft or even journeys to other planets.

Sixteen-year-old Marina recalls: **"In one experience I was in a spacecraft with other Star Seeds, children and teens all of different ages. It was like a 'classroom' teaching 'consciousness' humanity, evolution, spiritual consciousness, physics, geometry light. I remember being taught how to move objects with my mind. Even if we don't recall it the information remains in our subconscious until we need it and it will come back to us. One time on the craft [they] taught quantum physics but more about geometry and frequency, vibration, mathematics."** [30]

Amanda, a mother of four in Brazil, shared her experiences with "Beings" on another planet: **"In June 2019 the 'beings' took me with other 'beings' to a strange open field, they were guiding us. I knew all of them. I understood we were going to work together, I didn't see human, just different kinds of extraterrestrials. They talked about supporting Earth, I felt I already knew that I was part of them. Our mission was to help the children. I understood something was going to change soon."** Amanda was clear that she didn't feel separate from these "Beings," but one with them. The common goal was/is the Earth mission and its children.

Additional aspects of the FREE survey found that 90 percent of the people with conscious recall of their experiences **believed there was a grand plan; 86.42 percent felt they had a mission here; 85 percent experienced psychospiritual transformation; and 23.29 percent were told about a transition to a new Earth.** However significant this overview is, it does not include the new generations of children and their awareness. In my research speaking to many children under ten years old, they are not only conscious of their cosmic origins, but are fully cognizant of their interactions with many non-human intelligences, that is until they are compromised through education and the reprogramming of beliefs. The profound and stunning statements they can make as a young child are extremely compelling, as indicated by a long-term friend of mine, experiencer Mike Oram in the United Kingdom. In the 1950s, at just four years old, he shocked his mother by saying that she and his father were not his real parents. He said: **"Mum, you are my parents as far as bringing me onto this planet but my real parents are in space.' I pointed to the sky and said to my mother 'I have come from somewhere out there.' I continued by also telling her that: 'Something of great importance is going to happen on this Earth, not in your lifetime but mine. It will affect all units of consciousness whether they are mineral, vegetable, animal, or man. It is to do with global consciousness and that is why I am here at this time, to experience this change. The 'energy' is heading this way and the essence of that energy is light. The energy will repair our DNA, it will make us complete and who we really are.' My mother never forgot that conversation."**[31]

In my book *The New Human*, I particularly focused on the exceptional clarity of information coming from these new generations of children and teenagers. This included their understanding of themselves, soul mandates, their multidimensional abilities, and why they consented to be on Earth at this time. Cathy from Sweden at nine years old shared that she is being taught by her extraterrestrial guides to be a teacher to her family and other adults: **"My ET guides teach me different knowledge so I can teach**

adults! To help humanity to awaken."[32] These children not only have awareness of their role in bringing understanding and knowledge to this planet, they also know who we really are, as one eight-year-old said to her mother: "**Mum, we are the aliens.**"

Mike Oram's statement in the early 1950s was stunningly prophetic. The shift has already begun. We are all awakening to our cosmic ancestry. Once we have embraced our galactic origins and activate our full potential, we not only will we be able to transform this planet, we will return back to where we came from with the understanding and awareness. This will allow us to take our rightful place amongst the stars as cosmic citizens. As the late Sergeant Major Robert Dean stated after his time on the spacecraft: "**On board the spacecraft I was shown our future, we have power we haven't dreamed of. Higher cultures have intervened and are assisting us to be transformed into another species. I have been shown the future and it's glorious . . .**"

The New Human is awake and emphasizing that we are a species waking up to who we really are and the truth of our cosmic heritage. The future has already begun. I conclude with Robert Dean's assertion: "**They are family.**"

11

ET LINEAGES AND HUMAN EVOLUTION

Interview with Caroline Cory

ALAN STEINFELD: I am here with the lovely Caroline Cory, who at a very young age began *"making contact"* with otherworldly beings, when she spontaneously perceived various forms of subtle energy. From that point forward she developed a skill to discern and work with **"a cosmic roadmap for the structure of consciousness, the multidimensional configuration of the human body and mind."** She has used this gift to master, on some level, the constructs of Earthly reality. But one of the things that I feel is particularly special about Caroline is her ability to connect with different extraterrestrial beings. **So I want to start this interview by asking you if can you tell me what was your first memory being connected to the ETs, or maybe even being an ET?**

CAROLINE CORY: Those are two different questions. Being an ET is one thing and being connected to ETs while I'm here on planet Earth is something else entirely.

A: Okay. So the question is: When did you first realize you had an ET connection?

C: My first experience happened when I was five years old. Actually, it was Christmas Eve. I was in my parents' living room, decorating the Christmas tree and doing all that kind of stuff. And I was looking around and thinking: "**What does all this have to do with Jesus? What are all these humans doing?**" As I was having these thoughts, I was also hearing my parents arguing, which led me to ask, "**Isn't Christmas about love and where is Jesus in all of this?**"

As I'm thinking and saying these things to myself, all of a sudden, I see this group of beings. They were white light kinds of forms. I could feel, sense, and hear them. It was then that I found out that I could see what I would now call subtle energy. At the time I realized that I could see beings that nobody else can see. There was telepathic communication that seemed to start organically. They told me, "**We come from the same place. We will be with you for the rest of your life and we will continue to communicate with you. What we are doing now with you is how telepathic communication actually works.**"

They showed me how my brain was patterned in a particular way. It was like a bunch of little codes were being transferred from them to me and me back to them. I understood how they were speaking to my mind in codes and not in a language that I knew.

A: What did the codes look like?

C: It was like little geometric holograms. It's hard to

describe because it's not a human thing. It was more like a pure feeling sensation, as an experience. And I could hear everything they were saying. They showed me that you can have a whole book and condense it into one little code. When that code gets transferred to your brain, it's like a zip drive. The zip drive gets downloaded, and then unzips itself into the human language that you understand.

Even though I'm five years old, I am thinking, *"Oh, that makes sense. That's cool."* Then they said: **"We are here in spirit form, but you have to ask for the connection. It will not just happen. We will not impose ourselves on you."** Then I started to concentrate. I put my little face into this kind of concentrated mode and I said, *"I am asking to remember this. I'm asking to stay connected to them. I'm asking to know how to communicate telepathically."* And before I knew it, they were gone.

Since that time, I started asking the question: **"Where did they go? Where is the other side? How many different types of beings are there? And if I could communicate like this with them, could I do this with other beings?"** As I was asking these questions, I started to gain more and more an understanding of how consciousness works. That experience onward matured into my field of study. I wanted to understand the mechanics of consciousness between beings. That got me started in trying to understand how to utilize your mind to communicate, to perceive subtle energies and to discern the

different types of beings. It has all been about training my awareness. This has been my whole journey
in this life. But one more thing about that first experience: Those beings were not angelic; they felt
more like they were of a divine entity. Since then,
they would come back over and over. And it was only
later that I started to see "extraterrestrials."

A: When did the extraterrestrials start making contact?

C: That happened much later. But those beings stayed
around me, from that time of five years old until I
was in my twenties. At that point I started to sense
different types of beings, but they weren't the same
divine beings as before. They felt more "material,"
but still non-human.

At that time, I started to look around and ask,
"Is anyone else noticing this?" I would hear people
talking about little grey creatures, but I didn't know
what they were talking about. Eventually I started to
see them, but only when I was working with people
in helping them to understand their own consciousness and showing them how to communicate with
many types of beings. So in a way I was introduced
to other beings through the connection with the
people I was assisting. I would see an Arcturian or a
Pleiadian, or sometimes a little grey alien.

A: How would you know who these beings were and
where they were from?

C: Let me back up. There was something I developed
in studying the mechanics of consciousness. I started

to understand how consciousness could tap into different kinds of things, and I found that you can operate beyond the normal functioning of the human brain. I found I could activate what I call "**the full brain**." This is when the total capacity of the brain can merge with anything around you. This way you can gather any sort of information from any type of beings from other star systems. When you merge and become one with the other, there is no separation. I trained myself to do this. I call it "**the merging process**" and I teach people how to do this. When you use this process to consciously merge with another, you know right away who they are, where they come from, and whether they are benevolent or not.

A: Can you tell us how you do the actual process?

C: I teach people this. First you have to raise your vibrational field to a minimum of 734 hertz, between 734 hertz and 1,000 hertz. To do this you have to align your brain in a specific way with a meditation I call "**connecting to source**." This helps expand your energy field's frequency. When you do that you are in the full brain, and everything becomes an experience. There is no longer an intellectual process. You don't have to say, "What is that, who are you?" You feel/sense/understand everything all at once, all the senses come together and you fully experience the other being or person in their totality.

When you are at that frequency range it expands the greater part of you, the higher vibrational aspect. Then you create a tunnel and you wrap your energy field around the other being. You're not projecting any preconceived idea, because this does not come out of your human brain or personality. You are on this higher plane. It is like an objective knowing. This creates that funnel where you're merging with the other's higher consciousness—their pure form. It is like your pure form blends with their pure form— the knowing is instantaneous.

A: But how did you know which ETs were from certain places when they were showing up?

c: Because since I was five, I realized I could see them. I could see basically behind the veil. For instance, I can see right now who's standing behind you.

A: Who is it?

c: He is a very cool, old, tall teacher-like being. I like him. Oh, actually he's not behind; he's kind of merged with you right now. So when I see a person I see the subtle energy around someone; I know what they are going through, what issues they are struggling with, and what is going to happen to them. When those things would happen, I realized: **"Okay, well, what I saw was correct."** I kept getting validation about what I was seeing with the subtle energy, as a reflection of the consciousness of that person. It was a developmental learning process, so now I'm talking after twenty years of observations. If there are beings around, I know I can see them.

A: When was the first time an ET showed up?

c: I don't remember the exact age. Maybe it was about twenty years ago, a couple of beings showed that seemed more galactic. I want to call one of them a galactic light being and the other felt more of the divine order. They were helping me reprogram my brain, recalibrate it to sharpen certain skills so I could know how to receive greater information.

After that period, I was working with someone and I saw a being who I had no frame of reference for. But in the merging process I could tell they were from Arcturus. I had never heard of Arcturians before, and this person I was helping was struggling with a health issue and the being was there as their guide. They were telling me to tell that person that they were on the right path and it would be alright. This Arcturian being looked humanoid in the sense with a head and limbs. There are various races of Arcturians, but the unique feature of the one that I saw was a kind of strange forehead, big and rounded. He wasn't very tall, maybe 5'11", not huge. I've seen other beings who were very, very tall. This particular one had some sort of a suit on or uniform. That was how I could tell that he was a material being versus a purely divine being, who would have more of a light essence.

I started working with many people, and beings would just reveal themselves. And I noticed that each race had their own unique features. But a quality of the Arcturians is their advanced knowledge. They're like a walking library. Their energy is so strong they emanate a wealth of information. I feel like they hold the key to a lot of the wisdom and knowledge about all the races and the histories of planets, and how the material form functions. One of the other things I realized at that time was that different ET races work with particular individuals depending on the person's star lineage.

A: What other beings have made contact with you?

C: I did have a negative experience with some little grey beings, but the next day I saw these tall, gorgeous blue beings. They were almost seven feet tall. Even though they were humanoid-like with bodies of a head and limbs, they were translucent blue. They came from Sirius B. They also emanate knowledge and wisdom, but in a way that had more to do with energetics, whereas the Arcturians' wisdom feels more like data and timekeeping—in this sense, more administrative. But the Sirius B blue beings were more about moving energy, healing, very powerful in a loving way. It almost felt like they were the masters of energy as opposed to other ETs that we feel around us.

A: Are you feeling ETs around us now?

C: Oh, definitely.

A: Are they around everyone all the time?

C: They are there depending on you, depending on if you're open to it, if you're conscious of it, if you summon them. Don't forget my first lesson was, you have to ask. But a lot of them are here and most people are not aware of their presence, because they are not sensitive enough.

A: How do we become sensitive to that kind of contact?

c: It takes a little bit of training. If you do the meditation and connect to source—this begins an alignment
and then the merging. If you do that a few times,
then you are able to discern. In fact, I teach a course
called "**Cosmic Connections.**" I train the class to
come into energetic alignment and merge their consciousness. Then we all go to Saturn. And when we
get there we merge with the consciousness of the
beings on that planet. Then I ask them to feel what
that feels like. Then we would go to Jupiter and do
the same. By doing this you start to sense the subtle
differences. If you train yourself, you can feel the
difference of what it is like to be in the presence of
various life-forms. Are they material and how material are they? Some beings can be half material;
some not at all.

a: Would everyone in the class get the same read-
ings?

c: Yes, exactly. That is what was so fascinating. Let's
say we had fifty people doing this and we all go to
Jupiter. I would ask: "**Are there beings here? Do you
feel something—yes or no?**" If yes, then we merge
them. "**Do they feel humanoid or not? Do they feel
male, female, or neither?**" I would ask, "**What are
their main characteristics?**" I would ask questions
and let people feel the subtle difference of their experience. Then when we were done with the exercise,
we would compare notes. Usually, depending on the
class, between 62 to 98 percent of the students would
have the exact same answer.

A: Are there beings on all the planets?

C: Not all; some planets don't need them. But there are so many planets.

A: But the beings you saw on Saturn and Jupiter were physical beings?

C: Actually, on Jupiter we saw a future human. A very advanced but totally human being. He was just a lot more sophisticated. I'm talking about spiritually sophisticated, meaning wise, intelligent, altruistic.

A: Does Jupiter have a surface that is solid beyond, beyond all its gaseous clouds?

C: The place we tuned into felt like desert with white rocks. But other planets look very different. For example, we went to Venus as well and it felt very red and fiery. There were beings there too.

A: Were they aware of you when you showed up?

C: Yes, which is also fascinating. Because we could communicate with them telepathically. You have to realize that our current scientists tell us that on these planets there are no signs of life. This is because they're looking for a sign of life having to do with water. They think life cannot exist without water. If there's no water, that means no life. They don't realize that different life-forms require different things to survive. This is why they think there is no way we could survive on Venus—it's too hot. Well, the beings we saw didn't have the same breathing requirements that we do. They don't have a digestive system or any other physiological mechanism like humans.

Therefore, they don't function in the same way, but they can totally live on Venus.

A: Do you think now the awareness of scientists about other life-forms is changing? The title of the book is *Making * Contact*, so how are we, as a global population, going to make contact?

C: I think, again, it starts with you as the individual. You have to want it and believe it. Then you have to ask for it in the proper way. Because I sometimes hear people say: "**Hey, I would love for a UFO to show up and I can just hop on it, go for a ride, and meet all the ETs that are on it.**" Well, I would be careful. You have to ask for the right kind of beings that are relevant to you. This means the ones that are here to assist you on your higher journey. But you can only be in the right frequency to connect only after you've done the energetic preparation and protection.

A: Can you tell me about your negative grey ET experience? Because people might think it's like there's only good creatures out there. But I'm curious about the whole scope of beings.

C: I was in Atlanta at the time, and all of a sudden in the middle of the night I woke up. I will never forget it. The feeling was so strong—that there was definitely on my left two or three short beings. I call them Greys, because they were typical of what people have described. When I looked at them, they were emanating a very negative energy toward me, bombarding me with a vibration that really felt awful. I was rejecting, pushing it back, saying, "**No, no, I**

don't want this." At the same time, I was looking at them and I realized that they were not grey; they were blue. Actually, I saw that the color wasn't their skin; it was the tight-fitting bodysuit that covered their whole body. Their eyes were more like coverings on the face in the shape of eyes, maybe to cover or protect their eyes.

When I merged with them to find out what's going on, I felt into their skin that they were not able to breathe very well in our atmosphere. So they were wearing these suits with eye coverings or lens filters for eyes in order to sustain themselves in our atmosphere. I said, "**Oh, this is not their skin and these are not their eyes; it is protective gear.**" But it was the energy they were emanating that felt like they were trying to harm me. I kept rejecting them, saying, "**Go away. I don't want this, go away.**" At the same time, I could sense that there were about like thirty-five reptilian beings there too in another room, not tall, but short and very stocky. I felt like they were connected to the Greys and came together for some reason.

A: What do you think they wanted from you?

C: This was at the time when I was starting my public teaching and healing. I think they were just messing with me, maybe because they did not want this higher information to be out in the public.

A: I would call you an ET ambassador. When did you first realize that you were this go-between, between us and them?

c: My mission is more than ETs. The ET experience is just part of what I came to work on and reveal. I feel my main intent for being here is to have the experience on this place. Because knowledge only comes from experience. You know something, once you lived it. I believe that I had all of these experiences since I was five with different beings, in order to help others understand their roles within the bigger citizenship. I think this is the reason I have the ability to see, sense, and discern. This way I can speak about them from experience.

A: If the fabric of the universe is consciousness, how would you describe the purpose of existence?

c: The purpose of existence is to thrive. We are part of the universe itself. We are an individual consciousness, yet part of a much larger universal consciousness. It is not just that you are a cell in a body, you want to be part of the greater body. You want to sustain the body; you want the body to stay healthy so you can continue to experience. So, the purpose here is to expand yourself so that you can contribute to the expansion of the universe.

A: Why does the universe want to expand, though?

c: We're not talking physical expansion, although there is that. We're talking about expanding conscious awareness, like when a new experience is added to an original experience. The more experience you have, the more you expand and this way the more the mass consciousness expands. In an expanded consciousness, more becomes available for you to achieve. Every time you go through an experience, you gain a greater capacity to create, because you have acquired additional streams of knowledge and information.

A: In a previous interview with you, Caroline, you told me that there was some kind of limitation put upon the expansion of human thought. This came from a distortion in the energy grid around the planet. Can you talk about this crackdown on the expansion of human consciousness and how things are changing now?

C: I have to back up a little bit. When you come here in human form, you exist within parameters of the planet's grid system. This planetary energy is configured within a coherency to the larger solar, galactic, and universal systems. These levels of energy grids help us as a human on Earth to maintain constant communication with the rest of the universe.

In acquiring a human brain, we gain access to the geometric and mathematical coherency within the planetary grid. This can be seen as harmonizing with the energy field of the planet. You can visualize it as a larger patterned field that wraps around the planet from the surface to about 7,000 miles above the surface of the planet. All these grids are in perfect coherent alignment with the human brain. What I mean is that, geometrically, every point within the human brain correlates with a specific point within the greater grid structures. Therefore, when you focus on a specific point within your brain, you are also able to access a corresponding point in space within that grid. When that happens, then the human and

planetary grid are in vibrational resonance. This potential also exists within the galactic and universal
grids. In other words, a focused point in your brain
becomes resonant with all the layers of grids, meaning that our human brain has the power necessary
and the available pathways to connect anywhere in
the universe instantaneously. All you have to do is
tune into the grids on multiple levels.

The trick is to train yourself to maintain the harmony between your human brain, the grid pattern,
and the rest of the universe. In this way, no matter
where you may have incarnated on the planet you
are still in connection with the entire universe at any
point in time; that is how it was originally designed
to be.

When we talk about intelligent design, we're not
just talking about plants and apples and trees. We're
talking about the intelligent design of the consciousness level, which is geometrically based for all levels
of life. This is the way we are supposed to operate.
But if somebody comes along and stops you from
accessing the universal points within the grid, then
those pathways become blocked. Instead of going inside your brain, they just make the highway for the
planetary mind inaccessible.

A: Did somebody do this to us?

C: Yes, about 247,000 years ago. You know, humans
are still a juvenile species. We are like babies compared with the rest of the universe. There are some
beings who understand everything I just explained.

They're much more evolved in some ways; they've been around much longer. Yes, one group of beings said, "**We wonder what would happen if the human brain didn't have their pathways open to the rest of creation anymore? How would they behave?**" So, it started out as an experiment just to see what the little rats would do!

A: Didn't they do this on purpose to shut us down? Because there is that passage in the Bible that said "We don't want them to be us, to be gods."

C: It was an experiment that got out of control. These being saw that "**oh wow, humans will do what we tell them to do. Let's see how far we could go with this.**" So they kept that human brain cut off from the rest of the universe for longer and longer periods of time. Pushing the experiment to a greater and more intense degree, because it was feeding their egos.

A: They liked the feeling of control and manipulation.

C: They started to feed on that energy. Because when you have the feeling of power you want to stay with it. They said: "**Wait, I'm strong and powerful and let me see what else I can do!**"

Before you know it, we had thousands of years of manipulation of the grid, and by extension, the human brain. Because the exit point and the entry point for the human brain's greater connections were tampered with and dismantled. We actually got cut off from the rest of the universe. What happened next was that the experiment gained momentum. Finally,

292 MAKING * CONTACT

there came a point when humans didn't even want or know how to ask about their universal connection.

A: That is where religions came in, as a substitute for our connection.

C: Exactly.

A: But something is changing. What do you think it is?

C: Well, the experiment got out of control . . . But again, we think in terms of hierarchy, but an awareness came from the universe itself. It was not like people judging; it was more like within your body a few bunches of cells started to do something different that was not keeping with the whole body's health. They started to isolate themselves from the rest of the body. When this happens the immune system of the body kicks in and it's like, "**Whoa, wait, what's going on down there?**" In this way the universal order stepped in for a self-correction of the greater body bringing in various levels of correction patterns.

A: Why did they wait so long?

C: It actually was not so long. From a linear point of view, yes, because humans look at time and space from that perspective, it seemed like 230,000 years. But from a universal timeframe, it took only three and a half seconds for the main hub, the main brain of the universe, to kick in and say: "**Something's wrong down there; I am self-correcting now.**" Then the universal immune system sent a signal to planet Earth in order to correct itself and that is what is happening now. The first steps began 2,000 years ago, with the implanting of a new configuration that will bring us back into perfect balance. Now, since the year 2000, there has been an even greater unfolding. This will continue for another 250 years until the reparation of the system is completed.

A: As we gain this greater sense of balance, what do you feel is possible for the human race that was not possible before?

C: Well, first, this is happening on many energetic levels. For example, the planet herself has to reconfigure in terms of chemistry, electromagnetism, and its core cosmic and astronomical realignment. All this is needed for the planet to be whole again. It is the same thing for the human species. Since the brain had been blocked from the cosmic universal connection for thousands and thousands of years, and now suddenly becoming unblocked, there is a gradual retraining to open one system back up at a time to its original configuration. This means that the portals and communication highways that were meant to be open between your brain and the universe are now coming back online again.

A: So what's possible for us now?

C: Since it is a gradual process, you will begin to realize that you are more than your body. This is not just as a concept but as a real experience. You will start to feel, see, sense, and understand certain things beyond the human physical form. You will start to tap into frequencies and see more of the subtle energy as I was describing earlier.

When you begin to perceive subtle energies beyond the normal visible spectrum, you will have a
greater understanding about the truth behind the
physical form. It will be like you're reading a blueprint of what you are observing physically. For example, if you have a physical issue, something wrong
with your body, you will be able to perceive the information behind what you're struggling with. Say
it's your liver, or your stomach, or whatever, you will
see the information and be able to correct it yourself. I'm not talking just about energy healing; a lot of
people do that; that is still being done in an intuitive
way. No, I'm talking you literally see very clear information on what to do to heal yourself on a whole
other level of awareness.

A: Wow, that's fantastic.

C: This will be true with all kinds of knowledge. You
won't just need to read and learn through books or
through people. I mean, there will be that too, but if
you want you can now look at it and perceive it and
allow the information to flow through you from that
object. For example, you can look at the moon and
know exactly how far it is. What's behind it. Who's
on it. It's like you are pulling in all the information
that was not available to human consciousness before.

A: I love that. Can you talk about your connections
with different ET races?

C: My experience at five showed me how I was an
extension of those other beings. It's almost like I

was in physical form, but they were me on the other side of the veil. We are of the same consciousness stream. So, when I work with other people, I noticed that there were particular ET races around them, sometimes Arcturians, or Pleiadians, or Sirians, for example.

A: Why aren't we connected to all of them?

C: It is because we are connected to certain star lineages on the other side of the veil. There is a part of us that continues to exist there even though we're here in human form. We all have this invisible cosmic lineage that continues to stay connected to us. When I became aware of that I realized how purposeful it is to re-awaken the lineage connection in order to bring through information to the human aspects. So part of my purpose here is to awaken people to their individual lineages. When you begin to sense your connection to an Arcturian or Pleiadian lineage, you start to bring that information into your human experience. When that happens, you are then adding that to humanity, which adds to the totality of cosmic expansion. It is like when an American goes to France they are attracting all these French cultural vibrations, intellectually, spiritually, socially, and energetically. When they come back home, they bring back this additional information, which now is shared energetically as well as culturally in America. This adds to what other people can experience as well. Does that make sense?

A: Yes, because of my unique lineage I'm able to

bring something unique here and I contribute to the collective nature of human beings.

c: That's why awakening to a particular lineage is part of your mission. We are supposed to be bringing that through and remember all of that we are.

a: But something also seems different about you, I think.

c: Well, for me, it is that I came into this Earth existence already knowing my connection, and I opened up to my lineage faster than the average person. It's almost like I already knew that this was what I was supposed to do.

a: Can you talk about if have you been off-planet with your body?

c: I kind of go to certain places, not really in a spaceship, more with awareness of the grid boundary that pulls me toward my cosmic alignments and the lineages that I came from.

a: Could you talk more about this idea of lineages?

c: The more you bring through your connection to your star lineages, the more you become it. It starts to become a normal thing. We are not just a body in a human packaging; there is so much downloadable information available to us from what we are now connected to. This is how I am able to talk about the grids and the patterning of space and all kinds of stuff. I'm bringing that in from being it and experienced it. This is not information that somebody gave me. I feel that my lineage comes from a different place than most other people. It seems further away in the universe, because I feel I am related to beings who are more of a multiverse kind of knowledge, as opposed to lineages closer to human orientations.

A: Someone hearing all this might ask, how can you confirm any of it? I mean, it's your personal experience that you're sharing. I don't doubt that it's your experience, but for someone else—how can they know if it's true?

c: When you tell me you fell in love with someone, how do I know if you are lying? One person's experience is their truth. It is up to you to feel and see if their truth resonates with you. It will either feel truthful to you, or not. But it might be beyond your belief system.

A: But if something is beyond my belief system, how can I open up to experience it?

c: This is why my teaching style is experiential. I never just hear something and repeat it to others. I only talk and teach about things that I personally have experienced myself or realized through working with others. Experience is how you train yourself to discern the truth, which is very valuable nowadays.

I explained earlier that when you align your brain channels and raise your vibration above 734 hertz, you're outside your human analytical system. Then you're not projecting your ideas about something, because you have moved to an objective state, beyond the personality. If everyone put themselves in that state first, then they would feel and know what was truthful or not truthful. If you do that a few times, you will learn from your body's own physiological sensing what truth feels like and what doesn't feel quite right. When you align your brain channels and your energy field to this higher vibration you become aligned with those galactic and universal pathways that then can come through your body. This activates or allows you to do remarkable things like move objects with your mind, or you feel expanded sensations in your body.

When I speak, also I'm speaking from experience. It's almost like I am remembering the experience as I'm speaking. I feel like my brain is connected to my larger brain.

For example, a long time ago, I remember people were saying, "**Oh, I have this ecstatic feeling of oneness with the universe.**" I was thinking, how do they know? Maybe they just merged with the planet, but there is so much more expansiveness to them beyond that. It is virtually unlimited.

I understood this when I started to train myself. I would expand to the size of the planet, and I would merge with that and feel it. I felt every cell of my body knew exactly where it was in relation to this bigger field. Then it's kind of like it registered and clicked "**okay.**" Then I would expand to the solar system and then I would know "**oh, okay, it's a little bit different, but it still feels this way.**" I would do the exercise again; I would keep increasing my frame of reference. I expanded to the universe and I knew exactly what that felt like—for me. But everyone can train themselves to discern on all these levels of awareness.

A: What would you say your next level of work is now on planet Earth?

C: I would say my purpose is to continue to awaken more to my original being and bring that through. I want everything I think, say, or do in human form to be a reflection of my universal self. In this way my human aspect in the daily doing and thinking and being is reflecting the larger aspect of myself. When I do that I am bringing those universal vibrations to others and to the human collective—creating a pathway to that larger consciousness for them as well.

A: As we start to wrap up, is there anything you feel now from an ET being that you can bring in or channel through?

C: There is an Arcturian here and he's saying, "**It's safe for you to go out and be who you are. Speak your truth. They're saying don't buy into the collective programming.**" He keeps showing me it's safe to go about your work and your business. He is saying, "**Alan, you're bigger than what you think you are.**" He's saying that "**what Caroline was talking about as lineage—it is your time to explore that.**" He is saying, "**As you open up to your original universal self more, it will pour through into this book and all your work in a new way.**"

A: How do I open up to my universal self more?

C: He's saying, "**Use the tools that I've shared with you. Begin with that and then create your own ways on top of that. You will fine-tune your own style and you will gain access to your own universal aspects more at this time. Begin to ask the**

questions and the downloads will begin. It's time for you to remember more your universal aspects. Tune into your lineage."

A: I'm not sure what my lineage is, but I get downloads all the time. As you were talking and at times in my creative expression, I feel like I merge with these ET beings. I don't know where they are from, but it feels like we are the same being.

c: You don't have to identify a name or a place. It's more about the energy. Just ask the questions from a clear space, and you will know.

A: Thank you. Is there a message for the people reading this book and the world?

c: I feel like the people reading the book don't believe in themselves. I feel like they are still looking for validation outside themselves. I'm hoping this book will empower them to take back control over their own belief systems. I feel that the purpose of this book is to empower people to believe in their divine self. But they can do more than believe; they can try doing some of what I have talked about here. We are all part of this great cosmic intelligence.

A: What about this book, in general? Do you have anything to say about it from that higher place of ET being?

c: They are saying that **"you've approached the subject with wisdom and clarity. This imprint you're leaving behind in a physical paper form is very valuable at this time. Many people like paper form or digital; it doesn't matter, because it is still very relevant right now."** I feel like this is **a galactic, cos-**

mic lineage being imprinted through this effort.
They are saying thank you for making this platform
available to express themselves.

A: Thank you.

EPILOGUE

Alan Steinfeld

*A billion stars go spinning through the night, blazing high
above your head. But in you is the presence that will be,
when all the stars are dead.*
　　　　　　—Rainer Maria Rilke, "Buddha in Glory"

What does it really matter if there are aliens out there? Why have
you read this book, and what have you gained except a lot of
strange ideas? One answer is illustrated in the story Darryl Anka
shared about Benjamin Franklin. When asked about the practical use of a hot air balloon, which he was one of the first to witness, Franklin responded: **"Of what practical use is a newborn
baby?"** The reason for making contact is the same reason people
travel, learn a foreign language, or study the arts. It comes down
to a hardwired mechanism in the human mind to indulge in the
creative fire of *"making known the unknown."*[1] The American
psychologist William James called it *"the impulse toward better
cognition."*

　　For something new to begin, we must forge a path through
the forest of undetermined opportunities. T. S. Eliot wrote that
"each venture is a new beginning, a raid on the inarticulate,"[2]

implying that we must keep pushing the envelope toward the unfamiliar so that an awareness of a larger reality can be brought into view. This reminds me of one of my favorite comments by John Mack: "**The alien encounter experience seems almost like an outreach program from the cosmos to the consciously impaired.**"[3] Consequently, making contact is not just about rising to the occasion to meet something or someone alien, it is about discovering our own fundamental sentience that has long been ignored. This sort of notion is expressed by one of the deepest thinkers on the subject of alien contact, Whitley Strieber. In the book *The Super Natural*, he wrote: "*To make real contact work we must not forget what is actually the central reality of the whole matter: not only that we don't know who and what they are, but that we also don't know who and what we are.*"[4] Barbara Lamb, another longtime UFO investigator, feels from her work with contactees that "**we must believe we are so much more than just these human beings living in this human body for one lifetime.**"[5] Essentially, it seems that the whole investigation of the phenomena is to show us that the mysteries are not out there in the universe, but in us. In this way the effort of this book is to instigate a voyage on the sea of self-discovery.

In the final analysis, we must shift our notions about being an incidental aberration of a lifeless universe. A new generation of scientists are trying to solve the hard question of science about how life began. They are devising theories that state that "*life might just be an emerging property of existence.*" If this is true, then "*we ourselves are part of the mystery that we are trying to solve.*"[6] Such ideas align with the enlightened perspective of Eckhart Tolle in referring to our ultimate relationship with the universe: "*You don't have a life; you are life that is taking time to experience this now as a human or star or a blade of grass . . . You are the consciousness of the universe. How can*

you not be?[7] If we fail to get that message, we will miss that point of contact.

HUMAN EVOLUTION

Our destiny, our nature, and our home, is with infinitude—
and only there.

—William Wordsworth, *The Prelude*, Book 6 (1805)

By now, I am optimistic that the reader will realize that the writings collected here are more than a treatise about individual experiences and alien agendas. It is about the next stage of our evolution. In reimagining the human race, John Lash wrote: **"The perception of our kinship with all species allows us to become human in a total co-evolutional perspective . . . We cannot know our place in the cosmos through anthropocentric fixation, but disregarding the unique status of the human species is not valid either."**[8] Somehow embracing the non-human makes us more human. Like the floating fetus in space at the end of Stanley Kubrick's **2001: A Space Odyssey**, we are being born anew. The present moment is an embryonic gestation for the birthing of a cosmic consciousness.

Even though contact has already been made, according to the testimonies of people throughout this book, "Contact" on a larger scale is about a synergy of awareness that must come for the collective mind of humanity. This is key to our evolution as a species. The transformation was summed up by the evolutionary biologist Bruce Lipton. In my 1999 interview with him, he outlined the teleology of human destiny:

The next level of evolution for us is to recognize that we
are all cells in a larger community coming together to
share awareness in order to create one living organism

that would be called humanity. We are not humans
until we create humanity. This is when we all recognize
that we're all cells in the same living organism and work
in a coherent fashion—then humanity is complete.
When humanity is complete, the Earth as an organism
completes its evolution. It becomes a living, breathing,
pulsing Gaia . . . When we come together in a unity, with
a voice that will allow us to speak as one, this will allow
us to speak with other Ones.[9]

So, in the long run, this book is not about "them," whoever "they" are. It is about us, and how at this crossroad in history, we have an opportunity to become something more than
mind-controlled automatons unaware of our own sense of self
and *"the synergy of awareness"* that Bruce Lipton speaks about.
The coming of contact is not a preparation to go to the stars,
rather it is breaking the chains of enslavement to conditioned
thought. True freedom allows the imagination to wonder. And
since wonder always takes us onto an uncharted course, I feel
that *Making * Contact* has the ability to conjure up the most
exciting considerations to date concerning the future of the
planet.

As you come to the end of this opus, the hope is that you have
secured in the machinations of your reading mind the fact that
making contact is an inside job. From those least concerned with
the topic to those waiting in anxious anticipation for the next
chapter of humanity to unfold, KNOW we are part of the grand
intelligence about to meet more of itself.

Some evening when you have a chance to look at forever in a
starry night sky. Contemplate the potential civilizations throughout the Milky Way, and FEEL that you are part of all that.

Albert Einstein said: **"Still there are moments when one feels**
free from one's own identification with human limitations and

inadequacies. At such moments, one imagines that one stands on some spot of a small planet, gazing in amazement at the cold yet profoundly moving beauty of the eternal, the unfathomable: Life and death flow into one, and there is neither evolution nor destiny; only being."[10]

CONTRIBUTOR BIOS

DARRYL ANKA is best known for his trance channeling of Bashar, a multidimensional being and a friend from the future who has spoken through Darryl for the past thirty-five years. He has brought through a wave of new information that clearly explains in detail how the universe works, and how each person creates the reality they experience. Over the years, thousands of individuals have had the opportunity to apply these principles and see that they really work to change their lives and create the reality that they desire. Along with Edgar Cayce and Seth and Abraham Hicks, the Bashar material has been heralded as some of the most relevant, compelling, and dynamic channeled material delivered to the planet to date. Currently there are millions of people who have heard Bashar's messages on YouTube, Facebook groups, special videos produced by Bashar Communications, and in live appearances.

In addition to channeling Bashar, Darryl expresses his creative talents in the form of writing, directing, and producing films through his own production company, **Zia Films**. His first film, *Dearly Departed* (2012), was a fictionalized documentary based on near-death experience reports and shot as though the crew took the camera into the afterlife and interviewed spirits of people who've passed on to get their take on life after death. It was nominated for Best Faith-Based Feature and Best Visual Effects in the Action on Film International Film Festival in Monrovia, California. His second film was a documentary called *First Contact* (2016) that explores his life as a channel and the messages Bashar shares through him. It relays the true story of a UFO encounter that led to the channeling. Darryl's third film, *Alienated*, a sci-fi film that he co-wrote and co-produced with his wife, Erica Jordan, is soon to be released.

On the whole, his desire is that the information presented here and in his other work will expand the spirit, heighten the awareness of the limitless potential that life offers each and every day, and inspire us to follow our highest joy. As Bashar often suggests, *"Live your dreams, instead of merely dreaming about being alive."* His website is www.bashar.org.

GRANT CAMERON became involved in UFOlogy in May 1975 with personal sightings of a UFO that became known as *Charlie Red Star.* These sightings led to almost three decades of research into each US president's experience with UFOs. After experiencing a mental download event on February 26, 2012, he turned away from "nuts and bolts" research toward the role of consciousness in the phenomenon. This new research has expanded to the possible involvement of extraterrestrials in modern music, and in the aspects of inspiration in science, music, art, near-death experiences, meditation, and with individuals known as savants and prodigies. He lectures widely in Canada, the United States, and Europe and was one of the forty witnesses who testified before six former senators and congressmen in Washington, DC, at the **Citizen Hearing on Disclosure**. He has appeared in numerous UFO documentaries and has been a frequent guest on *Coast to Coast AM*. He is the author of *Inspired: The Paranormal World of Creativity, Tuned-In: The Paranormal World of Music*, and *Managing Magic: The Government's UFO Disclosure Plan*, among others. His website is beyondpresidentialufo.com and his YouTube channel is www.youtube.com/whitehouseufo.

CAROLINE CORY is a futurist, a visionary author, and the founder of an unprecedented approach to learning and teaching called the

OMnium Method,™ which includes the New Paradigm Education System. In 2012, she created OMnium Media and "Experiential Cinema," an entertainment and media platform that tackles thought-provoking topics on the human condition and the nature of reality, which supports her personal mission to uplift the human spirit through highly creative and artistic means. She is the producer, writer, and director of such cutting-edge films as *ET Contact*, exploring how ET encounters may be evidence of a greater phenomenon, which includes the hybridization of a new species. *Among Us* explores the phenomenon of non-human presence on Earth, from angels to extraterrestrials, and how they may be transferring subliminal information into our DNA. Her most recent film is *Superhuman: The Invisible Made Visible*, based on the jaw-dropping experiences of individuals with extrasensory powers that seem to defy the laws of physics known to man today. The film provides tangible evidence for the powers of the human mind over matter. See www.superhumanfilm.com.

Caroline continues to lecture and coach internationally on various mind-over-matter subjects and appears regularly as a guest expert on supernatural phenomena at major conferences and television shows including A&E's popular series *The UnXplained* with William Shatner and History Channel's *Ancient Aliens*. Her website is www.omniummedia.com.

LINDA MOULTON HOWE is an investigative journalist who has devoted her documentary film, television, radio, web, writing, and reporting career to productions concerning science, medicine, the environment, and Earth mysteries. Her TV broadcasts about environmental issues in Colorado were also recognized and honored by the Environmental Protection Agency with a Citizen Participation Award from actor and environmentalist Robert Redford at the EPA's regional office in Denver. She has received three regional Emmys, a national Emmy nomination, and was an honored producer for medical and science programming at WCVB-TV (ABC) Boston, winning a Peabody. Her award-winning documentaries have included *A Strange Harvest*, which explored the cattle mutilation mystery around the country. It was broadcast on KMGH-TV as a ninety-minute evening special on May 25, 1980, to the largest audience in the station's history for a locally produced documentary.

Linda's book *An Alien Harvest: Further Evidence Linking Animal Mutilations and Human Abductions to Alien Life Forms* was awarded best nonfiction by the Arizona and New Mexico Southwest Book Association in December 2015. Her other books are *Glimpses of Other Realities, Volume I and Volume II*, which concern U.S. military, civilian, and intelligence testimonies about an alien intelligence interacting with Earth life. Her fourth book, *Mysterious Lights and Crop Circles*, detailed her investigations of the complex crop formation phenomenon in England, the United States, and Canada from 1992 to 2002.

She has been interviewed during all fifteen seasons of *Ancient Aliens*, which has become the History Channel's second-largest-grossing and most popular show. Currently she is the chief reporter and editor for her award-winning website www.earthfiles.com, with an archive of nearly three thousand reports and thousands of images covering science, the environment, and the high strangeness of unexplained mysteries. Her YouTube channel, www.youtube.com/earthfiles, has more than 160,000 subscribers, and she continues to produce new programs weekly. Linda also speaks at many conferences each year and is currently writing a memoir about her extraordinary path at the edge of exploring this planet's relationship to the cosmos.

J. J. HURTAK, PH.D., and **DESIREE HURTAK, PH.D.,** are social scientists, futurists, and founders of the international organization **The Academy for Future Science**. They were science consultants for Sidney Sheldon's bestseller of an alien encounter titled *The Doomsday Conspiracy*. Upon the recommendation of the Hurtaks, Sheldon included astronaut Gordon Cooper's testimony of his own UFO sighting while in the military. Their public presentations on UFO phenomena go back to 1977, when J. J. Hurtak was a presenter at the First World Congress on UFOs in Acapulco, Mexico, along with J. Allen Hynek. In 1979, he was one of the first to give a briefing to the world press

(*El Universal*) on EBEs (extraterrestrial biological entities) in Mexico City. He was also a presenter at the first government-related UFO disclosure conference, When Cosmic Cultures Meet, in Washington, DC (1995), along with Dr. John Mack and Dr. C. B. "Scott" Jones.

Together, the Hurtaks were speakers at the Barcelona UFO Congress (2019), where they shared a panel with the physicist Michio Kaku. Their scientific papers include studies on *The Ontological Basis of Quantum Theory, Nonlocality, and Local Realism* (2019), *What Is Time? Time Is It?* (2018), and *Reexamining Quantum Gravity* (2017). *Examining the Existence of the Multiverse* (2015) was coauthored by nuclear and theoretical physicist Elizabeth Rauscher, Ph.D., formerly of Lawrence Livermore National Laboratory and the University of California, Berkeley. Rauscher also co-authored *Mind Dynamics in Space and Time*.

Dr. J. J. Hurtak is the author of *The Keys of Enoch*® (1973), with more than 100,000 copies sold in twenty-five languages, and numerous other writings. Together the Hurtaks have written ten books, including *The Overself Awakening*. They are also respected archeologists, having worked in Mexico and Egypt, where they were sharers in the discovery of the legendary tomb of Osiris on the Giza Plateau (1997). They are members of the board of FIONS (New York), which is associated with astronaut Edgar Mitchell's IONS (Institute of Noetic Sciences). They are also well known for their award-winning films on consciousness development, including *Merkabah*, *The Light Body*, *Extraterrestrial Realities*, *Gates of Light*, and *Voice of Africa: The Zulu Shaman Credo Mutwa*. Worldwide they are recognized for their provocative work affirming the science of consciousness within a multidimensional cosmology and humanity's destiny in space. Their websites are www.futurescience.org and www.keysofenoch.org.

DR. JOHN EDWARD MACK was an American psychiatrist, writer, university professor, and head of the department of psychiatry at Harvard Medical School. His clinical expertise was in child and adolescent psychology and the psychology of religion. He was also known as a leading researcher on the psychology of teenage suicide and drug addiction. In 1977, Mack won a Pulitzer Prize for his book *A Prince of Our Disorder*, on T. E. Lawrence.

In 1989 a colleague asked if he wanted to meet the UFO researcher and abduction specialist Budd Hopkins. Mack recalled: "I assumed that either there must be something the matter with Budd Hopkins or that Hopkins was encountering a new form of mental illness . . . I wasn't prepared for what I found." What Mack heard from Hopkins was so compelling that he spent over three years with nearly 100 self-proclaimed abductees contacting him at his office at Harvard University's Cambridge Hospital. In 1994, he published *Abduction: Human Encounters with Aliens*, a book containing cases from thirteen experiencer patients. A sequel, *Passport to the Cosmos: Human Transformation and Alien Encounters*, followed in 1999; it was as much about spirituality and the modern worldviews as it was about "experiencers" of alien encounters.

His accidental death in 2004 is still mourned as a great loss in the UFO field. Nevertheless, John remains probably the most esteemed academic to have studied the subject of "making contact." The Mack family still maintains the John E. Mack Institute website johnemackinstitute.org, which holds some of his most important work including the original audio of the 1995 talk that was transcribed and edited for this volume. A new book about John's life, *The Believer: Alien Encounters, Hard Science, and the Passion of John Mack* by Ralph Blumenthal, was released in March 2021.

NICK POPE is a freelance British journalist and media commentator. He was an employee at the British government's Ministry of Defence (MoD) from 1991 to 1994. While there, one of his responsibilities was to investigate UFO phenomena to determine if they had any defense significance. He's recognized as one of the world's leading experts on the unexplained and conspiracy theories. He is known as the go-to media person for UFOs, called by some the "real Fox Mulder." He's made appearances on numerous TV news shows and documentaries, including *Good Morning America*, *Nightline*, *Tucker Carlson Tonight*, and *Ancient Aliens*. Nick has also written for *The New York Times*, for the BBC News website, and for NBC's technology and science website, and has acted as a consultant/spokesperson on numerous alien-themed movies, TV shows, and video games. He gives talks at academic conferences, fan conventions, and debates all around the world. He's spoken at the National Press Club in Washington, D.C., the Royal Albert Hall, and the Global Competitiveness Report. He has debated at the Oxford Union and the Cambridge Union Society and currently lives in the United States. His website is nickpope.net.

MARY RODWELL is Australia's leading researcher and writer on the UFOs/contact phenomenon. She is the author of the highly acclaimed book *Awakening: How Extraterrestrial Contact Can Transform Your Life* (2002), republished by New Mind Publishers in 2010. Dr. Roger Leir said, **"In my opinion this book will become the Bible of the Alien Abduction Phenomenon."** She also produced the award-winning documentaries *Expressions of ET Contact: A Visual Blueprint?* (2000) and *Expressions of ET Contact: A Communication and Healing Blueprint?* (2004).

Her latest book, *The New Human* (2016), documents the next level of human development she calls "**star children.**" As a skilled regression therapist Mary brings contactees back to their time of encounters or before, helping them bring through ET messages. In this regard she founded the Australian Close Encounter Resource Network (ACERN) in 1997 to provide professional counseling, support, hypnotherapy, and information to individuals and their families with "anomalous" paranormal experiences and abduction—contact experiences. She has lectured in Hong Kong, the United States (including Hawaii), Canada, the United Kingdom, Ireland, France, Malta, and New Zealand. She has appeared regularly on national and international media news programs and in documentaries, including *The Oz Files*, *My Mum Talks to Aliens* (featured on SBS Australia in 2010, and now shown globally), *Paranormal Files* in the United Kingdom on BBC TV, and *Animal X* on the Discovery Channel. Mary also has participated in university debate forums on this phenomenon, including at Oxford University in 2006 and at Australian National University, Canberra, in 2010. Her website is www.alienlady.com.

ALAN STEINFELD is a contributor and the curator of this collection of essays on "making contact." This book is a product of his investigations and contact with the leading researchers and investigators into the UFO phenomenon and its connection to what has been called **the ET presence**. Ever since his own alien contact in 1987, he has been obsessed with the topic, gathering hundreds of books and attending conferences worldwide, from which he came to understand some of what making contact is about. He has since lectured on the subject from New York to California, as well as in England, France, Spain, Israel, and Australia. In a related field he is also an expert on the crop circles of England, which he feels are higher consciousness communications that have been laid out to shift our perceptions of reality. In addition, he has taught remote viewing to thousands online and in person, as it was shown to him by one of its founders, Russell Targ from the Stanford Research Institute. Over the past several years he has been one of the main emcees at the largest UFO gathering in the world, **Contact in the Desert**, near Palm Springs, California. He has produced two feature-length documentaries on UFOs: *The Hidden Hand*, directed by James Carman, and *Calling All Earthlings* by Jonathan Berman.

He has produced and hosted New York City cable program *New Realities* for more than twenty-five years, interviewing leaders in the fields of health, spirituality, and consciousness. Such guests have included **Deepak Chopra, Marianne Williamson, Ram Dass, Bruce Lipton, Joe Dispenza,** and hundreds of others. He makes these programs, as well as his panel discussions on UFOs, available on the *New Realities* YouTube channel, which has close to 25 million views and 70,000 subscribers. He is a board member of **FIONS** (Friends of the Institute of Noetic Sciences), which is associated with IONS (Institute of Noetic Sciences), an organization founded for research on consciousness by the astronaut Edgar Mitchell. Alan is also a member of the **Evolutionary Leaders**, a network of paradigm-shifting leaders around the planet. His next book promises to bring to the world the first documented case of ET contact that has never been revealed. Overall, he feels that "only when the inner explorations of the soul are combined with outer adventures of mind can we achieve, as planetary beings, a harmonious understanding of ourselves in relation to the greater cosmos." His websites are www.newrealities.com and www.youtube.com/newrealities.

WHITLEY STRIEBER is the author of more than twenty books of both fiction and nonfiction. He started his career with the novels *The Wolfen* (1978) and *The Hunger* (1981), both of which were made into feature Holllywood films. He also co-wrote *The Coming Global Superstorm* with Art Bell, inspiring the film *The Day After Tomorrow*. However, he is best known for his first nonfiction book, *Communion: A True Story* (1987), an autobiographical account of his contact experience of December 1985 at his cabin in upstate New York. It became a number one *New York Times* nonfiction bestseller (on the list for fifteen weeks) in both the hardcover and paperback editions, with combined sales of more than two million copies. It was turned into a feature film starring Christopher Walken. The painting on the cover of *Communion*, rendered by Ted Seth Jacobs, is considered one of the most widely recognized images of a "grey" alien. After the publication, Whitley and his wife, Anne, received more than 200,000 letters from people around the world describing similar close-encounter experiences. The highlights from these correspondences were compiled by Whitley and Anne into a book called *The Communion Letters* (1997). Other books in the Communion series are: *Transformation: The Breakthrough, Breakthrough: The Next Step, Confirmation: The Hard Evidence of Aliens Among Us, The Secret School: Preparation for Contact*, and *Solving the Communion Enigma: What Is to Come*. His more recent books, *Super Natural: A New Vision of the Unexplained* (2016) with Jeffrey J. Kripal, and *A New World* (2019), from which the essay in this book is derived, go further into exploring the personal and collective relationship between humans and "the visitors."

Since the Communion experience, Whitley has developed a unique relationship with whatever it is that is causing this outpouring of abduction and close encounter testimony. He says, "'They' **are in my life right now, thirty years later, as an intimate and deeply engaged presence. They have gone from being a terrifying presence in my life to one for which I am deeply grateful and which enriches me every single day of my life.**" He currently hosts the spiritual and science-themed internet podcast *Dreamland*, available on a weekly basis from his website www.unknowncountry.com.

HENRIETTA WEEKES is an actor, writer, and performer with a BA in art history from Manchester University, England, and acting training from Manchester Royal Exchange and Kimball Studio, New York. Having moved from London to New York City twenty-four years ago, she has produced numerous shows, events, and talks at prestigious venues such as Webster Hall, Ars Nova, Gotham Comedy Club, and the Highline Ballroom, and she was director of Harry's Loft, East 19th Street. Since 2006, she has worked for Evolver, a consciousness studies media platform founded by Daniel Pinchbeck, presenting their web series with thought leaders at the Learning Lab, as well as directing community relations. Her coming into ET awareness happened suddenly in 2019 at an Open Center New York presentation about the coming times. When she considered that "making contact" was a real possibility, a flood of memories came to her from her childhood that started to fit into patterns of abduction that have evolved her life to another level of awareness. Her piece in this collection is a montage of impressions, senses, and dreams dealing with the phenomenon.

Henrietta currently works with individuals, organizations, and production companies on special projects, which encompass theater, film, web series, and events. She offers to creatively connect people, advises on productions, and produces intimate in-depth retreats in San Miguel de Allende, Mexico, with Mexican partners. Henrietta founded The Vyne with a small team of women colleagues to foster her own art and the creativity and vision of others. Her website is www.vyneproductions.com.

ACKNOWLEDGMENTS

Kimberly Meredith for introducing me to St. Martin's.

Joel Fotinos for believing in me and for his vision and direction.

Beth Grossman for her support and friendship.

Gina Salvati for her connections and assistance.

Will Bueche for assisting with the John Mack essay.

Jean Marie Bauer for all her help throughout the years.

Henrietta Weekes for her poetry of being.

Paul Lowe for his years of encouragement.

Dr. George Steinfeld, my coach in cognizing new realities.

Paula Gloria Tsconas Barton, my muse in spiritual knowledge.

Irene and Cozy McFee for giving the space and freedom to create.

Victoria Jennings and Paul Andrews for bringing together a worldwide community of making contact at Contact in the Desert.

And **Evelyn Steinfeld**, my mother, whose questioning, "*If you really believe this ET sort of thing,*" not only helped me, but led me to find overwhelming proof that we are part of a greater reality.

NOTES

INTRODUCTION

1. From *The People's Edition of The Entire Works of W. E. Channing*, D.D., "The Union," 190, Belfast: Simms and M'Inty, 1843.

2. "Deepak Chopra Interview with Ben Bowler for World UNITY Week," June 22, 2020. www.facebook.com/watch/?v=2933883910072553.

3. John Dewey, "The Quest for Certainty: A Study of the Relation of Knowledge and Action," Gifford lectures, 1929 London, 294, https://archive.org/stream /questforcertaint029410mbp/questforcertaint029410mbp_djvu.txt.

4. Goodreads.com. www.goodreads.com/quotes/8868221-to-consider-the -earth-as-the-only-populated-world-in (accessed December 10, 2020). The original translation: "To consider the Earth as the only populated world in infinite space is as absurd as to assert that in an entire field of millet, only one grain will grow."

5. Edgar Allan Poe, "The Last Conversation of a Somnambular," *London Popular Record of Modern Science*, November 29, 1845.

6. Meredith Somers, "Existence of Aliens Unlikely to Shake Humans' Faith, Experts Say," *Washington Times*, June 19, 2014. www.washingtontimes.com /news/2014/jun/19/existence-of-aliens-unlikely-to-shake-humans-faith /#ixzz35CDfkvxh.

7. "Michio Kaku Foretells Humanity's Extraordinary Future" NBC News interview by David Freeman, March 2, 2018, www.nbcnews.com/mach/science /michio-kaku-sees-amazing-things-our-future-except-those-scary-ncna851226.

8. Somers.

9. Cheryl Costa and Linda Miller Costa, *UFO Sightings Desk Reference: United States of America 2001–2015*, synopsis at www.amazon.com/UFO-Sightings -Desk-Reference-2001-2015/dp/1544219237 (accessed December 10, 2020).

10. Max Planck, *Scientific Autobiography and Other Papers* (New York: Philosophical Library, 1949), 9, 33.

11. John Locke: "Of Wrong Assent, or Error," Book 4, Chapter 20 in "Concerning Human Understanding," https://www3.nd.edu/~afreddos/courses/439/locke0420.htm.

12. Elizabeth Howell, "Fermi Paradox: Where Are the Aliens?" Space.com, April 27, 2018. www.space.com/25325-fermi-paradox.html.

13. Ibid.

14. Memo from H. Marshall Chadwell, CIA Assistant Director, Scientific Intelligence Briefing the Fourth DCI (Director of Central Intelligence, 1950–53) General Walter Bedell Smith about UFOs, December 1952. From the CIA article by Gerald K. Haines, on the CIA's Role in the Study of UFOs, 1947–90. https://www.cia.gov/library/center-for-the-study-of-intelligence/csi-publications/csi-studies/studies/97unclass/ufo.html.

15. Ross Pomeroy, "12 Possible Reasons We Haven't Found Aliens," June 13, 2017, for Space.com: https://www.space.com/37157-possible-reasons-we-havent-found-aliens.html.

16. Ken Wilber, A Brief History of Everything (Boulder, Colorado: Shambhala Publications, 1996), 52.

17. Reed Tucker, "A Harvard Professor Says an Alien Visited in 2017—and More Are Coming," New York Post, January 2, 2021, https://nypost.com/2021/01/02/a-harvard-professor-says-an-alien-visited-in-2017/.

18. Ibid.

19. D. N. Perkins, The Mind's Best Work (Boston: Harvard University Press, 1981), 178.

20. Trigant Burrow, Preconscious Foundation of Human Experience (New York: Basic Books, 1964), 57.

21. Helene Cooper, Ralph Blumenthal, and Leslie Kean, "Glowing Auras and 'Black Money': The Pentagon's Mysterious U.F.O. Program," New York Times, December 16, 2017. www.nytimes.com/2017/12/16/us/politics/pentagon-program-ufo-harry-reid.html.

22. Mindy Weisberger, "Are UFOs a Threat? We Need to Investigate, Says Former Head of Secret US Program," Live Science, July 11, 2020. www.livescience.com/unidentified-ufos-history-channel.html?utm_source=notification.

23. Ralph Blumenthal and Leslie Kean, "No Longer in Shadows, Pentagon's U.F.O. Unit Will Make Some Findings Public," New York Times, July 23, 2020. www.nytimes.com/2020/07/23/us/politics/pentagon-ufo-harry-reid-navy.html.

24. Amanda Macias, "Pentagon Forms New Task Force to Investigate UFOs," CNBC, August 15, 2020. www.cnbc.com/2020/08/15/pentagon-forms-new-task-force-to-investigate-ufos.html.

25. Robert Hastings's testimony at "Military Witnesses of UFOs at Nuclear Sites" press conference, National Press Club, Washington, DC, September 27, 2010.

26. Jeffrey Kripal and Whitley Strieber, The Super Natural: Why the Unexplained Is Real (New York City: TarcherPerigee, 2017), 297.

27. Niall Boyce, "The Psychiatrist Who Wanted to Believe," *The Lancet* 380 (9848)(2012): 1140–1141. www.thelancet.com/journals/lancet/article/PIIS0140 -6736(12)61655-9/fulltext.

28. President John Kennedy, "We Go to the Moon" speech, Rice University, Houston, Texas, September 12, 1962.

29. Kripal and Strieber, 305.

30. William Bramley, "Can the UFO Extraterrestrial Hypothesis and Vallee Hypotheses Be Reconciled?" *Journal of Scientific Exploration* 6 (1): 3. http:// citeseerx.ist.psu.edu/viewdoc/download?doi=10.1.1.684.3518&rep=rep1&type =pdf.

31. Linda Moulton Howe has used this phrase many times in her nearly four decades of research to describe the sometimes confusing and contradictory nature of the phenomena.

32. Raymond Williams, *The Long Revolution* (London: Chatto & Windus, 1961), 35.

33. "John O. Brennan on Life in the CIA," *Conversations with Tyler*, podcast, December 16, 2020, https://conversationswithtyler.com/episodes/john-o -brennan/.

34. John Mack, *Abduction: Human Encounters with Aliens* (New York: Scribner, 1994), 20.

35. Rainer Maria Rilke, *Letters to a Young Poet*, #8, written in Borgebygard, Fladie, Sweden, August 12, 1904. www.carrothers.com/rilke8.htm.

36. Ralph Waldo Emerson, *Essays: Second Series, 1844*, https://archive.vcu. edu/english/engweb/transcendentalism/authors/emerson/essays/poettext. html.

37. Owen Barfield, *Poetic Diction: A Study in Meaning*, 2nd revised edition (Middleton, Connecticut: Wesleyan University Press, 1984), 28. First published in 1928.

38. Martin Heidegger, *The Question Concerning Technology and Other Essays*, translated by William Lovitt (New York and London: Garland Publishing, 1977), 11–12. www.rhondaholberton.com/research/wp-content/uploads/2016 /09/The_Question_Concerning_Technology_and_Other_Essays.pdf.

39. John Z. Young, quoted in Williams, *The Long Revolution*, 22.

40. Whitley Strieber, *Breakthrough* (New York: HarperCollins, 1995), 6.

41. Henri Bergson, *Creative Evolution*, translated by Arthur Mitchell (New York: Macmillan, 1964), 255.

42. "Kidnapped by UFOs? The True Story of Alien Abductions," *NOVA*, April 1, 1997. Mack quote in transcript. www.pbs.org/wgbh/nova/transcripts /2306tufos.html.

43. Johann Wolfgang von Goethe, *Maxims and Reflections*, translated by Bailey Saunders (1892). http://monadnock.net/goethe/maxims.html.

44. "Dr. Joe Dispenza 'Ask for a SIGN.'" Uploaded to YouTube by Manifest Yourself on July 22, 2020. https://youtu.be/E0mgL0jtMaU.

2: UFO Disclosure and the Theory of Wow

1. Transcribed and edited from a talk by Grant Cameron at the Los Angeles Conscious Life Expo, February 2019. Uploaded to YouTube by Grant Cameron Whitehouse UFO, December 23, 2019. https://youtu.be/aeVbtmOGcMk.

2. Sarah Scoles, "What Is Up with Those Pentagon UFO Videos? The Department of Defense Released Two Videos of So-Called UFOs. Or Did It?" *Wired*, February 17, 2018. www.wired.com/story/what-is-up-with-those-pentagon-ufo-videos/.

3: Extraterrestrials and Multidimensional Nonlocal Reality

1. The British Earth Aerial Mysteries Society, "August 17, 1992: The A70 UFO/Abduction Case of Garry Wood and Colin Wright," http://www.beamsinvestigations.org/A70%20abduction%20with%20Colin%20Wright%20near%20Tarbrax,%20Scotland,%20southwest%20of%20Edinburgh%20that%20occurred%20August%2017,%201992.htm (accessed November 4, 2020).

2. Ji-Gang Ren et al. "Ground-to-Satellite Quantum Teleportation," *Nature*, August 9, 2017.

3. University of Bristol, December 2019.

4. D. Llewellyn, Y. Ding, I. I. Faruque et al., "Chip-to-Chip Quantum Teleportation and Multi-Photon Entanglement in Silicon," *Nature Physics* 16 (2020): 148–153. https://doi.org/10.1038/s41567-019-0727-x.

5. Bill Chalker, *Hair of the Alien: DNA and Other Forensic Evidence of Alien Abductions* (New York: Simon & Schuster, 2005), 212–213.

6. "Kidnapped by UFOs? The True Story of Alien Abductions," *NOVA*, February 27, 1996. www.imdb.com/title/tt0976073/.

7. Svar Nanan-Sen, "UFO Sighting: Ex-US Navy Chief Reveals Moment Mystery Craft Vanished Before His Eyes," *Express*, April 28, 2020. www.express.co.uk/news/weird/1274902/UFO-sighting-video-US-Navy-aircraft-vanished-pentagon-latest-news.

8. Ibid.

9. Albert Einstein and Nathan Rosen, "The Particle Problem in the General Theory of Relativity," *Physical Review* 48 (73) (1935): 73–77. https://doi.org/10.1103/PhysRev.48.73.

10. Charles W. Misner and John A. Wheeler, "Classical Physics as Geometry," *Annals of Physics* 2 (6) (1957): 525. https://doi.org/10.1016/0003-4916(57)90049-0.

11. Michael S. Morris and Kip S. Thorne, "Wormholes in Space time and Their Use for Interstellar Travel: A Tool for Teaching General Relativity," *American Journal of Physics* 56 (5) (1988): 395–412. https://doi.org/10.1119/1.15620.

12. "Travel Through Wormholes Is Possible, but Slow," *Science Daily*, April 15, 2019. www.sciencedaily.com/releases/2019/04/190415090853.htm.

13. J. J. Hurtak, *The Book of Knowledge: The Keys of Enoch®* (Los Gatos, California: Academy for Future Science, 1973).

14. Robert M. Wood and Ryan S. Wood, *The Majestic Documents* (Redwood City, California: Wood and Wood Enterprises, 1998).

15. Linda Moulton Howe's testimony given on April 29, 2013, Citizen Hearing on Disclosure, National Press Club, Washington, DC.

16. J. J. Hurtak and J. Bozzoli, *Merkabah: Voyage of a Star Seed* (Los Gatos, California: Academy for Future Science, 1996). www.merkabah.org.

17. Christof Koch, *In Which I Argue That Consciousness Is a Fundamental Property of Complex Things . . . A BIT of Consciousness: Confessions of a Romantic Reductionist* (Boston: MIT Press, 2014).

18. E. A. Rauscher, J. J. Hurtak, and D. E. Hurtak, *Mind Dynamics in Space and Time* (Los Gatos, California: Academy for Future Science, 2016), 509.

19. H. Sherman and Ingo Swann, "An Experimental Psychic Probe of the Planet Jupiter," CIA Library, April 27, 1973. Approved for release on April 1, 2008, by the CIA and National Security Agency.

20. E. A. Rauscher and Russell Targ, "The Speed of Thought: Investigation of a Complex Space-Time Metric to Describe Psychic Phenomena," *Journal of Scientific Exploration* 15 (2001): 331–335.

21. *Calling All Earthlings,* directed by Jonathan Berman, executive produced by Alan Steinfeld. Los Angeles: Carpe Stella Productions, 2018.

22. Vladimir shCherbak and Maxim Makukov, "The 'Wow! Signal' of the Terrestrial Genetic Code," *Icarus* 224 (1)(2013): 228–242.

23. *The News,* July 16, 1979, Mexico City.

24. Elizabeth Klarer, *Beyond the Light Barrier,* 3rd edition (Flagstaff, Arizona: Light Technology Publications, 2009). Originally published in 1980.

25. J. J. Hurtak, *The Book of Knowledge.*

26. "Close Encounter with Alien Grays in California," UFO Casebook, September 1, 2013. www.ufocasebook.com/2013/grey-aliens-yuba-city-california.html.

27. Ibid.

28. Richard S. Ehrlich, "The UFO Seekers Flocking to a Remote Thai Hilltop in Search of Buddhist Aliens," CNN, October 5, 2019. www.cnn.com/travel/article/thailand-ufo-buddhist-aliens/index.html.

29. Ibid.

4: CONTACT IN THE IMPLICATE ORDER

1. David Bohm, *Wholeness and the Implicate Order* (London: Routledge & Kegan Paul, 1980), 221. The author added "in the implicate order" to the end of the quote as a way of referencing its definition. www.gci.org.uk/Documents/DavidBohm-WholenessAndTheImplicateOrder.pdf, 243.

5: STUDYING INTRUSIONS FROM THE SUBTLE REALM: HOW CAN WE DEEPEN OUR KNOWLEDGE?

1. Essay developed by John E. Mack, MD, from a talk given at the International Association for New Science Conference, September 16, 1995, Fort Collins, Colorado. This version of Mack's essay reincorporates selected remarks from the transcript that Mack originally omitted.

2. Margaret Mead, "UFOs–Visitors from Outer Space?" *Redbook,* September 1974.

6: THE RETURN OF THE VISITORS

1. The main part of this essay is from Whitley Strieber's *A New World*, "Chapter Seven: The Return of the Visitors" (San Antonio, Texas: Walker & Collier, 2019).

7: EXTRAORDINARY ACTUALITY: MY JOURNEY TO THE STARS

1. Joseph Greene, *Robots of Saturn (A Dig Allen Space Explorer Adventure, Book 5)* (Golden Press, 1962).

2. https://en.wikipedia.org/wiki/Harmonic_Convergence.

3. Andrew Fazekas, "2012: A Banner Year in the Hunt for Exoplanets," *National Geographic News*, January 2, 2013. www.nationalgeographic.com/news/2013/1/130102-top-exoplanet-discovery-space-science/#close.

4. Helene Cooper, Ralph Blumenthal, and Leslie Kean,"Glowing Auras and 'Black Money': The Pentagon's Mysterious U.F.O. Program," *New York Times*, December 16, 2017, https://www.nytimes.com/2017/12/16/us/politics/pentagon-program-ufo-harry-reid.html.

5. "Sgt. James Penniston," Rendlesham Forest Incident Official Website, www.therendleshamforestincident.com/Sgt_James_Penniston.html (accessed June 1, 2020).

6. Samuel French Morse, ed. *Opus Posthumous* (New York: A. A. Knopf, 1957).

7. Cathy Caruth, *Unclaimed Experience: Trauma, Narrative, and History* (Baltimore: Johns Hopkins University Press, 1996), 4. https://joaocamillopenna.files.wordpress.com/2015/03/caruth-unclaimed-experience.pdf.

8. Ibid, 11.

9. Peter Oehen, MD, "MAPS-Sponsored Swiss MDMA/PTSD Study: Discussion and Analysis," *MAPS Bulletin* xvii (1) (Spring–Summer 2007): 13. https://maps.org/news-letters/v17n1/mp2_study_analysis-oehen.pdf. Although Oehen's study was about using certain psychoactive drugs (MDMA) to gain access to trauma, hypnosis in many cases works the same way.

10. Ibid, 14.

11. Notes taken from Linda Moulton Howe lecture, "They Are Doing Something Different and No One Can Explain It," Conscious Life Expo, Los Angeles, California, February 2016.

12. *Missing Time* by Budd Hopkins was published in 1981 and chronicled the loss of memory during the abduction experience. In many cases, the person would later also find body scars resulting from some sort of alien medical procedures; in some cases metallic-like implants were put in the body purportedly as tracking devices. Whitley Strieber has talked about his implant on many occasions.

13. John Mack, *Abduction: Human Encounters with Aliens* (New York: Scribner, 1994), 48.

14. Whitley Strieber, "Black Swan Ghosts and Other Discoveries on the High Strangeness Trail," *Dreamland* podcast. Uploaded to YouTube by Whitley Strieber, May 29, 2020. www.youtube.com/watch?v=hMnghUYEMq8.

15. "Kidnapped by UFOs? The True Story of Alien Abductions," *NOVA*, April 1, 1997. Mack quote in transcript, www.pbs.org/wgbh/nova/transcripts/2306tufos.html.

16. Neil Young, "After the Gold Rush," verse three. Written and performed by Young on the 1970 album of the same title.

17. May Pang's official website relays the conversation she had with John. She says, "This was one of John's favorite songs, because it literally came to him in a dream. He woke up and wrote down those words along with the melody. He had no idea what it meant, but he thought it sounded beautiful." https://web.archive.org/web/20100116073030/http://maypang.com/?page_id=6.

18. *The Beatles Bible*. The Lennon quote taken from a 1980 interview with the BBC. https://www.beatlesbible.com/people/john-lennon/songs/9-dream/.

19. *The Beatles Bible*. The Lennon quote taken from a 1980 interview with David Sheff.

20. John Lennon, verse from "#9 Dream," *Walls and Bridges* album, 1974.

21. May Pang's official website.

22. Linda Moulton Howe's witness testimony at the Citizen Hearing on Disclosure, April 29, 2013.

23. William Blake, *The Marriage of Heaven and Hell* (circa 1790).

24. B. D. Sharma, *Holistic Health Healing and Astrosciences* (Noida, India: B. Jain Publishers, 2003), 170.

25. According to The Mind Sublime on YouTube, Christopher Mellon posted classified AATIP documents on Twitter and his website on August 6, 2018. They were taken down soon after, but were reposted in many places, like "Episode 5: Advanced Aerospace Threat and Identification Program (AATIP)," https://youtu.be/l24bPVlX4rI. Uploaded to YouTube by The Mind Sublime, June 10, 2020.

26. H. G. Wells, *The Open Conspiracy* (1933), from https://en.wikiquote.org/wiki/H._G._Wells (accessed November 4, 2020).

27. William James, *The Varieties of Religious Experience* (1902).

28. Private conversation with Aboriginal Elder Paul McClough, in Jarvis Bay, NSW, Australia, 2014.

29. Henry David Thoreau, "Chapter 18—Conclusion," *Walden* (1854). http://eserver.org/thoreau/walden18.html#more.

30. Although this quote has been attributed to Thoreau because it is found in *Walden*, "Chapter 18—Conclusion," he borrowed it from William Habington (1605–1664) in the last lines of his poem *To My Honoured Friend Sir Ed. P. Knight*, www.poetrynook.com/poem/my-honoured-friend-sir-ed-p-knight.

8: SOMETHING MOVING

1. https://quotefancy.com/quote/762857/Albert-Einstein-Nothing-happens-until-somethingmoves.

2. Satprem, *Mother or the Divine Materialism* (India: Macmillan India Press, 1977), 303.

3. Darin Stevenson in conversation with the author.

4. William Shakespeare, *A Midsummer Night's Dream*, Act V, scene i.

5. Rainer Maria Rilke, "The Guardian Angel," *The Book of Images*, revised bilingual edition (New York: North Point Press, 1994), 33.

6. Satprem, *Mother or the Divine Materialism*, 264–65.

7. On the opening page of Whitley Strieber's *A New World* (San Antonio, Texas: Walker & Collier, 2019), he quotes from Colonel Philip J. Corso, who asked one of the aliens what they can offer us, if we let them into our lives; the answer was "**A new world, if you can take it.**"

9: TELEPATHIC CONTACT WITH EXTRATERRESTRIAL INTELLIGENCE

1. C. C. Gillispie, *The Montgolfier Brothers and the Invention of Aviation 1783–1784* (Princeton, New Jersey: Princeton University Press, 1983), 92–93.

10: AWAKENING TO OUR COSMIC HERITAGE

1. Zecharia Sitchin, *The Complete Earth Chronicles* (Rochester, Vermont: Bear & Company, 2014).

2. Genesis 1:26, *The Good News Bible: Today's English Version* (Edinburgh, Scotland: Thomas Nelson, 1992).

3. Mary Rodwell, *The New Human: Awakening to Our Cosmic Heritage* (Australia: New Mind Publishers, 2016), Chapter 14.

4. Ann Krielkamp, "Francis Crick on DNA: Intelligent Design," *Exopermaculture*, April 14, 2011. www.exopermaculture.com/2011/04/14/francis-crick-on-dna-intelligent-design/ (accessed 2018).

5. Dr. William Brown, letter to the author, 2010.

6. Rodwell, *The New Human*, Chapter 19.

7. Jo Sheval Iskra, letter to the author.

8. Vladimir I. shCherbak and Maxim A. Makukov, "The 'Wow! Signal' of the Terrestrial Genetic Code," *Icarus* 224, Issue 1 (2013): 228–242.

9. Jayesh Shinde, "Just One Gram of DNA Can Potentially Hold All the Data Stored on the Internet," *IndiaTimes*, April 3, 2017. www.indiatimes.com/technology/science-and-future/just-one-gram-of-dna-can-potentially-hold-all-the-data-stored-on-the-internet-274786.html (accessed 2018).

10. Rey Hernandez, Jon Klimo, and Rudy Schild, eds. *Beyond UFOs: The Science of Consciousness and Contact with Non-Human Intelligence* (Volume 1) (Dr. Edgar Mitchell Foundation for Research into Extraterrestrial and Extraordinary Experiences, 2018), Chapter 8 (406).

11. Rodwell, *The New Human*, Chapter 14.

12. "The Universal Energy of Vibrations," *Bibliotecapleyades*, www.bibliotecapleyades.net/ciencia/esp_ciencia_universalenergy01.htm (accessed 2018).

13. Dr. Lena Ohlson, e-mail message to author (2015).

14. Dr. Maree Batchelor, e-mail message to author (2016).

15. Ibid.

16. Rodwell, *The New Human*, Chapter 14.

17. Mary Rodwell, *Awakening: How Extraterrestrial Contact Can Transform Your Life* (Agnes Waters: New Mind Publishers, Republished 2010), Chapter 8.

18. Rodwell, *The New Human*, Chapter 14.

19. Ibid.

20. "Robert Dean Interview," *Project Camelot*, interview by Kerry Cassidy, 2014. www.youtube.com/channel/UC2na0DRywwQrXeodGmCt63Q.

21. Rodwell, *The New Human*, Chapter 10.

22. Ibid., Chapter 15.

23. Marina, in personal letter to the author, Mary Rodwell.

24. Amanda, e-mail to the author (2019).

25. Rodwell, *The New Human*, Chapter 8.

26. From the author's notes in a personal interview for *The New Humanity*, 2016.

27. John, conversation with the author for *The New Humanity*, 2016.

28. Lea Kapiteli, letter to the author (2019).

29. Jimmy Jones, letter to the author.

30. Marina, in a personal letter to the author.

31. Mike Oram, *Does It Rain in Other Dimensions?* (O Books, 2007), 36–37.

32. Cathy from Sweden, e-mail to the author.

EPILOGUE

1. This is a frequent call to action by the entity Ramtha, channeled by J. Z. Knight. www.ramtha.com.

2. T. S. Eliot, "East Coker," *Four Quartets* (London: Faber & Faber, 1943).

3. "David Jay Brown Interviews John E. Mack," *Mavericks of the Mind*, November 19, 2011, www.davidjaybrown.com/blog/p_264.

4. Kripal and Strieber, 321.

5. Barbara Lamb interview with Alan Steinfeld, December 29, 2020, https://youtu.be/xiO9F-tfIKA.

6. Max Planck, in *Where Is Science Going?* (1932). www.goodreads.com/author/quotes/107032.Max_Planck.

7. Eckhart Tolle, in *Stillness Speaks* (2003). www.goodreads.com/work/quotes/2782954-stillness-speaks.

8. John Lamb Lash, *Not in His Image* (White River Junction, Vermont: Chelsea Green Publishing, 2006), 320. www.academia.edu/16360159/John_lamb_Lash_Not_in_his_Image?auto=download.

9. "Bruce Lipton on the Synergy of Awareness," *New Realities*, 1999. Uploaded to YouTube by NewRealities on January 21, 2020. www.youtube.com/watch?v=kOcw57ihj5s.

10. Jeremy Bernstein, *Einstein* (New York: Viking Press, 1973), 11.

INDEX

We may say we
want to see them.
We may even beg
them to come.
But actual contact
is apocalyptic.